How Much Is Enough?

How Much Is Enough?

Buddhism, Consumerism, and the Human Environment

Edited by Richard K. Payne

WISDOM PUBLICATIONS

Wisdom Publications
199 Elm Street
Somerville MA 02144 USA
www.wisdompubs.org

Library of Congress Cataloging-in-Publication Data

How much is enough? : Buddhism, consumerism, and the human environment / edited by Richard K. Payne.
     p. cm.
 Essays from an international conference jointly sponsored by Ryukoku University, Kyoto, and the Institute of Buddhist Studies, Berkeley.
 Includes bibliographical references and index.
 ISBN 0-86171-685-X (pbk. : alk. paper)
 1. Consumption (Economics)—Religious aspects—Buddhism—Congresses. 2. Consumption (Economics)—Moral and ethical aspects—Congresses. 3. Human ecology—Religious aspects—Buddhism—Congresses. 4. Environmental ethics—Congresses. I. Payne, Richard Karl. II. Ryukoku Daigaku. III. Institute of Buddhist Studies (Berkeley, Calif.)
 BQ4570.E23H69 2010
 294.3'4212—dc22

                              2009054246

14 13 12 11 10
5 4 3 2 1

Cover design by Rick Snizik. Interior design by Gopa & Ted2, Inc. Set in Diacritical Garamond Pro 11.25/14.2.

Wisdom Publications' books are printed on acid-free paper and meet the guidelines for permanence and durability of the Production Guidelines for Book Longevity of the Council on Library Resources.

Printed in the United States of America.

Dedicated to the members of the International Brigades,
volunteers from fifty-three nations, who fought for freedom
and democracy in the Spanish Civil War.
"No passaran!"

Table of Contents

· · ·

Editor's Preface

"How Much Is Enough?"
Buddhism and the Human Environment

■ ■ ■

Richard K. Payne

In the twenty-first century, the Buddhist tradition exists in a social environment radically different from any previous era. The global horizon of contemporary Buddhism creates new questions, questions that the tradition had never in fact confronted previously. In the Western cultural context, two of these are the therapeutic culture and the social activist culture. While the therapeutic culture, which presumes a psychological orientation, can tend to be highly individualistic, the social activist culture has the opposite orientation. In the second half of the twentieth century, Buddhism became involved in several struggles for social justice—perhaps most memorably the opposition to the war in Vietnam, opposition that included Buddhist monks using self-immolation as a means of protest.

Closer to the end of the twentieth century, environmentalism became an increasingly important part of the social activist world, and as a consequence Buddhism also became involved in the issues of environmentalism. One of the key ideas for all forms of Buddhism is the absence of any eternal, unchanging, or permanent essence to be found either in people or in the objects of our daily experience. For many contemporary Buddhists, this notion of "no-essence" is interpreted in a more positive form to mean that the existence of each and every thing, including people, is causally interconnected. Thich Nhat Hanh has coined the term "interbeing" in an attempt to express how deep mutually interdependent existence is.

It was out of this sense of mutually interdependent existence that the international symposium on "Buddhism and the Environment" was organized by Mitsuya Dake and David Matsumoto, members of the faculties of

Ryukoku University, Kyoto, and the Institute of Buddhist Studies, Berkeley, respectively. The conference was held in the Alumni House, on the campus of the University of California, Berkeley, on Sunday, September 14, 2003. Keynote speakers for the symposium were Lewis Lancaster, University of California, Berkeley ("Buddhist Strategies and Discourses: The Views of Causation and Contemporary Problems"), and Ryusei Takeda, Ryukoku University ("Where Should the True Encounter between Religion and Science Take Place?"). Panelists included Stephanie Kaza, University of Vermont; Duncan Williams, University of California, Irvine; Ryugo Matsui, Ryukoku University; Ruben Habito, Southern Methodist University; Tetsunori Koizumi, Ryukoku University; Malcolm David Eckel, Boston University; and Mitsuya Dake, Ryukoku University.

The emphasis that the symposium placed on the human environment highlights the interdependence of our human social reality with the encompassing and supporting natural world. By becoming aware of this interdependence we can see that the distinction between social and natural is itself an intellectual construct, an analytic tool for looking at things in one particular way. It is not a "natural" distinction, and we can look at things differently. Seeing the interdependence of the social and natural, we can experience more directly the karmic relations between our actions and the human environment around us, both social and natural.

ACKNOWLEDGEMENTS

The editor would like to thank the Open Research Center of Ryukoku University for its support of both the conference and the publication of this work. The generosity of their support, both financial and personal, is deeply appreciated. I would like to particularly thank Prof. Mitsuya Dake for his interest in seeing this project through to completion. Thanks are also due to the conference participants and to the other contributors to this volume. Without the assistance, support, and encouragement of the staff of Wisdom Publications—particularly Tim McNeill, MacDuff Stewart, Joe Evans, and Laura Cunningham—this would never have been converted from a heap of papers on the floor next to my desk into the book you now hold.

Just How Much Is Enough?

• • •

Richard K. Payne

Having grown up during the Great Depression, my parents maintained a set of values based on frugality, rather than expendability and overconsumption. From the early 1960s on, my father became increasingly concerned with organic farming, a commitment that simultaneously brought together our family background in agriculture and his own radical politics. When he visited me in Japan in the early 80s, there were two things he insisted on doing. One was to visit a leading figure of organic farming in Japan, Masanobu Fukuoka, and the other was to see the memorial at Hiroshima.

My mother shared these values, and I grew up eating homemade bread and home-canned fruit. Where my mother learned this story, I have no idea, but at an early age she told me the following tale:

> Once two Zen monks were traveling from one temple to another. As they approached the temple, they discussed the question of whether it would be an appropriate place for them to pursue their practice. Passing over a bridge near the temple, they noticed a cabbage leaf floating downstream. They paused and began to reconsider whether a temple that would allow such waste could possibly be a true hall for training in the way. Just then, the temple gate opened and a monk with a long pole came rushing toward them. Startled, they watched as the monk caught the cabbage leaf, bowed to them and returned to the temple. Nodding to one another, the two monks entered the gates of the temple, confident that they had found a place where they would indeed be able to make progress on the path.

While she may have only intended to reinforce the importance of frugality, her story also laid the groundwork for my own conviction that Buddhism is a religion committed to respecting all life, not simply in some abstract sense, but concretely through individual actions.

The environment—what can Buddhism tell us about our relation to it? Frequently it seems that the environment is something distant—melting glaciers, or loss of habitat for polar bears. It can also seem abstract—average change of the oceans' temperatures as measured over the last half century, or increasing concentration of pollutants as parts per million. Or at least, the environment is something separate from us—the natural world that we go to visit beyond the city's edge. We need, however, to move beyond any idealized conception of nature in order to avoid having that socially constructed conception of "nature as separate from human" be the object of our concern. The idea of nature as something separate from the human, as either a material or spiritual resource for us to draw upon, maintains a dualistic separation between the human and the natural—a dualism that is itself at the very heart of our present ecological fiasco. The same is also true of the other polarity common to this discourse, that between nature and culture.

One of the things that Buddhism can tell us is that these images of the environment—distant, abstract, separate—are all mistaken conceptions of the way things are. The environment is right here around us; it is the air we breathe and the water we drink, and it is intimately interconnected with each and every one of us. The mistaken conceptions of the environment—distant, abstract, separate—are themselves based on a mistaken conception of the self. The self is not an isolated, independent, unchanging reality distinct from other people or the world around it. It is itself an ongoing process and an open system.

Perhaps as a consequence of our evolutionary history, the personal human self is motivated by a deep sense of insufficiency—the theme of this collection of essays. The Buddha's diagnosis for our suffering, unease, and dissatisfaction is this pervasive feeling of existing in a state of insufficiency. Insufficiency (*tanha*, sometimes translated as craving) is not simply need. Needs can be fulfilled, but as long as we cling to the sense of self as a separate, independent, unchanging reality there will be a disparity between the actuality and the imagined—a disparity that is experienced as an insufficiency.

Modern consumerist society tells us that our felt insufficiency can be filled by acquiring things—the latest consumer technology, the latest automobile, the latest, most recent, best, improved, newest, rarest, most fashionable, as seen being worn/driven/eaten/drunk by some celebrity/ fashion model. Consumption, whether we need the whatever or not, drives the engines of our contemporary society, which itself needs to keep us ignorant of or at least distracted from attending to our own needs. The human drive to acquire more is not only doomed to fail, but because we have gotten so clever at trying to fulfill our insufficiency, our manic drive to feel fulfilled now poses a serious threat to our environment, which is to say we are a threat to ourselves.

GLOBAL PERSPECTIVES ON THE ENVIRONMENT

It may seem obvious that environmental concerns require us to have a global perspective. But while we may think about the environment globally—climate change, for example—we also need to have a global perspective on our thinking about the environment. In other words, while we may be thinking about a global environment, our thinking may not be global, it may remain constrained by our own societal location. This collection of essays on the relation between the lived practice of Buddhism and contemporary concerns about the environment includes the work of both American and Japanese scholar-practitioners. In doing so, it broadens the perspectives available to the contemporary discussions, and in some cases challenges presumptions previously unexamined.

This collection is concerned with the question, How much is enough? The authors draw on the teachings of Buddhism as a resource for answering this question. They do so within a context that understands "the environment" as including the human, as the entirety of the human domain, both social and natural. At first glance, it might seem that "human environment" is a smaller category than nature or ecology, a kind of subset within one of those larger categories. One of the goals of this work is to point out the mistaken character of such a conception—the human environment is a broader category because it includes nature, society, and individual.

By identifying the object of concern as the human environment, the point is also being made that there is a single human environment—not an American one that is different from a Chinese or Indian or European one. At the same time, there is not a Buddhist environment, nor a Christian environment, nor a Jewish, Muslim, or Hindu environment, but only the human environment.[1]

The need for working with a conception of the human environment as a single totality is demonstrated by the consequences of what might be called the American myth. Key to the American myth is the equation of prosperity and happiness. The occasional sentimental narrative of "poor but happy" aside, Americans seem to be quite cynical about the causal link that points from prosperity to happiness. But it is the second part of the national myth that makes it particularly problematic for the human environment. This is the self-image that America is a prosperous nation and that as a consequence Americans are happy. The inverse of this is, then, that if you are not happy or if you are not prosperous, there is something wrong with you individually. It is from this perspective that social action programs that relieve suffering carry with them a social stigma—consider the stigma attached to public transportation in much of the nation, a stigma so great that there is a refusal to fund it adequately since it "only helps the poor."

The Buddhist perspective, however, is that suffering is universal. If we are aware of suffering as universal—as something affecting ourselves as much as the farmer in Bangladesh whose fields are flooded, or the inner city drug addict, or any of those "others" upon whom we can project our own suffering so as to protect ourselves from experiencing it—then the stigma of social programs intended to assist everyone can be diminished, the individualism that isolates each person, not only from others in the society, but also from the natural environment that supports and sustains us all, can be diminished. Each in its own way, the different perspectives offered by the essays gathered here contribute to creating a broader perspective on both the nature of the human environment and the ways in which Buddhism may relate us to that environment.

CONTENTS OF THE COLLECTION

Duncan Williams' opening contribution to this collection, "Buddhist Environmentalism in Contemporary Japan," examines a number of programs undertaken by Japanese Buddhists to protect the environment. The opening vignette regarding an action to protect trees by the chief priest of

Gyōzenji Temple in greater Tokyo demonstrates one strategy for employing Buddhist ideas in the service of the environment, a strategy related to the doctrine of buddha nature. Asserting that plants and trees have buddha nature makes sense in the context of East Asian Buddhism where not only is the idea of buddha nature itself a well-established part of Buddhist thought, but the extension of the idea of buddha nature to plants and trees, pebbles and stones has long been part of the tradition.

Other actions discussed by Williams demonstrate the sophistication of the Japanese Buddhist community, not only in terms of the scientific aspects of environmental issues, but also in their ability to create effective volunteer campaigns and their initiative in utilizing the economic potentials of environmental actions. For contemporary Western Buddhists, the issues of the relation between social and economic privilege and environmental responsibility is raised by the work of Rev. Ōkōchi. His travels to areas of the world torn by strife and warfare—places such as Rwanda, Palestine, Cambodia—heightened his awareness of the palpable reality of suffering. The conditions that the people in these countries suffered from reminded Ōkōchi of the conditions current in medieval Japan when Hōnen, founder of the Jōdo sect to which Ōkōchi belongs, was active in establishing a form of Pure Land Buddhism.

Ōkōchi's analysis of suffering provides us with a perspective important for contemporary Western Buddhists generally, not just in relation to environmental issues. As Williams puts it, "Ōkōchi interprets suffering as existing not only on a personal level, but at a deep structural level in the modern socioeconomic system."

Our current socioeconomic system has been identified by the name "consumerism." Economically, consumerism focuses on the consumption of goods and services. The public display of such consumption for the sake of demonstrating one's social status was identified by Thorstein Veblen (1857–1929) who referred to it as "conspicuous consumption."

Consumerism is the focus of the second essay, Stephanie Kaza's "How Much Is Enough?: Buddhist Perspectives on Consumerism." As Kaza makes clear in her opening, consumerism is driven by the creation of artificial needs by means of advertising. The purposeful stimulation of the Three Poisons—delusion, anger, and greed—in order to get someone to purchase an item is quite clearly contrary to Buddhist teachings. The Eightfold Path includes, for example, the ideas of right speech, right action, and right livelihood. The pursuit of economic gain by creating an artificial need that the product being promoted promises to fulfill would certainly appear to be a breach of all three of these aspects of the Eightfold Path.

Kaza develops a Buddhist critique of consumerism by first examining the global consequences of the kinds of wasteful overconsumption that consumerism encourages. She then goes on to examine specific ways in which consumerism has been critiqued, including those developed on the basis of Western ideas, as well as newly developed ones that draw on Buddhist concepts. Kaza closes her discussion with a set of proposals of her own for moving toward liberation by the reduction—or elimination—of desire.

Several of the environmental activists discussed by Williams are members of the Pure Land traditions of Japanese Buddhism. Mitsuya Dake presents a Pure Land Buddhist perspective on environmental issues in his contribution to this collection. In an analysis that moves beyond an understanding of suffering as private, Dake challenges the standard conceptions of Buddhism prevalent in the West, which he describes as "forms of Buddhism that emphasize self-cultivation and that are usually connected with some sort of cognitive, personal, and empowering experience." The representation of Buddhism as commonly found in the West is informed by the West's own preconceptions about the significance and goal of religion as formed by Romanticism. Dake points out, however, that "for many Buddhists in East Asia, this image represents only part of the Buddhist belief system, which as a whole comprises more than just meditation or mental cultivation."

The Pure Land tradition focuses its attention on the Buddha Amitābha, known in Japanese as Amida. Prior to his awakening, Amida vowed that when he became a buddha he would manifest a buddha-land that was pure, or as interpreted by some Chinese Pure Land masters, a land that purifies. Although the Sanskrit name of Amida's buddha-land, Sukhāvatī, means "land of bliss," it has come to be referred to as "pure land" (jōdo), or more typically in Buddhist English, "the Pure Land." The significance of being a land that purifies is that in contrast to our present world, it is one in which not only is it easy to hear the teachings—the birds there sound the phrase "Buddha, Dharma, Sangha"—but also one can understand the significance of the teachings, put them into effective practice, and become awakened.

Analogies between Amida and the Pure Land, on the one hand, and the Christian God and his Heaven, on the other, have been made frequently and—as Dake discusses—quite erroneously. The Pure Land is not conceived to be an ontological absolute, but is rather identified with the state of nirvāṇa as being uncreated—a technical philosophic concept that is often, if not usually, misunderstood in the West as implying an absolute state of existence, but which actually refers to something simply not existing, in the same way that a candle flame when extinguished simply does not exist.

Dake then goes on to develop an interpretation of the Pure Land symbolism as signifying "interconnectivity and harmony in diversity." He points out, however, that as valuable as such perspectives may be, they are not themselves solutions to our urgent environmental concerns. "In order to solve the environmental problems we face, it will be necessary to develop a connection between that method of thought and concrete norms of behavior in this modern age." Turning to the teachings of Shinran, founder of the Shin school of Japanese Pure Land Buddhism, Dake suggests that such "concrete norms of behavior" can arise out of Shinran's view of human nature in which "despair as to the self and one's awakening to truth and reality" are understood to be mutually identical.

Here we encounter an aspect of East Asian Buddhist teachings that is important for Western, particularly American, Buddhists to hear. Implicit in our understanding of human nature in the West is a kind of simplistic optimism about individual self-sufficiency, encouraging us to believe that "Through my own efforts, I can attain whatever I really set myself to, including awakening." (How many of us were raised with the children's book *The Little Engine That Could*?) The Pure Land teachings confront this idea directly, pointing out the self-contradiction in the idea that the ego can overcome the ego. This is the "despair as to the self" that Dake speaks of, and this—contrary to many Western treatments of Pure Land— places Pure Land firmly in the mainstream of Mahāyāna thought. It may be a different approach from the more familiar emphasis on the emptiness of the self found in Mahāyāna, but it is making exactly the same point, and can provide a critique of consumerist culture like that developed by Kaza in her paper. The challenge to the concept of an autonomous self here again brings us to conceptions of suffering as something that cannot be simply located in the private realm of the individual person. This broadens the relation between Buddhism and environmental concerns to an "ecosocial" dimension.

The ecosocial perspective brought to our environmental concerns by Gary Snyder is presented by David Barnhill. Barnhill identifies three strains within Snyder's thought that are themselves interdependent—Buddhism, ecology, and radical politics. These three themes are interwoven through Snyder's poetry from an early period, Barnhill beginning with an examination of *Myths & Texts*, which dates from 1960. One theme that runs continuously through Snyder's poetry from this early period is American labor history, a history that—like the histories of other disenfranchized peoples—has been "placed under erasure."

Snyder also connects his radical social, environmental, and political ideas with the vows of Amida, the ones that created the Pure Land. The connection between the symbolic representation of what the world could be—the Pure Land—and the ideals of an environmentally motivated Buddhism that relates to broader social issues as integral to the personal/social/environmental totality is asserted by Snyder's use of the image of the Pure Land.

Barnhill then goes on to examine the anarchist roots of Snyder's politics. Although largely ignored—placed under erasure—in contemporary political discourse, anarchist thought has deep roots in Western political thought, dating from at least the end of the eighteenth century, and having informed social reform movements in the United States for almost the entirety of its history.

In addition to the imagery of the Pure Land, the Buddhist strains of Snyder's environmental thought are largely drawn from Huayan ideas, such as the image of Indra's net. This is by now a familiar image for Buddhist environmentalism, one that promotes a nondual relation between individual and whole, a "mutual interdependence," or as Barnhill calls it, a "relational holism."

It is then from this complex of radical politics and Buddhist cosmology that Snyder develops his critique of contemporary society's role in environmental degradation. Snyder's mix of environmental and social concerns makes it possible for him to see the relations between the two. How, in other words, do we take action that is simultaneously protective of the environment and of people?

Snyder's answer is, at least in part, that of bioregionalism. Places are not simply interchangeable units in an abstract Cartesian space. Rather, they form a living, integrated whole. Bioregionalism looks to the "natural divisions created by soil, climate, topography, river drainages, etc.," rather than to the relatively arbitrary divisions of political units, such as nation or state.

Bioregionalism is, however, a way of thinking that, while promoting an awareness of interdependence in a very concrete way, does not define appropriate courses of action. Just as Dake discussed in relation to Shinran's thought, it is another step to go from a vision of reality to action based on that vision. Barnhill first emphasizes the nonviolent dimension of Snyder's message of the liberatory effects of creating a new awareness. This task is partly through meditation and study of the Dharma, but also by critical reflection on the power of "key images, myths, archetypes, eschatologies, and ecstasies."

Where Snyder's suggestion focuses on control of the cognitive dimensions of the culture to recast not only ways of thinking but also actions, Shinichi Inoue gives his attention to the development of economic relations based on Buddhist principles. In contrast to an economics of exploitation, in which the dominant attitude is one of taking as much as we can from the natural world, Inoue proposes what might be called an economics of restoration, one in which the dominant attitude is one of borrowing—that is, temporary use of those resources we need before restoring them to their proper place.

Turning to more specifically economic aspects of dealing with environmental concerns, Inoue presents us with a schema develop by Mitsuru Tanaka (Kawasaki Environment Agency). Tanaka proposes a four by four matrix that charts the environmental impact of both production and consumption. Production of essential goods with only minimal environmental impact would score a 1, while producing unnecessary or frivolous goods by highly polluting means would score a 16. Absolutely essential goods, such as medical supplies, whose production involved pollution would score much better than frivolous goods, such as many "luxury" items, even if the latter were produced with little pollution. Such a scale would allow for a system of environmental taxation that takes into account both production practices and the nature of the goods produced. Inoue suggests that such policies are "increasingly important as we begin to understand that environmental destruction carries with it an economic price that may not become evident until much later."

Inoue examines two agricultural industries that are economically, environmentally, and culturally significant for Japan—rice and dairy farming. Consideration of the production practices involved in these two kinds of farming connects to the issues of bioregionalism discussed by Barnhill. Japanese dairy farmers, for example, use pasturage in the mountains. This is similar to the practice of another mountainous country, Switzerland, but in sharp contrast to dairy farming in the United States, which is done on open plains.

From this perspective Inoue considers the importance of Buddhist values as they relate to economics. The areas he considers are: unconstrained greed, the presumption of competition as the sole fundamental economic principle, an appropriately positive evaluation of money as an opportunity for mindfulness, and the avoidance of waste. These are the positive principles that Inoue highlights as the Buddhist contribution to an environmentally sensitive economics.

Drawing on the structure of the Eightfold Path, Tetsunori Koizumi takes a more systematic approach to developing a Buddhist environmental program. Taking as his point of reference general systems theory, Koizumi reexpresses the elements of the Eightfold Path in such a fashion as to provide us with a practical guide for action, a prescription for sustainable living. He begins by interpreting the Buddha's teachings as being structured by a metaphysical dualism. He uses the terms "manifest world" and "latent world" for saṃsāra and nirvāṇa, respectively. This is based on what seems to be a quasi-Aristotelian interpretation in which "name and form" (Skt. *nāmarūpa*) are "projected" from the latent into the manifest world.

Koizumi then further divides the manifest world into three—biosphere, sociosphere, and psychosphere. All existing entities in all three spheres are understood by Koizumi as evidencing the quality of impermanence, and as such, they move through three phases of creation, preservation, and decay.

Having set up this philosophic background, Koizumi is then ready to examine the specifics of the Eightfold Path. His first step is to group the eight into mental or physical activities, forming two complementary sets. When viewed in terms of the Middle Path, the elements of the Eightfold

Path constitute a systemic balance, a balance of potential and kinetic energies. In this way Koizumi equates latent world, nirvāna, mental actions, and potential energy on one side, and sets them in opposition to manifest world, saṃsāra, physical actions, and kinetic energy on the other.

Viewing the injunctions of the Eightfold Path in terms of the conservation of matter and energy in the service of physical, mental, and environmental health provides a way of integrating ecology, economics, and ethics. Echoing Dake and Barnhill, Koizumi says in conclusion, "translating the Buddha's insight into an agenda for individual action and social policy is the challenge that confronts us today."

It is just such daily, lived expressions of the Buddha's insight that Ikuo Nakamura discusses in his "The Debate on Taking Life and Eating Meat in the Edo-Period Jōdo Shin Tradition." By the Edo period (1600–1868) concepts such as karma and rebirth and the six realms of existence had become integral to Japanese conceptions of the ethical relation between humans and the environment—"the indigenous Japanese view of animals and the Buddhist concept of not taking life mutually influenced each other and brought about the creation of a unique understanding of the relation between humans and animals."

The idea of buddha nature as extending to include not only humans but also animals, and even trees and grasses—found in the modern Japanese Buddhist environmental activists discussed by Williams—has its roots in early medieval Japan. Nakamura discusses how such ideas produced in Japan a "culture of memorialization" in which religious services and memorials allowed for the expression of remorse over killing and consuming animals. The merging of Buddhist and Shintō beliefs also led to the popularity of some Shintō deities, such as Suwa, who were believed to pardon hunters for having taken the lives of their prey.

Shinran, founder of the Shin sect of Japanese Pure Land Buddhism, mentioned previously, took a radical ethical stance on these issues. Rather than accepting the widely held ideas regarding purity and pollution, he asserted that we all share the same ethical status as hunters and fishermen, that is, those directly responsible for taking life. In contemporary terms we might say that Shinran saw how we are all complicit in a system of economic, ethical, social, and environmental relations.

In early modern Japan the issue of vegetarianism was closely linked with the issue of celibacy. Thus, debates about meat-eating simultaneously involved the question of clerical marriage. The Shin view of these issues drew together three ideas. First, that the practice of austerities such as vegetarianism and celibacy conferred no special ethical status. Second, the idea that in this period of the decline of the Dharma (Jpn. *mappō*) in which we live, we are incapable of effecting our own awakening through our own individual efforts. And third, the idea that Amida had vowed that even the worst of us—such as hunters and fishermen—could be born into the Pure Land. Thus, based on a kind of "nonduality of good and evil," meat-eating and clerical marriage came to be positively valued in the Shin sect. One expression of this is the ritual preparation and consumption of a carp at New Year's in the Hōonji Temple. Nakamura's examination of this practice draws attention to the confluence of indigenous Japanese conceptions of the sacrality of animals and Buddhist conceptions of karma as understood in the Shin tradition.

These ideas and practices confront us with very different conceptions of the relation between the human and the natural from those that commonly inform eco-Buddhist discussions in the West today. At the same time, our presumptions regarding what Buddhism teaches in relation to these issues are also challenged. This encourages us to think through more carefully, from a more globally Buddhist perspective, the question of appropriate Buddhist responses to our present environmental situation. In his "Is 'Buddhist Environmentalism' a Contradiction in Terms?" Malcolm David Eckel makes just such reconsiderations explicit.

Eckel begins by pointing out the pervasive role of Orientalist stereotypes of the West as exploiting nature and of the East as protective of nature in forming many of the presumptions about Buddhism and the environment. Calling these presumptions into question, Eckel suggests the importance of the origins of Buddhism in the yogic culture of ancient India. He also suggests other aspects of Buddhism that can serve to question the presumptions about environmental commitments. The issue of social location is intimated by a story that leads to the question of whether or not conservation is another form of attachment. When upper-middle-class American Buddhists want to protect natural environments that they themselves make use of for recreational purposes—skiing, hiking, camping, rock climbing—is this not simply another instance of concealing from ourselves our own egocentric motivations? This is just the kind of issue that Snyder raises when he points toward the importance of thinking about the lives of lumbermen who cut down trees, as well as about the lives of spotted owls who live in those trees. To fail to think about both leads to just the kind of oppositional conflicts that have become all too familiar in recent years. These kinds of questions lead Eckel to conclude that "'Buddhism' and 'environmentalism' may not be contradictory in the strict sense of the word, but they make an uneasy combination, and each raises awkward and difficult questions about the other."

Eckel appears confident, however, that this "uneasy combination" is not the end of the matter. Like Inoue, he turns to the idea of the Middle Path as a balance between two extremes, explaining this as a three-step process going from one extreme to its opposite, and then finally correcting back toward some midpoint between the two. In his analysis of the relation between Buddhism and the environment Eckel suggests that the naive assumption that "of course Buddhism respects the environment" comprises the first extreme. The second extreme comes as a reaction to the first when careful consideration throws the naive assumption into doubt. Eckel points out, however, that "the original problem remains: What to do about the environment, and what to do about the environment from a Buddhist point of view?"

Eckel raises a question that usually remains unasked, that of the location of awakening. Is the location of awakening Bodh Gaya? Or is it, as the highly psychologized interpretation that dominates the Western understanding of Buddhism would tell us, the mind? But mind, of course, is an abstraction, a construct. Eckel turns instead to the concrete character of embodied human existence, which is necessarily always located in some particular place. "While emptiness, in a sense, is everywhere, it is realized only in *this* moment, *this* place, and *this* body." One can also see that this undermines the easy avoidance of realizing the way by thinking of it as something that happens someplace else. Eckel suggests that by attending to the immanence of awakening, a Buddhist sensibility regarding the environment can be developed and sustained. As others in this collection also have, Eckel closes with the image of the Pure Land as signifying the potential inherent within our own present world: "I wonder whether this could be a time for Buddhists to rediscover the utopian aspiration embedded in this concept—to purify this buddha-field and turn it into a Pure Land."

The essay by Lambert Schmithausen reprinted here, "The Early Buddhist Tradition and Ecological Ethics,"[2] has attracted a host of misunderstandings, often criticisms based on the idea that a close, scholarly examination of early Buddhist teachings and attitudes toward the natural world should not be done in an intellectually neutral fashion. Rather it seems the expectation of scholarship is partisan, that is, providing already interpreted representations of early Buddhism that support the idea that Buddhism is "eco-friendly." Schmithausen has been criticized personally for being anti-ecology. If one reads the essay included here, one discovers that nothing could be further from the case. His personal commitment to both the environment and to honest, accurate intellectual inquiry is evident.

What Schmithausen's work does contribute to the consideration of the relation between Buddhist thought and environmentalism is, first, clarity about the nature of early Buddhist thought on the issues involved. Second, his research challenges some of the characterizations of the Buddhist tradition that have become unquestioned presumptions in modern Western Buddhist thought, apparently largely as a consequence of the dominance of the Mahāyāna tradition and the consequent uncritical acceptance of Mahāyāna polemics. One small gem is embedded in a note, where he critiques the characterization of the goal of becoming awakened oneself as in some sense "selfish."

Through a very detailed philological analysis, Schmithausen examines the question of just what the early Buddhist tradition did think about the environment. The intellectual approach that Schmithausen takes has as its intent the sincere desire to understand what the Buddhist tradition has been. Such an approach avoids a neocolonialist gesture of exploiting Buddhism as a resource for our own purposes. It is only by finding out what Buddhism actually says, rather than what we want it to say, that an intellectually honest, and therefore sustainable, eco-Buddhism can be created.

FINAL THOUGHTS

This collection does not seek to create a single answer to the question of Buddhism and the human environment, much less a master narrative about what all Buddhists should think or how all Buddhists should act. More humbly, it simply seeks to contribute to the discussion of how Buddhist thought—the variety of ideas, of concepts that are widely shared by

Buddhists—can inform a contemporary Buddhist worldview that integrates in an authentic fashion a wider environmental awareness. Much of what has informed environmentalism in the West to date, including "deep ecology," has been Western cosmology and religious belief.[3] Simply adopting that version of environmentalism into a Buddhist context—simply repackaging it as Buddhism—would introduce, as unexamined presumptions, values and beliefs that may not only be foreign to the tradition itself, but might actually subvert the critical perspective that Buddhism can provide to the global concerns with the environment. As the essays in this collection indicate, there are a variety of Buddhist concepts that can be brought to bear on environmental issues.

Impermanence is fundamental to the Buddhist perception of existence. As understood by many contemporary Buddhists, the opposite face of impermanence is interdependence—this is seen not as a logical consequence, but simply as a different way of expressing the same insight; the two are simply synonymous with one another. This provides one Buddhist approach to realizing—making immediately real for oneself—the environment as a religious issue: being impermanent, a person is not autonomously separate from his or her environment, but rather interdependent with it.

Understandings of the bodhisattva vow provide another immediate lived connection between the environment and one's own Buddhist insight and practice. Personally, it has seemed to me that given the interdependence of all being, the bodhisattva vow—the vow to put off one's own final awakening in order to assist all living beings to equally realize awakening—is not an ethical injunction. It is not some kind of external rule that one needs to adhere to, to force oneself to follow, a command. Rather, if we take interdependence seriously, the bodhisattva vow is instead simply a statement of fact. In other words, if we take interdependence seriously, no one obtains full and final awakening until all do. So, the bodhisattva vow is not something in addition to one's life, it is not something external to oneself that one takes on, but rather it is a realization of one's own actual existence as an interdependent being—and there is no other kind of existence. This is not optional.

In the essays that follow, various other Buddhist ideas are explored for their value in relation to our contemporary environmental concerns. The Buddhist voices that can be heard in these essays offer the opportunity to think critically about both Buddhism and the environment, allowing us a chance to move beyond our preconceptions into a deeper, richer engagement with the living potential of the Buddhist tradition in today's world.

NOTES

1 Such divisions, whether ethnic, political, or religious, are inherently antihumanistic, and may all-too-easily be put to the service of authoritarian or fascist regimes. See Luc Ferry and Alain Renaut, *Heidegger and Modernity*, trans. Franklin Philip (Chicago and London: University of Chicago Press, 1990), 2–5.

2 Reprinted with the author's permission from the *Journal of Buddhist Ethics* 4 (February 1997): 1–74. Available online at http://www.buddhistethics.org/4/current4.html.

3 See particularly Luc Ferry, *The New Ecological Order*, trans. Carol Volk (Chicago and London: University of Chicago Press, 1995), for a critique of deep ecology as antihumanistic.

Buddhist Environmentalism
in Contemporary Japan

Duncan Ryūken Williams

"To the Honorable Mitsui Real Estate Company: Plants and Trees Have Buddha Nature"

Riding Tokyo's Den'entoshi Subway Line due west, one emerges from the underground section of the train line just before Futako Tamagawaen Station. Before reaching the station's platform, one can see a large temple on the hill to the left side. During the mid-1990s, for a period of several years, one would have also noticed a series of massive signboards along the temple hillside that collectively read "Mitsui fudōsan dono, sōmoku busshō ari" (To the Honorable Mitsui Real Estate Company: Plants and Trees Have Buddha Nature).[1]

This prominently displayed message to one of Japan's largest real estate conglomerates had been put up by Shunnō Watanabe, the chief priest of Gyōzenji Temple. This Jōdo sect temple had been established in the 1560s on this hilltop in Tokyo's Setagaya Ward and in the centuries that followed became well known for its view of the plains below. The priest had launched a campaign against the construction by Mitsui Real Estate Company of a massive apartment complex right next to the temple that would not only obstruct the view from the temple, but would involve clear-cutting 130 of 180 ancient trees.

Watanabe not only rallied his temple members, but also over the course of several years organized a major petition drive (eventually collecting over twelve thousand signatures submitted to the ward office) opposing the destruction of one of Tokyo's few remaining wooded sanctuaries. Employing the slogan, "Plants and Trees Have Buddha Nature," the Buddhist priest appealed to the conscience of the residents in the ward (serving as the new head of the "Seta no Kankyō Mamoru Kai," the Association to Protect Seta's Environment), the ward officials, and Mitsui Real Estate Company. Declaring that his group was "not anti-construction, but simply for the preservation of trees," the campaign successfully pressured the company to build the apartment complex with minimal environmental impact.

Today, most of the ancient trees next to Gyōzenji Temple still stand and the view from the temple over the region is still panoramic. This case highlights the increasing role of Buddhist priests, temples, and lay associations in environmental activism in Japan. Historically, environmentalism and concern with consumers' rights had been associated with local citizens' groups and environmental organizations that came out of the left and labor movements of the 1960s and 70s.

Buddhist temples have often served as stewards for much of the natural landscape of Japan since the early medieval period. But explicitly linking Buddhist doctrine with environmental protection is relatively recent. Beginning in the late 1970s, a number of Buddhist priests, temples, and lay associations dropped their traditional resistance to what had been perceived as a leftist cause, developing new forms of Buddhist environmentalism that resonated with a more conservative worldview. For example, in the 1980s Shōei Sugawara, a forward-thinking abbot of the Sōtō Zen Senryūji Temple in Komae, proposed to his parishioners a way to make the temple more ecological.[2] Sugawara was appalled to learn of a major development project right next to his temple that would destroy the forest that his temple had protected for over four hundred years. With a keen sense of responsibility as the caretaker of this forest, which was partly on temple land and partly on private land, he was determined that the successive prior abbots of Senryūji Temple who had guarded the forest as a sanctuary would give him strength and guidance so that it would not be destroyed during his tenure as abbot.

During 1981–82, he was one of the leaders in a citizens' movement to promote a vision of the town's future development that would be more "green" (*midori no machizukuri*). The group collected the signatures of nearly 10% of the entire town's populace (7,800 signatures) on a petition demanding a halt to the project. Their efforts won widespread support—ranging from the most left-wing activists to the most conservative town assembly members—by appealing to both the local citizens' groups and those concerned about preserving the traditional landscape of the Senryūji Temple. Not only was the development severely restricted, the twenty thousand hectare (approximately fifty thousand acres) forest and temple grounds were designated a nature preserve (*ryokuchi hozen chiku*) by the Tokyo Metropolitan Government, which bought the section of the forest that had been privately owned. Today, this nature preserve is open to the public only once a month to minimize human impact (unlike a park designation, a nature preserve under Japanese law is much more highly regulated). Roughly one to three hundred people visit the preserve on those days to enjoy nature and educate themselves about the forest ecological system. The August open preserve day draws many more people, since it has been arranged to coincide with the temple's famous O-Segaki, "Hungry Ghost Festival."

Once environmental awareness at Senryūji was raised in the 1980 campaign, the abbot followed up with a proposal to make the temple itself more ecological. Since one of the main characteristics of a Japanese Buddhist temple is the large roof on the main hall (*hondō*) containing the primary image of worship (*honzon*), Sugawara thought if that broad space were used for solar paneling, most temples should be energy self-sufficient. He explains that even though Buddhism has traditionally advocated friendly relations between humans and nature, the modern world has disrupted this relationship. His idea for a solar "temple," using energy friendly to both nature and humans, took many years before it would be actualized. In the year 2000, his advocacy of solar temples among those in his sect culminated in a regional meeting of four hundred Sōtō Zen temples in western Tokyo. The gathering had, as its plenary speaker, Kōichi Yasuda (abbot of Eisenji Temple), who spoke on the practical steps to install solar paneling at Buddhist temples.

When Senryūji Temple finally installed the solar panels on top of the abbot's quarters, it produced more than enough energy for the electrical needs of the entire temple complex. The excess energy was sold to Tokyo Electric Power Company at its daytime peak rate, while the temple bought back energy when necessary (cloudy days and nights) at the cheaper off-peak rates. This arrangement proved to be beneficial to the environment (no pollution), the temple (cheaper energy costs), and the power company (which was in power deficit during the peak hours, which is precisely when solar energy produces the most energy). Today, the temple is working with an architectural firm, Taisei Kensetsu, to develop solar roof tiles made in the traditional Japanese Buddhist temple style. This is because many abbots who suggest placing solar paneling on temple roofs face strong resistance from parishioners who prefer the traditional architecture of their temple. With nearly fifteen thousand temples affiliated to his sect, Sugawara sees the solution to this problem as the key to a majority of Buddhist temples, not only of his sect, adopting solar energy in the future.

These two success stories of a Buddhist priest spearheading a local environmental initiative represent a small portion of the many individuals who understand their commitment to Buddhism and the traditions of temple life as requiring engagement in environmental issues. This paper will provide an overview of this type of "Buddhist environmentalism" in Japan and offer some preliminary ideas on how the Japanese case can be understood primarily as a "conservative conservationism."

ESTABLISHMENT BUDDHISM AND SECT-WIDE ENVIRONMENTALISM: THE CASE OF THE SŌTŌ ZEN "GREEN PLAN"

While the energy advocacy of Sugawara stemmed from his personal interests, they were not out of line with the sect to which he belongs. Since 1995, the Sōtō Zen have maintained a nationwide campaign for the environment, taking up key issues of energy use and consumer waste. The earliest of Japanese Buddhist sects to promote environmentalism on a sect-wide basis, they developed a comprehensive "Green Plan" and promoted it to the more than fifteen thousand temples of Sōtō Zen Buddhism.

The "Green Plan" has been part of the official Sōtō Zen strategy to engage pressing contemporary issues under the slogan "*Heiwa, Jinken, Kankyō*" (Peace, Human Rights, and the Environment). Through pamphlets, books, and symposia, the sect has encouraged both individual priests and temples and sect organizations (such as regional districts, women's and youth associations) to take up the environmental cause as a part of affiliation with the Sōtō Zen sect. The promotional materials emphasize the teachings of Dōgen and Keizan that promote sensitivity to the natural world (such as Dōgen's view that grasses, trees, and forests are manifestations of buddha nature). They also point to conservation measures (such as monastic rules on not wasting water and food).[3] In one pamphlet, the 1998 *Green Plan: Kōdō no tame no Q&A* (The "Green Plan": Q&A for Action), the question is asked, "Why does a Buddhist sect like Sōtōshū get involved with environmental issues?" In response, the official doctrine highlights eco-friendly teachings of Śākyamuni Buddha, Dōgen, and Keizan that encourage increasing wisdom and decreasing desire, for example, Keizan's "heijōshin" or "mind of equanimity."

The Plan also draws on teachings from the traditional lay-oriented manual, the *Shushōgi*.[4] Mimicking the traditional five-line verse (*gokun*) used by monasteries before a meal, the sect advocates the following verses for reflecting on the environment:

> (*Green Plan gokun*):
> Save the Earth! Five Verses to Living the Green Plan
> in Everyday Life
> 1] Let's Protect the Green Earth. The Great Earth Is the
>   Home of All Life.
> 2] Let's Use Water Sparingly. Water Is the Source for All Life.
> 3] Let's Limit Our Use of Heat. Heat Is What Propels All
>   Life.
> 4] Let's Maintain Clean Air. Clean Air Is the Open Space for
>   All Life.
> 5] Let's Live in Harmony with Nature. Nature Is the Buddha
>   in Form.[5]

The pragmatic character of these verses reflects a general tendency of the Green Plan to focus on everyday acts at the individual or temple level, rather than doctrinal justification for its advocacy of green thinking. Green Plan pamphlets for sect households and temples include items such as checklists to monitor the use of television and other electrical appliances (meet a sect-wide goal of reducing energy use by 1%), information on purchasing "eco-products," warnings on genetically modified foods,[6] and detailed guides on how to properly separate recyclables from general garbage. As a sign of the times, the sect manufactured and distributed to sect households over 1,500,000 cell phone straps with the slogan "Sōto Zen Buddhism, Green is Life."[7]

To chart progress on these initiatives, the sect established a fund, the Sōtōshū Green Plan Kikin, to raise money for nonprofit environmental groups in Japan. To measure carbon emissions output, the sect headquarters distributed a chart to calculate the amount of CO_2 each household produces per year. For each activity such as washing dishes, car idling, bath use, and aluminum can recycling, the member household is encouraged to calculate the amount of CO_2 reduced and to donate the equivalent savings to the fund (e.g. 10.2 kg of CO_2 reduced is equal to 2,010 yen). Based on the Buddhist teachings of using less (*chisoku*) and donating (*fuse*), the fund has been a way to link Buddhist practice, environmental awareness and action, and fundraising. By focusing on carbon emissions reductions, the Sōtō Zen Green Plan supports the goals of the Kyoto Protocol, addressing consumption concerns in a global warming context.

Individual temples have also been sites of Buddhist environmental practice. At a 1997 Green Plan symposium attended by 1,600 people in Ōmiya City (Saitama Prefecture), one participant stated that, "The temple should be a 'kakekomidera' for environmental problems."[8] From the medieval period, a "kakekomidera" ("a temple to run away to") was a temple where women seeking a refuge from their husbands ran away to seek a divorce. However powerful the husband might have been in the secular world, the temple served as a sanctuary for desperate women seeking refuge. The speaker at the symposium might have meant that the Buddhist temple was the last refuge for the environment in a time of crisis.

Whether it be the establishment of a green corridor and biotope at Kōzen'in Temple (Kawaguchi City, Saitama Prefecture), collaboration with forest ecologists in the large-scale reforestation campaign at the head temple Sōjiji (Yokohama City) as part of the "Sennen no mori" (the Thousand-Year Forest), or the installation of a nationwide acid rain monitoring system at 650 Sōtō Zen temples, the Buddhist temple as a site for environmental practice has become increasingly accepted.[9] As the abbot of Kōzen'in Temple, Hayafune Genpō, has suggested, "A temple is not only a sanctuary for future human life, but for all living beings."[10]

In the case of Sōtō Zen, while individual households and temples have made efforts to implement the Green Plan, probably the most active group in promoting the campaign has been what are called Fujinkai (women's associations) that are organized at most temples and in various districts across Japan. Over a hundred districts have been involved in "street campaigns" promoting the Green Plan in front of schools and shopping areas, riverside trash clean-ups, promoting the use of kenaf[11] and other eco-friendly products for housewives, and tree-planting projects.[12]

JAPANESE ENGAGED BUDDHISM AND THE SEARCH FOR AN ALTERNATIVE PARADIGM: THE CASE OF JUKŌIN TEMPLE

In contrast to sect-wide activities of established Buddhist organizations, a number of individual priests and their temples have developed alternatives outside the sectarian establishment and the mainstream economic system. A good example is Ōkōchi Hideto, a Jōdo sect priest, a leading figure in the Japanese "engaged Buddhism" movement. As abbot of Jukōin Temple, founded in 1617 and with a current parish membership of 250 families, he could easily have settled for the life of a typical parish priest performing funerary rites and organizing annual services around the temple calendar.[13] But over the years, he has served in all kinds of social and environmental justice movements including the JVC (Japan Volunteer Center), Kokusai Kodomodomo Kenri Center (JICRC, a children's rights group), and ARYUS (Bukkyō Kokusai Network), and has authored a number of books on small-scale development. Though some of the groups are Buddhist-inspired, many are secular, nongovernmental organizations working on social welfare issues in Japan and around the world.

The key to Ōkōchi's engaged Buddhism is his interpretation of the Buddhist teaching of "suffering." Over the years, he has made numerous trips to Southeast Asia, the Middle East, and Africa. From the effects of warfare in Rwanda and Palestine to genocide in Cambodia, coming into contact with the palpable suffering of people encouraged Ōkōchi to reflect on the relative comfort of Japanese Buddhists. For him, Buddhism is based on feeling the teaching of suffering not as an abstract concept, but as something in one's guts. In war-torn countries and poverty-stricken regions, Ōkōchi experienced the type of conditions that inspired Hōnen, founder of the Jōdo sect, to develop a Buddhist approach to suffering for the common people. Hōnen was responding to the severe socioeconomic conditions of medieval Japan, which left many people starving and impoverished.

Working with suffering, Ōkōchi draws on Buddhist teachings such as the Four Noble Truths for inspiration. In an essay explaining his involvement with a local environmental group, he states:

When Shakyamuni Buddha (Siddhartha Gautama) gained enlightenment, his first teaching was the Four Noble Truths, that is, first, get a solid grasp of suffering (the problem), second, ascertain its causes and structure, third, form an image of the world to be aimed for, and fourth, act according to correct practices. Then, one gains a sense of the meaning of life in modern society as a citizen with responsibilities in the irreversible course of time. The suffering of the southern peoples and nature, from which we derive support for our lives even as we exploit it, has caused the Edogawa Citizens' Network for Thinking about Global Warming to think, and therefore we have achieved concrete results. The problem is structural in nature, so by changing the system and creating measures for improvement, we achieve results.[14]

Ōkōchi interprets suffering as existing not only on a personal level, but at a deep structural level in the modern socioeconomic system. This brings him in line with the analysis of many engaged Buddhists such as Sulak Sivaraksa or A. T. Ariyaratne. For Ōkōchi, Buddhism is not simply a religion for transforming oneself, but a religion for transforming society. "The 'awakening' sought by the Buddha was an awakening to the entire universe. The Buddha is someone who lives responsibly based on this self-awareness of the universe, that is, as a 'citizen' of the world."[15]

Ōkōchi combines this emphasis on a "return to the original teachings of the Buddha" with Pure Land Buddhist rhetoric about making *this* world the Pure Land. Many in the Jōdo and Jōdo Shin traditions interpret Amida's Pure Land to be a heavenly land where believers transfer after death. In contrast, Ōkōchi believes that heavens and hells are manifest in this world and that this world is itself the locus for the development of the Pure Land. This notion is, of course, not original, but it is nevertheless a minority tradition within the Pure Land sects. Another well-known advocate of this Pure Land approach is Keisuke Aoki, Jōdo Shin priest and abbot of a temple in Himeji. Aoki was one of the first Buddhist priests to get involved in environmental issues.[16] He has long advocated a Pure Land Buddhist theology in which hell (*jigoku*) can be found in the human mind and in a society based on competition and oppression, while the Pure Land (*jōdo*) can be found where the interconnectedness of life is celebrated and filled with infinite light (muryō kōmyō do). In his 1997 book, Edo to kokoro: Kankyō hakai kara jōdo e (The Impure Land and One's Mind: From Environmental Destruction to the Creation of a Pure Land), he emphasizes human responsibility in "the destruction of the earth, which is the creation of hell."[17] Well known locally for protecting the sea from overdevelopment, he has energetically campaigned for many years against oil refineries and other industrial production that caused the "red-lake phenomenon" in Harima Bay, ruining the local fishing industry. According to his theology, this hell, which he describes more globally as the "shadow of a society centered on money," can be replaced by an "ecology of the Pure Land," where the Buddha, enlightenment, infinite light, and compassion permeate this world.[18]

In his environmental work, Ōkōchi linked this concept of building a Pure Land on Earth with his critique of existing social structures. As an increasing number of Japanese became aware of global warming issues through the 1997 Kyoto conference (officially, the Third Session of the Conference of the Parties to the UN Framework Convention on Climate Change, or COP3), Ōkōchi was mobilizing citizens in his locality in Tokyo. He helped establish the Edogawa Citizens' Network for Thinking about Global Warming (an offshoot of an earlier organization, Group KIKI), which was dedicated to alternatives to nuclear power, garbage recycling, and other energy and waste issues. After a study tour to Sarawak, Malaysia, to document the destruction of the rain forest by Japanese multinationals, the group successfully pressured the local council to not use wood from tropical rain forests. In addition to small projects such as collecting aluminum cans, the Citizens' Network raised funds for CFC-recovery equipment to donate to car demolition businesses in their local Edogawa Ward, a district responsible for 60% of CFC emissions in the twenty-three wards of Tokyo.

By far their most ambitious project was to establish an alternative energy power plant in the ward to end their neighborhood's dependence on Japanese fossil fuel and nuclear energy. In 1999, the Edogawa People's Power Plant No. 1 was constructed as a citizens' effort to withdraw from the energy companies and the financial institutions that funded them, as well as further environmentally destructive investments. The power plant was located on the roof of Jukōin Temple.

The temple name, consisting of the Chinese characters Ju (life) and Kō (light), reflected the Jōdo tradition's teachings that existence is the unlimited life and light of the Buddha. In his rationale for the power plant project, Ōkōchi proclaimed, "Human life as well as all life existing in nature is mutually interlinked and dependent on each other. This Buddhist concept aims at creating a global society of coexistence and co-prosperity. Jukōin, in solidarity not only with Buddhists but also with other citizens, NGOs, and various other groups, is dedicated to ecological development and human rights issues."[19] This dedication meant that the four-hundred-year-old temple faced a radical rebuilding in terms of temple architecture. After obtaining the understanding of his parishioners, the temple was completely modernized using eco-friendly concrete and wood building materials. The traditional roof tiles were replaced with two sets of fifteen large solar panels that would generate 6,000 kw/hour. This was enough to receive official recognition from the local government as the first of several planned People's Power Plants in Edogawa Ward.

The funding for this project—six million yen—came from local environmental groups, individual donors, and loans from an independent bank that the group established, the Mirai (or Future) Bank. Ōkōchi adapted a temple fundraising strategy from the premodern period when donors bought roof tiles for a new temple's construction over and above the actual cost. He asked locals to buy solar panels as a gift to the temple power plant. The "taiyō kawara" or "sun tiles" were sold at Yen 5,000 per panel and the funds deposited in the new bank.

The model for the Mirai Bank was based on medieval and early modern Buddhist mutual aid societies (kō) with the goal of supporting environmental sustainability. Instead of giving their hard-earned money to the big national banks (which often use people's savings for environmentally destructive projects), the Edogawa citizens chose to invest in building and protecting the future (mirai). Inspired by microcredit banking in Third World countries, Mirai Bank not only criticized the existing capitalist system, but offered an alternative economic model for a new kind of sustainable society in Japan. In addition to funding the power plant, the bank embarked on a consumer campaign to encourage the purchase of eco-products. Because 60% of energy in Japanese households is consumed by refrigerators, air conditioners, and lights, the bank decided to focus on environmentally friendly refrigerators. Understanding that average families cannot take up new alternatives if they need to sacrifice comfort or pay exorbitant fees, the bank provided interest-free loans to buy environmentally friendly refrigerators. These refrigerators could reduce energy consumption by 400 kw/hr per year (equivalent to Yen 9,000), thus a bank loan of Yen 50,000 could be paid off in 5 years.[20]

The solar power plant not only generated alternative energy, but it also generated new, small-scale economics. Excess energy beyond the temple's energy needs was sold to Tokyo Electric Power Company at Yen 22/kWh with the income plowed back into paying off the initial investment. The Edogawa Citizens' Network for Thinking about Global Warming decided to encourage local citizens to "buy" this excess energy at a premium (using the green energy standard in Germany of Yen 55/kWh) with Green Power Certificates. By selling 200 certificates for Yen 1,000/30kWh, the power plant could return its initial investment in just nine years. To emphasize the involvement of the local community and to build a more mutually dependent society, each Green Power investor also receives Edogawatt bills, a local currency the size of a calling card that can be used to pay for babysitting, translation, and other services "deepening interpersonal relationships and trust."[21] Since solar energy has the lowest maintenance costs associated with energy production (almost zero), the idea is that each People's Power Plant can be profitable within a decade, generating clean, zero-emissions energy, and building a more intimate society at a time when modern Japanese society has grown increasingly impersonal. As the power plant enters the consciousness of the local community and attracts media attention, the temple has continued efforts to link grassroots activism with community development. On the third-year anniversary of the plant in October 2002, the temple organized a community-wide workshop on how to implement a low-energy, low-consumption lifestyle.

Ōkōchi's approach has been very practical and reflects his Jōdo sect background in his belief that ordinary Japanese citizens can participate in this type of "engaged Buddhism" without engaging in asceticism or sacrificing comfort. His ideal of "engaged citizenship" or the spirit of volunteerism in society is active social reform:

> A volunteer, according to Jukōin thinking, is not a person who provides his/her cheap labor to fill in cracks left by the administration, or a person looking for his/her own satisfaction. Volunteers look for the true nature of the problems and

promote movements oriented toward social reforms. . . . They should take the side of the weaker (the people) and not the strong side of the system. They begin by experiencing problems of suffering. Then, they move to reflect on the structures and the mechanisms concerning those issues. . . . Those volunteers rich in work experiences with NGOs show us the face of the Buddha and famous Buddhist saints.[22]

Thus, Ōkōchi aligns himself with ordinary citizens, disdaining what some might consider elitist asceticism. His approach differs from the Sōtō Zen establishment Buddhism because it is based in a critique of the current sociopolitical and capitalist system. With much of mainstream Buddhism aligned politically with the right and big business, Ōkōchi's leftist rhetoric of siding with the poor and oppressed offers an important, but marginal, voice in the contemporary Japanese Buddhist landscape.

CONSERVATIVE JAPANESE BUDDHIST ENVIRONMENTALISM IN LOCAL AND GLOBAL CONTEXTS

In contrast to the type of progressive politics of Ōkōchi, Japanese Buddhist environmentalism is by and large conservative. While it is undoubtedly true that socially engaged Buddhism is generally characterized by forms of progressive politics, many Japanese Buddhists involved with environmental issues come out of a strain of conservatism that celebrates local tradition and involves Japanese nationalism on the international stage.

A good example of an environmentalism based on the rhetoric of "conservation" is that of Shinchō Tanaka, the Shingon sect abbot of Shimyōin Temple in Kyoto. Born in 1940, Tanaka became the abbot of the ancient Shimyōin Temple in 1967 after training at the Shingon headquarters temple of Kōyasan. Located in the Kumogahata district of Kyoto at the very source of the Kamo River, which runs through the old capital, Shimyōin Temple has served as the protector of this important watershed since the medieval period. Taking pride in the temple's role of the centuries, the temple abbot has viewed it as a calling to help maintain the cleanliness of the water source and protect a site that in times past was considered a sacred zone in which only the initiated and purified mountain ascetics could enter. Indeed, over the years, Tanaka himself notes that many

Kyotoites would say that "the abbot of Shimyōin is picky" because of his strict rules about banning visitors from eating and drinking in or bringing bags of any kind into the temple area. He says he did this to correct the bad manners of visitors and tourists, whose numbers probably went down because of the rules, to keep the watershed pure and free of trash, as "the river is born from the mountain."[23]

The environmental activism of this priest began in the spring of 1988 when a proposal was made to build a major dam on the Kamo River between Kamigamo (the Lower Kamo) Shrine and Shimyōin Temple. Knowing that both the river that defined the character of Kyoto and the mountain on which his temple stood would be destroyed, he became determined to fight the dam project. It was a noble thought, but in the postwar history of dam building in Japan, once a decision to build a dam was made, even with protests and petitions, to this point not a single project had been halted.[24] In this seemingly impossible task, Tanaka put his faith in the protective deity of Shimyōin Temple, Fudō Myōō (the Immovable One), a deity in the esoteric Buddhist pantheon. Drawing on the esoteric Buddhist tradition's emphasis on the nonduality of body and mind, form and formlessness, Tanaka claims that "unlike other sects which focus on the other world, esoteric Buddhism focuses on this world," which is composed of the six elements (earth, water, fire, wind, space, and mind) that manifest the enduring truth of Dainichi Nyorai (the cosmic Buddha, Mahāvairocana).[25] With esoteric Buddhism as his philosophical ground and Fudō Myōō as his protective deity, Tanaka decided that "the anti-dam movement would start from our mountain temple."[26]

In his 1992 book, *Damu to oshō: Tekkaisareta Kamogawa damu* (The Dam and the Buddhist Priest: The Abandonment of the Project to Construct the Kamo River Dam), Tanaka chronicles the meetings and development of the anti-dam movement which began as a small group in January 1989, holding its first meeting at the temple. The group, with Tanaka as its spokesperson, began attracting supporters among civic groups, artists, and scholars, raising enough money to initially hire a consultant company to assess the potential for environmental damage. Raising its profile through such events as sponsoring anti-dam classical music concerts in the mountain temple or large demonstrations in Kyoto City, the movement drew the attention of local, national (including the NHK), and even international media (an August 16, 1989, article on the movement appeared in the *Los Angeles Times*). By June 1989, the movement had joined forces with ten other groups concerned with protecting Kyoto's water and greenery and began to exert political pressure on the governor and assembly. With opposition to the dam across the political spectrum, the campaign to "conserve" traditional Kyoto (its temples, the Kamo River, and greenery) managed to stop the project and become the first of several major campaigns to block the damming of Japanese rivers.

The appeal to tradition and conserving the old ways proved effective for this local campaign, which needed the support of conservative politicians. Conservatism of another strain marks the Buddhist environmentalism of Seiei Tohyama. Born in 1906 into a Jōdo Shinshū temple, Daishōji (Fuji Yoshida City, Yamanashi Prefecture), Tohyama and his son, Masao, are well known around the world among environmentalists working on desertification.

The Tohyamas trained as agriculturalists focusing on recovering desert regions for productive agriculture. Seiei began his work in Japan with the Tottori Sand Dunes Project, experimenting with various trees and plants to make desert conditions blossom. With nearly sixty thousand square kilometers transformed into desert every year, the Tohyamas believe that there is an "important link between greening of the world's deserts and world peace" given the increasing number of global conflicts over water.[27] Going global with their techniques, Tohyama looked at the massive desertification in China and decided to focus his efforts there. In 1979, he joined the Western China Scientific Inquiry Tour for an inspection of Chinese deserts. Describing why he focused his attention not on Japan, but on China, he states:

> Sino-Japanese relations are said to go back two thousand years. In ages past the Japanese were avid students of Chinese culture. The Chinese priest Jianzhen (688–763) took a set of Buddhist precepts to Japan, living out the rest of his days in Nara. Even during the centuries of Japan's self-imposed isolation from the rest of the world, its government made special efforts to acquire classical Chinese texts. Then there were the tragic years of the Sino-Japanese War of 1937–45. China received nothing in reparation for Japan's invasion. As a Japanese and a devout Buddhist (born and raised in a Pure Land sect temple), I feel

deeply aware of Japan's debts to China. My efforts to contribute to the development of China's deserts is just a small gesture
of gratitude, one person's endeavor to make amends.[28]

Here we can see the Buddhist motivations to Tohyama's work. Several
years later, with the support from China-Japan Friendship Association,
Academy of Sciences of China, and the Chinese government, Tohyama
began his project of greening the world's deserts at the Shapotou Experimental Station in the Tengger Desert using kudzu (the fastest growing
vine in Asia) to hold the ground together.[29] Not knowing if the techniques
he developed in Japan would work in China, he began the project "with
a simple purification rite, scattering grains of rice that had been part of an
offering to the image of Jianzhen at Yakushiji temple in Nara, Japan. We
prayed that the spirit of Jianzhen, the virtuous eighth-century Chinese
high priest, would bless the model vineyard at Shapotou."[30]

The Shapotou project was a great success, and by 1986 he was invited
to begin the Lanzhou Desert Research Facility. This project required
massive numbers of kudzu seeds, which only matured in the fall when a
flat pod would contain two or three seeds. Thus, he approached Nikkyō
Niwano, the founder of the lay Buddhist organization Risshō Kōsei-kai,
who nostalgically remembered his mother weaving kudzu cloth, and who
respected Tohyama's project.[31] Mobilizing the Risshō Kōsei-kai young
people's groups in autumn 1986, by February 1987, two hundred thousand Risshō Kōsei-kai members collected 550 kilograms of kudzu seeds
for the project. This project to green the desert along the Yellow River was
a major success and attracted great media attention. Tohyama reflects, "my
kudzu idea and our meeting [with Niwano] might have been part of the
Buddha's plan."[32]

These beginnings led to Tohyama's volunteers planting over a million
poplars (to promote a local Chinese species) and willows in the Mu Us
Desert in Inner Mongolia and over 2.4 million poplars in the Kubuqi
Desert (also in Inner Mongolia) during the 1990s. The hard work of volunteers and a ten million yen donation from Risshō Kōsei-kai Fund for
Peace helped to actualize these projects. Success brought with it increased
media attention and Tohyama began to talk of these greening projects
in terms of the slogan, "Sekai no sabaku ni Amida no mori o tsukurō"
(Let's Create Forests of Amida Buddha in the World's Deserts). As a Jōdo

Shinshū Buddhist, he believed that these forests could serve as manifestations of Amida Buddha's vow to save sentient beings in all ten directions (*jippō shujō*). Inspired by a Jōdo Shinshū temple, Kyōsenji (Hiroshima Prefecture), which had come up with the term "Amida no mori" (Forests of Amida Buddha), Tohyama drew on the tradition discussed above of Pure Land Buddhists' attempting to "build the Pure Land" on Earth.[33] The initial staff of seven volunteers developed into a large movement which raised over fifty-two million yen during a fundraising campaign between September 1997 and May 2000 (used to buy 440,000 poplar trees). The effort, which began in China as an attempt to repay China for transmitting Buddhism to Japan as well as for Japan's aggression during World War II, has gone global: Tohyama's group has become involved in "greening the desert" projects in Iran, Mexico, and Egypt.

Although the Tohyama project is couched in terms of creating "world peace" through these environmental efforts, we should also note that Tohyama is an ardent nationalist who joined the Japanese military in 1928 believing in the East Asia Co-Prosperity Sphere (in which he has said he still believes, because Ōtani Kōzui, the leader of the Jōdo Shinshū Honganji tradition, promoted it during the war). He continues to support the notion of the twenty-first century as an "Asian century" led by Japan, and has upset some observers with his denial of the Nanking massacre and his advocacy of the Yasukuni Shrine (in which are enshrined the spirits of the Japanese war dead, including a number of war criminals).[34]

Without delving into the details of the politics of the Tohyama case, what is of interest here is the preponderance of politically conservative Buddhist environmentalists. While engaged Buddhism, particularly in the West, tends to draw from the progressive end of the political spectrum (as with convert Buddhists in general), Japanese engaged Buddhism is far more complex. The leading Buddhist economist in the postwar period, Shinichi Inoue, is another case in point.[35] Although his work on developing "a Buddhist economics to save the earth"—the title of one of his books—can be understood as part of a Schumachian tradition of a "small is beautiful" economics and a critique of American economics, Inoue was a well-known nationalist and former member of the kamikaze corps during World War II. As a leading banker (Bank of Japan and Miyazaki Bank) and board member of several major lay Buddhist organizations, he had deep connections to powerful members of the conservative Liberal

Democratic Party (he was a cousin of former Prime Minister and Finance Minister Miyazawa). His model for a uniquely Japanese form of capitalism—to be a counterbalance to what he thought was an immoral American model (he had respect for the German model and Tony Blair's British model)—was an attempt to recast capitalism in a kinder, gentler Japanese mode based on the morality of Buddhism. Rather than developing a new theory of economics, Inoue was a firm believer in capitalism and a critic of leftist movements like labor unions. Inoue and Tohyama both have had extensive influence in the Japanese political world through either the media or personal connections. They represent an important strand of Buddhist conservationism that is truly conservative.

CONCLUSION

To conclude, let me raise the case of Rinnōji Temple (a Sōtō Zen temple in Sendai City, Miyagi Prefecture), whose abbot has been active in volunteer efforts such as a Thai AIDS hospice and earthquake relief for victims in Turkey and Taiwan, setting an example with its recycling and environmental education programs.[36] From the idea that the Buddhist spirit of attention to small things and "not wasting" starts at home, the temple looked to its own practices leading to waste and overuse of natural resources.

As a typical, though large, parish temple, the primary activity of the temple was not Zen meditation but the performance of funerary and memorial services for its parishioners. These services take place at death and in subsequent intervals over a period of thirty-three years. In addition, parishioners would visit the temple, with flowers and other offerings for the deceased, during the annual summer ancestral festival of Obon. At this season, when the spirits of the deceased are thought to return to the temple graveyard or to the memorial tablet (ihai) normally kept in the family altar (butsudan), the abbot noticed that an enormous number of flowers were being donated at the temple graveyard—nearly five thousand flower bundles during the Obon season alone—and then were simply discarded into the landfill. The temple conceived of a plan to take these flowers and develop a high quality composting system, the fertilizer from which would be donated to local farmers. By 2000, the temple had expanded this recycling project to include the composting of leftover temple food. They also recycled into charcoal from the bamboo offering stands used at gravesites. Once every two months and more frequently during the Obon season, the monks of the temple undertake the process of making organic fertilizer for the farmers.

Environmental education has also become a big part of the temple's activities since 2001. Each year the monks offer a presentation on recycling to the local middle school students using the temple recycling system as a model. In 2003, the temple produced a home video for its parishioners entitled *Kankyō no tame ni* (For the Sake of the Environment) that gave instructions on home composting and how to "not waste" water used to clean rice. The video targets housewives, who are most often responsible for cooking rice and monitoring recycling at home. By working with housewives and young teens, the temple reinforced the message that environmental education must begin early and at home.

The Rinnōji example illustrates antiwaste activism that functions within the traditional boundaries of what some have termed "funerary Buddhism based on the parish system."[37] This system, which characterizes mainstream Buddhism in contemporary Japan, tends to emphasize the continuity of tradition and customary/formalistic relationship between parishioners. The fees paid for funerary and memorial services constitute the vast majority of a temple's income. For the most part, any Buddhist consumer or environmental activities in Japan have had to operate within this system, which has been the mainstay of Japanese Buddhism since the beginning of the Tokugawa period (1600–1868). Thus, rather than an environmentalism that would be a radical departure from social and political norms, the Buddhist institution in Japan represents a conservative bastion from which it is not easy to move forward on environmental issues. For example, several years ago, the Japanese Sōtō Zen environmental division produced a CD of songs encouraging sect members to avoid disposable chopsticks. The message was to carry around "my chopsticks (*mai ohashi*)" as a way to save forests. Upset by this anticonsumerist message, the national chopstick manufacturers' association pressured sect headquarters to block the CD release. The project came to a halt. In Japan, when competing interests of labor/industry and environment come to a head, Buddhist organizations almost always side with industry. Institutional Buddhism in Japan not only tends to support the establishment, but it is perhaps the most conservative pillar in contemporary Japanese society. The result has been that despite the exception of the Sōtō Zen

Green Plan, most Buddhist environmentalism in Japan has had to remain small-scale, localized, conservative, and organized primarily on the initiative of an individual or (at times) at the level of an organization like the Buddhist women's association.

At the same time, whether it be empowering consumers through temple education (Rinnōji), creating energy off the grid through solar roof panels (Jukōin), or making use of sect-wide organizations to promote "green Buddhism" (the Sōtō Zen Green Plan), Japanese Buddhists are beginning to make structural changes that directly impact the environment. Precisely because establishment Buddhism is a pillar of mainstream Japanese society, even small changes at the over one hundred thousand temples have the potential to make dramatic changes not only at local temples, but in the environmental patterns of the millions of lay Buddhist members of those temples. In this way, a "conservative conservationism" seems to be one model for a hypercapitalist Japan and generally conservative Buddhist establishment.

NOTES

1   Much of the discussion of the Gyōzenji Temple case comes from an interview with its abbot, Shunno Watanabe (Gyōzenji Temple, Tokyo, June 26, 2003).

2   The discussion of the Senryūji Temple case comes from an interview with its abbot, Shōei Sugawara (Senryūji Temple, Komae, August 8, 2003). Today, the maintenance of the nature preserve is jointly conducted by Komae City and a volunteer citizens' group.

3   The pamphlet, Sōtōshū Shūmuchō, ed., *"Jinken, heiwa, kankyō 'Green Plan'" no susume* (Tokyo: Sōtōshū shūmuchō, 1996), highlights Dōgen's appreciation of nature.

4   See Sōtōshū Shūmuchō, ed., *Green Plan: Kōdō no tame no Q&A* (Tokyo: Sōtōshū shūmuchō, 1998), Questions 3, 4, 6–14, 30.

5   These verses can be found on most pamphlets, including Sōtōshū Shūmuchō, ed., *Chikyū o sukue!: Seikatsu ni ikasu Green Plan gokun* (Tokyo: Sōtōshū shūmuchō, n.d.).

6   See Kyara, "Idenshi kumikae shokuhin no hyōji gimu settei," *Kyara* 44 (2001): 29–33.

7   See Sōtōshū Shūmuchō, ed., *Green Plan: Kōdō no tame no Q&A* (Tokyo: Sōtōshū shūmuchō, 1998), Questions 15–30.

8   See Hayafune Genpō, "Biotopu sōsei: Sōtōshū 'Green Plan' no jissen rei to shite," *Komazawa daigaku bungakubu kenkyū kiyō* 58 (2000): 18.

9   The figures on the cell phone straps and the temples involved in the acid rain monitoring project come from an interview with Rev. Shungen Itō of the Green Plan section at the Sōtō Zen Headquarters, Tokyo (July 28, 2003). The acid rain project measures the average ph. level of the rain in nine regions of Japan as a basis for future work on bettering water quality; see Kyara, "Chikyū kankyō o mamoru zen Sōtōshū no undō: Green Plan," *Kyara* 37 (1998): 26–27.

10 See Hayafune Genpō, "Biotōpu sōsei: Sōtōshū 'Green Plan' no jissen rei to shite," *Komazawa daigaku bungakubu kenkyū kiyō* 58 (2000): 17. The biotope at Kōzen'in, "Kōzen'in Furusato no mori" (the Kōzen'in Temple Hometown Forest), is an experiment to maintain a mixed species forested area on temple grounds, which include not only foxes and owls, but reminders of the Buddhist character of the project (stone Buddha and bodhisattva statues and a monument memorializing the life of plants and trees [a "sōmoku kuyōtō"]). The temple has also collaborated with ecologists to maintain the ecological balance of the two ponds in the forested area: the Benten Ike (the Pond of Benten) and Tombo Ike (Dragonfly Pond).

The abbot's inspiration for maintaining a pond where dragonflies and butterflies can flourish came from the abbot of the Jōdo sect temple, Tokushōji (Ashigara City, Tochigi Prefecture), who was the head of the Association Against the Use of Aerial Pesticide Spraying to Prevent the Outbreak of Insects that Eat Ashigara's Pine Trees, a local environmental group.

11 [Ed. A fibrous plant in the Hibiscus family, similar to jute. The fiber can be used in a variety of applications, including paper, engineered wood, cloth, insulation, as well as rope and twine. The seeds also produce an edible vegetable oil high in antioxidants. Kenaf produces a higher grade of paper than does tree fiber, and being lighter in color requires less bleaching. Kenaf can produce seven to eleven tons of usable fiber per acre per year, while tree forests only produce 1.5 to 3.5 tons of usable fiber per acre per year.]

12 For the role of the women's associations in the Green Plan, see Kyara, "Green Plan jicchi hōkoku," *Kyara* 39 (1999): 20–21; "Shuzai, Green Plan katsudō," *Kyara* 40 (2000): 31–39; "Green Plan: Campaign jicchi hōkoku," *Kyara* 43 (2001): 29–33. The riverside cleanup campaigns in Shizuoka Prefecture were organized by the women's association of Chōrenji Temple. Nomadera Temple in Ehime Prefecture also started a "recycle shop" selling second-hand products. Honkōji Temple in Saga Prefecture sponsored workshops on how to use kenaf products for the kitchen and shopping bags.

13 The biographical data on Ōkōchi comes from an article he wrote, "NGO to jiin no tachiba kara," *Bukkyō Times*, May 14, 1998, as well as from interviews I conducted with him in July and August 2003 at Jukōin Temple.

14 See the second page of "The Citizen's Strategy for Creating a New World," http://oa145309.awmi2.jp/page-262.html. [Ed. URL no longer in service. Accessed October 24, 2009.]

15 Ibid.

16 On Aoki's work protecting the Harima Bay, see his *Edo to kokoro: Kankyō hakai kara jōdo e* (Tokyo: Fujiwara shobō, 1997), 59, 73.

17 This can be found as a subsection of chapter 2 of his book.

18 See Aoki, *Edo to kokoro*, 146, 229.

19 See the first page of http://oa145309.awmi2.jp/page-261.html. [Ed. URL no longer in service. Accessed October 24, 2009.]

20 Many of the details on the solar panel power plant project can be found in Ōkōchi Hideto, "Shimin ga tsukuru taiyōkō hatsudensho: Shiminritsu Edogawa daiichi hatsudensho, tada ima kensetsuchū," *Shigen kankyō taisaku* 35, no. 3 (1999): 44–46.

21 See the third page of "The Citizen's Strategy for Creating a New World," http://oa145309.awmi2.jp/page-262.html. [Ed. URL no longer in service. Accessed October 24, 2009.]

22 See the second page of http://0a145309.awmi2.jp/page-261.html. [Ed. URL no longer in service. Accessed October 24, 2009.]

23 See Tanaka Shinchō, *Damu to oshō: Tekkaisareta Kamogawa damu* (Tokyo: Hokuto shuppan, 1992), 21–22.

24 Ibid., 38.

25 Ibid., 152.

26 Ibid., 38.

27 Tohyama Seiei and Masao Tohyama, *Greening the Desert: Techniques and Achievements of Two Japanese Agriculturalists* (Tokyo: Kōsei Publishing, 1995), 14.

28 Ibid., 121.

29 Kudzu root is a tuber (1 meter long, 20 centimeters thick) used for viticulture.

30 Seiei and Tohyama, *Greening the Desert*, 144.

31 Ibid., 121.

32 Ibid., 145.

33 Tohyama Seiei, "21 seiki wa sabaku no jidai: Ajia wa hitotsu, sekai wa heiwa," http://www3.justnet.ne.jp/~tanahara/mourio3.html. [Ed. URL no longer in service. Accessed October 24, 2009.]

34 Ibid.

35 For Inoue's work in English, see his *Putting Buddhism to Work: A New Theory of Economics and Business Management,* trans. Duncan Williams (Tokyo: Kodansha International, 1997), and "A New Economics to Save the Earth: A Buddhist Perspective," *Journal of Japanese Trade and Industry* 18, no. 2 (March–April 1999): 20–25; reprinted in *Mindfulness in the Marketplace: Compassionate Responses to Consumerism,* ed. Allan Hunt Badiner, trans. Duncan Williams (Berkeley: Parallax Press, 2002), 49–58.

36 On the Rinnōji case, see the fifteen-minute video *Kankyō wo tawe ni* (Sendai: Rinnōji, 2003) and their website, http://www.rinno-ji.or.jp.

37 See Tamamuro Taijō's classic work on "sōshiki bukkyō" or "funerary Buddhism," *Sōshiki bukkyō* (Tokyo: Daihōrinkaku, 1963).

How Much Is Enough?
Buddhist Perspectives on Consumerism[1]

■ ■ ■

Stephanie Kaza

INTRODUCTION

Modern industrial nations have unleashed on the world a frenzy of product manufacturing, resource exploitation, and consumer shopping, which is having unprecedented impact on local cultures and ecosystems. Fast food, biotechnology, sweatshop clothing, and global trade in oil are all taking their toll on human, plant, and animal communities around the world. Advertising permeates almost every facet of modern urban life. It appears the ethic of greed is fast overtaking any other morally based ethics that might serve the sustainability of the planet.

Choosing what and how much to consume can be informed by ethical guidelines, such as those promoted by environmentalists and consumer advocates. Religions have also held a traditional role in critiquing materialism on moral grounds. As capitalist values penetrate more and more regions of the globe, there is a fresh call for ethical inquiry and religious reflection on the impacts of these values.[2] To what degree are capitalist values harmful to human health, spiritual development, or the environment? Christian, Quaker, and Jewish groups have taken up issues of consumerism related to holiday shopping, global climate change, and spiritual materialism. Do Buddhists have anything to add to this discussion? As a new religion in the West with growing popularity, I believe Buddhism offers a distinctive critique with liberating methods that may be useful in challenging the Western habits of overconsumption.

The primary goal of Buddhist practice, as the Buddha taught, is to reduce suffering. In his classic teaching of the Four Noble Truths, the Buddha pointed to desire as the source of suffering or dissatisfaction. In modern globalized society, desire is central to economic function: desire for goods, desire for energy, desire for entertainment, desire for "a better life." Over a matter of a few decades, the economy of manufacture has been replaced by an economy of desire whose object is arousal, manipulation, and the creation of human want to serve profit-making ends. At its 1997 international meeting in Japan, the Buddhist Think Sangha defined consumerism as:

> the dominant culture of a modernizing invasive industrialism which stimulates—yet can never satisfy—the urge for a strong sense of self to overlay the angst and sense of lack in the human condition. As a result, goods, services, and experiences are consumed beyond any reasonable need. This undermines the ecosystem, the quality of life and particularly traditional cultures and communities and the possibility of spiritual liberation.[3]

Reducing suffering in today's world calls for examining both the proliferation of desire and its ecological and social impacts. This essay first provides background on the scope of global consumption, asking: how much do we consume and who is most responsible for the impacts of consumerism? Some of the environmental, cultural, and psychological impacts of consumerism, as well as the traditional critiques of consumerism, are then reviewed. Subsequently, three Buddhist critiques will be explicated. In closing, liberative methods that lead to the opposite of suffering—a sense of well-being and contentment—will be offered. This paper is part of a much larger political and economic critique of the dominant paradigm of materialism and capitalism that is ravaging the Earth's organic systems to the point of severe instability. As Buddhism evolves in the context of North American consumerism, I believe it has tremendous intellectual and practical gifts for people concerned with these problems.

The Scope and Impact of Consumption

How much do people in northern industrialized countries consume? Here are some indicator figures: Americans consume their average body weight (120 pounds) *every day* in materials extracted and processed from farms, mines, rangelands, and forests.[4] In the United States, the number of shopping malls (close to 35,000) eclipsed the number of high schools in 1987. The Disneyland in Japan attracts as many people as the Vatican or Mecca.[5] Since 1950, Americans have used up more resources than everyone who ever lived on Earth before then. In an average lifetime, each American consumes a reservoir of water (43 million gallons, including personal, industrial, and agricultural uses) and a small tanker full of oil (2,500 barrels). The 102 million households of the United States currently contain and consume more stuff than all other households throughout history put together. Americans spend more for trash bags than 90 of the world's 210 countries spend for *everything*.[6]

In a 1991 report, the United Nations Human Development Program divided world economic activity into five income sectors. The top or richest fifth accounted for 85% of global income, trade exchange, and savings. After that it dropped dramatically, forming the so-called "champagne glass" figure. Members of the top fifth are mostly from the northern and western industrialized nations, where comfort and choice are everyday privileges. Countries in the expanding second fifth—parts of Brazil and Costa Rica, much of Eastern Europe, and East Asian nations such as Thailand and Malaysia—are approaching consumption levels of the top fifth due to international development investments. The remaining three fifths contribute much to the global population but relatively little to the global economy.

Alan Durning categorizes these income sectors into three broad socio-ecological classes based on degree of environmental impact: he calls these the *consumers* (top fifth), the *middle income*, and the *poor* (bottom fifth). The table on the following page summarizes the types and scale of consumption for each of the three classes.[7]

In Durning's assessment, the top and bottom groups create the greatest ecological impact—the top for its extravagant use of resources (luxury foods, expensive cars, throwaway materials, comfort-controlled shelters), the bottom by its desperate poverty and overuse of limited local resources.

Specific indicators show that the consumer class is responsible for most of the environmental impact to the planet. For example, in the arena of climate change, the poor release one tenth of a ton of carbon dioxide emissions/person/year, the middle income group one half of a ton/person/year, but the consumer class releases seven times this, or three and a half

Type of Consumption	Consumers (1.1 billion)	Middle (3.3 billion)	Poor (1.1 billion)
Diet	meat, packaged food, soft drinks	grain, clean water	insufficient grain, unsafe water
Transport	private cars	bicycles, buses	walking
Materials	throw-aways	durables	local biomass
Lodging	climate-controlled electrified buildings	some electricity	huts and shanties
Income/year	above $7,500	$700 to $7,500	below $700
% of World Income	64%	33%	2%

FIGURE 1. CONSUMPTION AND CONSUMER CLASSES

tons/person/year. Americans comprise only 4.7% of the Earth's people yet they produce 25% of greenhouse gas emissions. The global consumer class is responsible for 90% of the chlorofluorocarbons destroying the ozone layer, and 96% of the world's radioactive waste.[8] Fossil fuel use is conspicuously highest per capita for the United States. The total number of cars producing carbon waste has gone from 50 million in 1950 to 500 million in 1990, and is projected to double again by 2015.[9] Consumption of fossil fuels links directly to atmospheric destabilization, causing large-scale swings in global climate patterns.

Most products sold to the consumer class generate significant ecological damage to plants, animals, ecosystems, and people in the process of production. Some describe this as casting an ecological shadow on the middle income and poor classes who bear the burden of the hidden economic and moral costs to the environment. Very few items in Western countries have not drawn on labor or natural resources from the global reaches of the world. One metaphor for the load imposed by a given population on nature is its "ecological footprint," or the land necessary to sustain current levels of resource consumption and waste discharge. If we divide the Earth's biologically productive land and sea by the number of people on the planet, the average use is five and a half acres per person (with nothing set aside for all other species). Five years ago, the average world citizen used seven acres as his or her ecological footprint. That is over 30% more than what nature can regenerate. In other words, it would take 1.3 years to regenerate what humanity uses in one year. The average American has a thirty acre footprint. If all people lived like this, we would need five more planets.[10]

A consumer society is characterized by its use of leisure time for spending money (shopping, travel, entertainment) and for its belief that owning things is the primary means to happiness, which is itself assumed to be the primary goal in life. Individual lifestyles and identity become linked to consumption activities; "consumerism" is then based on accepting consumption "as the way to self-development, self-realization, and self-fulfillment."[11] What are some of the cultural impacts of consumerism? Americans now spend six hours a week shopping, and only forty minutes playing with their children. In another poll, 93% of teenage girls cited shopping as their favorite activity; fewer than 5% listed "helping others."[12] In each of the past four years, more Americans declared personal bankruptcy (often due to credit card debt) than graduated from college.[13] Western culture has become inundated with advertising, causing some degree of psychic numbing. The average American is exposed to three thousand advertisements per day, and will spend nearly two years of his or her lifetime watching just the commercials on television.[14] From 1980 to 1997 the amount spent on children's advertising alone rose from $100 million to $1.5 billion per year.[15] It is not uncommon for households to have a personal television set for each child in the family.

David Loy, Buddhist philosopher, considers whether consumerism has impacted culture so much that it has surpassed the influence of traditional religions and become its own religion.[16] The cultural power of this new religion lies in its extremely effective conversion techniques. Seductive product messages replace religious approaches to the pursuit of meaning in life. Loy expresses the concern that this consumerist religion actually depletes rather than builds moral capital. Producers evade moral responsibility in the name of profit maximization, exploiting people as laborers and consumers, eroding the health of ecosystems and species populations. Consumers also evade moral responsibility as they rationalize their choices to spend and collect endless products of materialism, professing ignorance of their sources.

Consumerism produces psychological as well as cultural impacts. Self-identity for consumers is tied strongly to material possessions; consumer goods are symbols of economic status, political or religious views, social group, or sexual orientation. In the consumer society, "I am what I have" is the unstated slogan that defines self. Advertising actively promotes a climate of self-involvement, playing on people's needs for happiness, acceptance, and security. By setting up idealized role models, advertisements foster envy, anxiety, health fears, and at root, a sense of dissatisfaction and inadequacy. When self-identity depends on products, addictions arise—to brand names, styles, tastes, and even to shopping itself. "Shopaholism" is a widespread chronic problem, allowing people to escape from suffering in the same way people use drugs and alcohol. Consumerism can have a negative effect on self-identity, eroding psychological capacities that could be engaged in more life-affirming activity. Filmmaker John de Graaf defines *affluenza* as "a painful, contagious, socially transmitted condition of overload, debt, anxiety, and waste resulting from the dogged pursuit of more."[17]

A central root-cause of overconsumption is the ideology of consumerism, promulgated by those who stand to benefit the most from it. In a society based on capitalist ideology, consumerist psychology serves those in power by generating wealth for those who promulgate the ideology. For those in power it is a lucrative equation; for those at the bottom of the economic ladder, it usually means poverty and debt. Consumerism rests on the psychological assumption that human desires are infinitely expandable; if there are an infinite number of ways to be dissatisfied, there are infinite opportunities to create new products to meet those desires.

Psychological values associated with consumerism are clustered around the human need for security and happiness. Marketers want people to think that buying products means buying happiness. Similarly, some products assert their worth through associating with values that emphasize freedom and individuality. Perhaps strongest of all are the values associated with affluence: having enough to be able to throw away what others could use, having so much that others cannot threaten you, having enough to generate and guarantee certain privileges (entry to exclusive clubs, for example). This ideology is now so effectively ingrained that it has become part of the internalized social order in the United States. But such strong conditioning calls forth critics, and over the past century there have been many who have challenged the tenets of consumerism.

TRADITIONAL CRITIQUES OF CONSUMERISM

Most critiques begin with the assumption that material goods drive our lives, and that a materially simpler life would allow more engagement with moral or aesthetic concerns. Defining the simple life and distinguishing between necessities and culturally conditioned needs is not an easy task. Sociologist Michael Schudson lists five traditional critiques, the first of which is the "Puritan" critique.[18] This line of thinking refers to the early New England colonists who believed people should invest less meaning in what they owned and more meaning in their religious practices. Goods should serve practical human needs, but should not be objects of desire themselves. Acquisitiveness was thought to corrupt the person, impairing his or her capacity for spiritual attainment.

The "Quaker" critique focuses less on people's attitudes toward material goods and more on the wasteful nature of the goods themselves. From this perspective, unlimited choice and excess proliferation of products is seen as luxurious and unnecessary. Planned obsolescence, as in the development of new models of cars and cell phones, is particularly objectionable. If goods cannot be designed to endure, keeping the limits of the Earth in mind, then they should not be produced at all.

What Schudson calls the "republican" critique addresses neither the attitudes toward goods nor the wastefulness of goods, but the impact on public society as a whole. In this view, a consumerist approach shifts attention to private involvement with personal goods and away from public engagement with politics. It also shifts a person's identity away from work (how one contributes to society) and toward lifestyle (what one consumes), thereby undermining the political task of making our work lives more just and sustainable. Further, a consumerist orientation turns people away from social activity. "People abandoned the town square for the front porch, and then later the front porch for the backyard or the television room."[19] Schudson does point out, however, that there are good counterexamples of consumerist engagement on behalf of political and moral principles. An iconic instance from American history is the Boston Tea Party.

To these three, Schudson adds the Marxist critique and the aristocratic critique. The "Marxist" or socialist critique objects primarily to the exploitation of labor under the economics of capitalism. Consumerism can even be seen as an opiate or distraction, leading workers to seek satisfaction in shopping rather than improve the abusive workplace. The "aristocratic" critique focuses more on aesthetics, attacking mass-produced cheap goods as ugly and in poor taste. Items that are rare or exclusive hold the greatest value, thus reinforcing a sense of class privilege.

Buddhist Critiques

What can Buddhism contribute to these critiques of consumerism? Are Buddhist critiques simply a variation on the critiques expressed above? Or can Buddhism offer new insights that could be helpful in today's accelerating rush to consume the planet?

To date, Buddhist initiatives in this conversation have been modest. Several popular books have brought Buddhist perspectives to bear on consumption issues, most notably E. F. Schumacher's *Small Is Beautiful* and Gary Snyder's *The Practice of the Wild*.[20] Both works popularize practices of simplicity and restraint, inspired by Western fascination with Eastern thought. Several Buddhist teachers in the U.S. have taken up particular themes relating to overconsumption. For example, early on the Zen teacher Philip Kapleau sounded a call for vegetarianism. Robert Aitken, another Zen teacher, has written about reducing wants and needs. Thich Nhat Hanh interpreted the fifth precept—"no abuse of delusion-producing substances"—to include junk television, advertising, magazines, and candy.[21]

As for Buddhist analysis of consumption, the field of literature is still relatively small. Rita Gross developed Buddhist positions on population, consumption, and the environment.[22] From Thailand, Sulak Sivaraksa has campaigned tirelessly for economic development linked to spiritual development, based in Buddhist principles of compassion and skillful means.[23] And philosopher David Loy has produced in-depth work on the concept of "lack" as it applies to both self-development and globalization.[24] Two recent anthologies bring together essays on consumerism with a Buddhist focus.[25]

Building on these commentaries, I suggest three primary critiques based in Buddhist understanding. First, consumerism can be seen as a central force in the process of identity formation or production. As Buddhist activist Jonathan Watts points out, consumerism as it has developed has given "corporations, governments, and other powers a tool which takes advantage of our dispositions to concoct 'me' and 'mine.'"[26] From a Buddhist perspective, identity formation or ego-based views of self promote ignorance, which means attachment to false views of self and the world. This generally refers to either of two extremes—that things are separate, fixed, and permanent *or* that things are insubstantial, lacking in reality.

Material accumulation strongly reinforces the first view, that things are separate, fixed, and permanent. The more we relate to material objects as real and permanent, the more deeply we tend to think of ourselves as a fixed object (or self) with specific identity. This confusion prevents us from experiencing the world as interdependent, co-creating, and in dynamic flux. Attachment to a false view of self as object can lead to more and more need for self-reinforcing possessions. The view that things lack any reality at all can itself be used as a rationalization for consumerism. Since nothing is real, then nothing matters, so why not indulge in whatever offers some momentary pleasure? This confusion prevents us from fully engaging the actual relationships of the world that shape and condition our lives. Attachment to insubstantiality can lead to false reasoning and undervaluing of the relations behind what is consumed.

The second critique is that consumerism promotes, rationalizes, and condones harming. Consumer products of all kinds depend on loss of animal and plant life, unpleasant or even debilitating factory conditions, increased climate impact from trade, and harmful behavior between people. Slavery in the name of product manufacturing is not uncommon even today.[27] Tremendous harm to many forms of life is justified for the sake of profit and gain. Buddhist ethics would seriously question such a justification. The foundational principle behind all Buddhist ethics is nonharming or *ahimsa*; this is expressed as the first of the five prohibitory precepts—"do not kill," or "do no harm." Following this precept as a guiding principle would mean investigating the origins of all consumer products and doing the best one could to choose those for which no harm has been committed.

A third Buddhist critique of consumerism is that consumerism promotes desire and dissatisfaction, the very source of suffering as described in the second of the Four Noble Truths. Other words for dissatisfaction are: clinging, craving, thirst, discontent, attachment. Craving in its most comprehensive sense is the fundamental desire for existence. Just to want to be alive is the most deep-rooted biological drive. Often identified in terms of karma and rebirth, this is said to be the "thirst that gives rise to repeated existence." Marketers play on this strategically, stimulating the desire to feel alive through delicious foods, powerful cars, or exotic vacations. Another way to think of this is the suffering that comes from wanting something other than the present experience. This can take endless forms as one strives continually for some new state, new feeling, new experience, or for satiety and permanence. But because of the ever-changing nature of reality, this striving is always frustrated. Craving also includes aversion, the desire for *non*-existence. In this case, one craves relief or escape from what is unpleasant or undesirable—a headache, for example, or a wilting heat wave. Marketers take advantage of this too, offering a parade of products that profess to relieve almost any form of human suffering.

Early Buddhist texts teach that desire results in four types of clinging or attachment.[28] One kind of clinging is to sense-objects or the experience of sensing. Consumer addictions offer graphic examples of this clinging, such as the need for tobacco or alcohol and their attendant sensory pleasures. Sexuality as consumption generates attachment to the stimulation of touch. A wide range of consumer products depend on constant restimulation of sensory experiences—fast food, sport vehicles, films and videos, even the consumption of energy in response to temperature fluctuation. This critique can also be seen to apply self-reflexively. Buddhist materialism in shops and catalogs promotes "Tibetan Treasures," Zen bells, and various meditation accoutrements from bamboo screens to prayer flags, all to help provide the "right" kind of sensory experience in support of one's practice.

Another type of attachment is clinging to views and values. Here a view or value can become objectified as something "right," which one identifies with a sense of self. Promoters as well as critics of consumerism can be strongly attached to their views on the subject. In today's world, views about wealth and poverty, scale and speed, knowledge and freedom have become objectified as absolute ends to be sought after through material means. Consumerism has an entire set of values that are now being promulgated internationally as central to the promotion of globalized trade. Economic development often incorporates consumerist ideology as fundamental to social well-being. Buddhists too can be attached to attitudes about poverty or simplicity, developing an identity around their Buddhist views.

Clinging can also take the form of clinging to rules, methods, or actions. Here attachments develop around behaviors seen as necessary to support the views described above. Choosing what clothes to wear, which foods to eat, and whom to impress can all become part of the consumer's identity, as analyzed by market specialists. Buddhist consumers have their own identifiable marketing behaviors well known to modern advertising firms. They are by now a defined market niche, vulnerable to marketing psychology designed to create good feelings associated with the identity of "being Buddhist."

Lastly, *self-clinging* means literally clinging to one's own experience of personal identity. This represents a futile attempt to bridge the sense of separation, fragmentation, comparison, and inadequacy, which arise from the experience of objects as separate from one's self. Paradoxically, this can never bring satisfaction because such identity building exacerbates the gap it is trying to eliminate.

These three critiques—that consumerism facilitates the formation of a false identity, promotes harm to other living beings, and impels clinging and attachment—overlap to some extent with the five traditional critiques identified by Schudson. Yet there are also some new contributions to this discussion. The Buddhist critique that consumerism promotes a false sense of self might be parallel to the Puritan critique of material goods as distractions from true spiritual development. A Buddhist concern for nonharming would reinforce the Marxist critique regarding worker exploitation. However, I believe the greatest strength of the Buddhist contribution is its analysis of the fundamental role of desire in promoting an endless cycle of suffering. Awakening or enlightenment rests on realizing the all-pervasive nature of this existence-based drive. To the extent that we ignore the role of desire, we are easy prey for the marketers and the expansion of consumerism as the dominant set of social values across the globe. Taking up the study of desire in its myriad consumer forms offers endless opportunities for spiritual insight.

BUDDHIST METHODS FOR LIBERATION

The Buddhist teaching of the Four Noble Truths provides a useful and relevant approach to investigating consumerism. This teaching is phrased literally in terms of a medical diagnosis: suffering is the disease, craving is the cause of the disease, there is a cure for the disease, and that cure is the Eightfold Path to enlightenment. In the Buddhist view, all craving is a manifestation of three basic tendencies known as the Three Poisons: greed, aversion or hate, and delusion. In terms of consumerism these become wanting more of something, wanting less of something, and wanting something that does not exist. Each of the three is key to marketing strategies, whose purpose is to generate endless desire.

The way out of this craving or dissatisfaction lies in cutting through the root causes. This is the third Noble Truth—that liberation from ceaseless suffering is possible. For the oppressed and deluded consumer, the third Noble Truth is the shining jewel in the Buddhist cure for consumerism. One can choose to remain sick with the disease or one can choose liberation and healing. Ethically acceptable choices for liberation from consumerism are those that bring personal and environmental healing. Ethically unacceptable actions are those that perpetuate the socially and environmentally destructive activities of consumerism.

In everyday terms, the effectiveness of the cure for the disease could be evaluated in terms of "well-being." Development ethicist David Crocker has formulated a definition of well-being based on Aristotle's ethic of human flourishing. "To have well being, to be and to do well, is to function and to be capable of functioning in certain humanly good ways."[29] He describes physical, mental, and social dimensions of well-being, with the good life being that which achieves a certain balance among them. Sustaining well-being is seen as more important than momentary experiences of well-being.

The Buddhist concept of *santuṭṭhi*—or contentment, satisfaction— expresses this goal succinctly. The opposite of suffering is to be free from desire and attachment, to be content with what one has and is. Thai scholar Pibob Udomittipong describes how deeply this concept challenges modern consumerism.[30] Soon after the first Thai National Economic Development Plan was drafted in the 1960s, the government banned Buddhist monks from teaching about contentment. The official governing body of the monks sanctioned this decree, apparently accepting the reasoning that *santutthi* was a barrier to economic growth. The late Buddhadasa Bhik-khu, a revered Thai monk, argued against the ban, pointing out that contentment leads to the development of wisdom and, as such, is necessary for real human progress.

The second concept of well-being is *metta*—the capacity to offer positive well-wishing or loving kindness on behalf of one's self and others, to help create a world of less suffering. Traditionally, the *metta* meditation is taught as an antidote to fear and other expressions of the error of separateness. Loving kindness is the first of the four *brahmaviharas*. The other three are compassion, sympathetic joy, and equanimity. One of the traditional phrasings goes:

> *May I be free from danger*   (safety)
> *May I have mental happiness*   (peace of mind)
> *May I have physical happiness*   (health)
> *May I have ease of well-being*   (manifesting loving kindness)

This is said first for one's self, then extended to family and friends, to enemies, and to all beings in the world. This way of framing well-being emphasizes the second element of Crocker's definition: being capable of taking positive steps to create a world of well-being.

What, then, are useful liberative methods to extinguish desire and thereby be relieved of the suffering of consumerism? Methods consist of insight into the nature of desire and practices that embody this insight in action. Here I will look briefly at aspects of Buddhist philosophy as they address the three Buddhist critiques: the fallacy of the false self, the ethics of the precepts, and the links of co-dependent causation. Right conduct provides guidelines to expose the process of identity formation. The bodhisattva vow offers a paradigm for the practice of nonharming. Co-dependent origination addresses the root work of breaking the links that perpetuate desire.

Exposing Identity Formation. The first Buddhist critique points out that the problem with consumerism is its constant reinforcement of ego-identity. Misunderstanding the self as either fixed or insubstantial misses the empty nature of self. This is almost impossible to grasp through armchair reflection. You need a more vigorous method to challenge the false views of the consumer self.

In Dōgen's well-known verse from the *Genjō kōan*, we find one approach to dismantling these false views:

> To study the Buddha way is to study the self
> To study the self is to forget the self
> To forget the self is to be confirmed by the myriad things
> To be confirmed by the myriad things is to drop off
>   body and mind of self and others.[31]

Zen priest Shohaku Okumura explains that the original Japanese word for "study" in Dōgen's text was *narau*. This derives from *nareru*, which means "to become familiar or intimate with."[32] Dōgen approaches this in the biggest sense—studying one's mind, body, sense organs, speech, and social relations as deeply conditioned by self-centered needs. Studying and forgetting the self, in Dōgen's view, is fundamental to becoming human.

How does one study the consumer-constructed self? Suppose, for example, you really love coffee. You can study how your identity is constructed around drinking coffee. You can observe your preferences for certain brands or coffee shops. You can study what pleases you about the act of drinking coffee. It might be the flavor, the stimulation, or the social company. You can study your history of experience with coffee and see how over time it adds up to your identity as a coffee drinker.

Looking closely at any one of these aspects of self, you can see how dependent your idea of self is on outside conditions. Time of day, quality of coffee, source of the beans, the staff at the coffee shop—all of these contribute to your experience. There is no such thing as a separate self enjoying a separate cup of coffee. It is all happening at once. Observing the endlessly connected web of conditions and relations, you can go beyond the small self to see yourself as part of the co-creating universe. The delusion of separate self crumbles.

"Self and others are working together. The working done by self and all others are called our actions."[33] Okumura points out that we think "we" are "driving" a "car." But actually the "car" is "driving" "us." The car we drive is being driven by the oil economy, its parts produced across the globe. Our driving is the action of highway builders, car designers, city planners, and congressional policymakers. All these beings contribute to our existence, nudging us to let go of confused views of a separate self.

But how is this "dropping off body and mind"? Dōgen's teacher Nyojo said, "Dropping off body and mind is zazen. When we just practice zazen, we part from the five desires and get rid of the five coverings."[34] The five desires come from contact with the five sense organs; they generate a false sense of self that is attached to the pleasures or aversions we experience with our senses. The five coverings are the hindrances of greed, anger, sleepiness, distraction, and doubt that keep our minds from functioning in a healthy way. Parting from sensory attachment and hindrances is one path to deflating the consumer self. Studying deeply the myriad aspects of consumer identity, you see into the delusion of self as consumer, of self as anything separate from anything else.

The insights from studying one type of attachment can be applied from one context of consumerism to another. Studying yourself as coffee lover gives you practice in studying yourself as a clothes shopper, for example. Seeing how self construction works, you become less gullible to the consumer industry and its endless hooks. As you consider various purchases, you can check your conditioning and attachment to self. This self-examination is not in itself the experience of enlightenment but it may open the door for awakening to the actual experience of the selfless state. This more profound level of insight can only strengthen your capacity for seeing through the lures of the consumer self.

Practicing Nonharming. The second Buddhist critique of consumerism is that it promotes harming. This critique raises questions of right and wrong—how do you decide what is harmful in the realm of consumerism? The Buddhist texts on ethical behavior offer specific guidance in the form of right conduct or the five precepts: not killing, not stealing, not abusing sexuality, not lying, and not using or selling intoxicants.[35] The precepts represent practices of restraint, calling for personal responsibility in reducing environmental and human suffering. Taken together they indicate choices one can make to avoid harming others.

I will work primarily with the first precept here, though each precept can apply to aspects of consumerism. The first precept is the injunction to abstain from "destroying, causing to be destroyed, or sanctioning the destruction of a living being."[36] A living being is anything that has life, from a small insect to a complex forest. Clearly, every act of consuming raises the issue of harm—just to stay alive we have to eat food that has been killed or harvested. Accepting this paradox, we nonetheless can choose *how much* harm we want to be responsible for. For example, many people practice vegetarianism because they don't support the harming of animals from industrial agriculture.[37] Others eat organic fruits and vegetables to reduce harm to soil from chemical fertilizers and pesticides. Some avoid fast food because of labor exploitation and human health impacts.

Consumer awareness movements are now promoting "chain of custody" verification that can document the source and treatment of material goods. Forest certification and green building are two arenas where knowledge of production processes have given consumers the option to choose the more ethically produced goods. Buying locally often shortens the chain, making it easier to track harmful impacts. Under pressure from student activists, for example, many university campuses are now constructing green buildings and buying fair trade coffee.

Traditionally the precepts have been oriented toward individual conduct; the Buddha Śākyamuni did not offer a counterpart set of moral guidelines for institutions. Because social structures (governments, schools, churches, etc.) contribute significantly to consumer-related harming, ethical guidelines for social structures would also be useful. Individuals and institutions influence each other. More conscious standards of restraint in public arenas (such as no advertising in schools) can encourage greater personal practice of nonharming, and the reverse can also happen. This means holding social or institutional agents accountable for the impacts of their actions. By taking initiatives in this arena, consumers can reclaim moral integrity that has been eroded by consumerist agendas. It is not necessary for one to have perfected moral practice before asking others to consider their own actions. The point of the precepts is to reduce harm and to practice interrelationship rather than self-interest.

Breaking the Links of Desire. The third Buddhist critique of consumerism is that consumerism promotes desire and dissatisfaction, the cause of suffering. A classic liberative method for working with desire is the twelve limbs (or links) of co-dependent origination, sometimes portrayed as a wheel of becoming. This cycle has been used to analyze the process of reincarnation and rebirth, but here I use it to describe the patterns that arise over and over in every moment of desiring or grasping. Consumerism utterly depends on this process, from beginning to end, in a relentless drive that spans generations and ecosystems.

The twelve links follow each other in order: ignorance, karmic formations, consciousness, name and form, six sense fields, contact, feelings, craving, grasping, becoming, birth, death, ignorance, and so on.[38] The pull of each link, based on the strong experience of the one that precedes it, is so powerful that people (and other beings as well, in their own ways) are said to be continually in the grip of this meta-pattern. Because each of the twelve limbs is a condition upon which the others depend, if any of the conditions cease to exist, the entire cycle ceases to function. Release from this cycle of grasping and suffering is what the Buddha called *nirvāṇa*. As consumerism is a never-ending field of desire, it offers an ideal platform for studying the twelve links.

One can begin at any point in the cycle; for this discussion, it makes sense to start with consumer *craving*—for new shoes, the latest camera, specialty chocolate, and so on—the list is endless. Craving is the experience of being hooked by an object, a thought, a need, and then yearning to grasp it.[39] In the twelve-link cycle, craving depends upon *feelings*, which arise following contact with objects in the sense fields. Feeling states in Buddhist psychology are categorized as positive (pleasant), negative (unpleasant), or neutral (indifferent). It doesn't matter so much whether one is angry, sad, joyful, or affectionate; for each feeling, one either wants to perpetuate it (usually the positive feelings) or get rid of it (usually the negative feelings). Since feelings are transitory, advertisers must continually restimulate potential buyers to keep the pleasant feelings going. This is done by generating an endless assault of *contact* points for the sense organs: bright and colorful signs, mood music playing, tantalizing aromas in the air. The point of contact is where the object of perception, the sense organ, and the sense consciousness all come together. The purveyor of goods provides the object; the consumer provides the already-conditioned sense organ and consciousness. Where consumers have become resistant to excess contact, advertisers are forced to try harder to get their attention, using shock images outside the morally acceptable realm, such as nudity and violence.

The six *sense fields* of the eye, ear, nose, tongue, body, and mind are gateways for consciousness. They themselves are conditioned by *name and form* or the actual material and immaterial aspects of a specific being. What one perceives in the sense field is completely conditioned by one's experience. A young child who has not yet learned to differentiate sound or shapes has not yet developed a coded sense consciousness to explain what he or she perceives through a specific cultural lens. Thus the young toddler watching hours of television can develop a consciousness dominated by products rather than living beings. With such an avalanche of products and sales pitches entering a child's sense fields today, parents must take very seriously their role in influencing what a child comes to recognize as real.[40]

Name and form are conditioned by previous experiences that mold *consciousness* and the material form it comes to take. Such conditioning is well documented for alcoholism, gambling, and other abusive addictions. Repeated use of alcohol or drugs can change people physiologically so they are more attracted to the highs induced by the substance. Apply this conditioning to other forms of excess consumption, and the addictive cycle extends to luxury foods, brand name clothing, and television serials. Advertisers do their best to capture teenage consumer consciousness by imprinting brand name loyalties for clothing, pizza, and hygiene products at an early age. Teen-product companies even hire teen trendsetters, passing out free samples to establish brand loyalty. Resisting the slogans of consumerism becomes one way to break the conditioning that is being so aggressively promoted.[41] Culture-wide consumer consciousness eventually results in long-term *karmic formations*, which will require culture-wide attention to transform.

Turning back to craving, we can see how craving perpetuates the other links. In craving pleasant experiences, one yearns for their continuation, and in craving the absence of unpleasant experiences, one yearns for their cessation. These forms of grasping are especially strong where the ego or sense of "I" attaches to what is craved or avoided (as for example, "I avoid meat, I'm a vegetarian"). Marketers are masterful at using human grasping to create specialty niches—even green consumers and dharma practitioners are well-established market groups.[42] *Grasping* generates *becoming*: the more one grasps after consumer goods or values, the more one becomes a consumer, leading to "*birth*" of the self-identified ego that sees life primarily as consumption. Thus, we have the phenomena of suburban "mall rats," tupperware queens, and eBay treasure hunters.

Eventually, of course, even the consumer must face *death*—when the self can no longer be propped up by possessions. Fueled by ignorance of the nature of dependent origination (compounded by massive denial in consumer culture), karmic traces carry over from previous actions or lifetimes. Consider the alcoholic father who models the pattern of alcohol abuse to his son, or the shopaholic mother who fosters an appetite for fashion in her daughter. From generation to generation, consumer consciousness flourishes, taking new and diverse forms year after year.

Observing the nature of co-dependent origination can provide a penetrating tool for analyzing consumerism. The cycle can also be studied in terms of cessation as well as origination. Breaking the driving energy from one link to the next slows down the desire-generating cycle. If you reduce contact with consumer stimulants such as television, your sense fields are less flooded with product messages. If you overcome a debilitating addiction, that craving has less impact on your consciousness. The point here is not that the cycle of causation can be brought to a halt, since beings keep taking form and are conditioned just by existing. But by applying mindfulness, one can observe the process and even learn to unhook from the craving. Each moment of consumption can thus be an opportunity for insight, tasting, if only in a small way, the freedom from grasping and dissatisfaction.

Buddhist Consumer Activism

Extreme suffering calls for strong and committed ethical response. There is no question that consumerism is rapidly depleting what remains of our global ecological heritage. Buddhist consumer activism could contribute a significant voice to this much needed ethical response. Thus far, socially engaged Buddhist activism in the industrialized world has focused more on social problems: AIDS, death and dying, prison work, gay liberation, etc.[43] Environmental concerns have been left to environmentalists to solve. I believe that consumerism may provide an appropriate and easily accessible arena for Buddhist activists eager to engage environmental concerns. This may involve personal lifestyle change or structural change within Buddhist institutions. Or Buddhist activists may take up social or political initiatives based on Buddhist principles. In some cases it may be most effective to work collaboratively with non-Buddhists, practicing Buddhism with a small "b."[44]

We would like to offer here a few suggestions for launching a Buddhism consumer activism movement. First, Buddhist centers could make it a priority to model the reduction of consumption, promoting a lifestyle based on simplicity and restraint. In California, Green Gulch Zen Center and Spirit Rock Meditation Center already have strong commitments to vegetarianism, waste recycling, and land stewardship.[45] As visitors come to these centers for teaching, they pick up the culture of the place; interpretive booklets and signs could be added to make such practices more obvious. Buddhist centers could also take up structural policy change by developing green operations principles and green mission statements. Very few centers have taken these first steps of codifying their consumer practices as an institution. A small working group representing a range of lineages and cultures could develop a peer alliance code to raise the standards and expectations among centers.

Green ceremonies could be developed at Buddhist centers or as interfaith projects to strengthen commitment to ethical principles of consuming. Such gatherings offer community-building alternatives to shopping or watching television. For example, in addition to the regular Buddhist events, a few centers celebrate Earth Day, Arbor Day, and Thanksgiving as Earth holidays. To catalyze institutional action, members could establish social action groups to take up particular consumer issues, such as fair trade coffee or sweatshop labor, to increase awareness of the implications of consumer choices. They might advocate that their center serve only organic produce, for example, as a way of demonstrating the importance of farming ethics.

Second, Buddhist activist organizations can support Buddhist resistance to consumer values. The BASE program (Buddhist Alliance for Social Engagement) of the Buddhist Peace Fellowship already offers training for socially engaged activists. Members meet regularly for meditation, discussion, and mutual support. The program is organized somewhat to parallel the Catholic base community model; it could easily be extended to encourage consumer activism groups. The International Network of Engaged Buddhists based in Southeast Asia has been very active in hosting several conferences on the theme of "Alternatives to Consumerism."[46]

The issues raised in these discussions need to be shared more actively with Buddhists in the privileged and overconsuming industrial world.

Third, Buddhist journals such as *Turning Wheel* and *Seeds of Peace* could publicize stories of individuals or organizations who have taken on consumer education projects. Every activist movement needs its stories and heroes. Buddhist publications could help promote those who have shown leadership in questioning runaway consumerism. These might eventually be collected in a guidebook to consumer activism from a Buddhist perspective. Such stories might inspire other Buddhist leaders to write or speak on consumer issues, using examples that illustrate the Dharma in action.

The Buddha Śākyamuni told his followers that his teachings should offer pragmatic relief for their suffering. If they weren't useful in everyday life, then the teachings were not of value. It seems to me that Buddhist methods of working with consumerism offer very practical methods to address the suffering it generates. Consumerism is a dominant practice field of our times; if the Buddha's teachings have merit, they can be used to untangle the complex web of all-consuming relations.

It seems not only possible but desirable for Buddhist activists, teachers, and thinkers to take up the ethical challenges raised by consumerism. I believe that such a consumer activist movement would engage many aspects of the traditional Buddhist enlightenment path: eliminating desire and attachment, seeing through the illusion of separate self, choosing to reduce the suffering of others, and acting from an understanding of co-dependent arising. The liberative methods of the Dharma provide powerful tools of analysis and practice that can help with this task. We have the choice to wake up in the midst of this planetary suffering. The beauty of this work is that it is so accessible and there are opportunities for awakening everywhere.

NOTES

1 This paper builds on a previous paper published in *Buddhist-Christian Studies* (2000) and includes revisions from my chapter in *Hooked! Buddhist Writings on Greed, Desire, and the Urge to Consume* (Boston: Shambhala, 2005).

2 See, for example, *Theology for Earth Community*, ed. Dieter Hessel (Maryknoll, NY: Orbis, 1996), and *Subverting Greed: Religious Perspectives on the Global Economy*, ed. Paul Knitter and Chandra Muzaffar (Maryknoll, NY: Orbis, 2002).

3 Jonathan Watts, "Concocted Death: A Buddhist Deconstruction of the Religion and Consumerism," in *Santi Pracha Dhamma* (Bangkok: Santi Pracha Dhamma Institute, 2001), 126.

4 John C. Ryan and Alan Thein Durning, *Stuff: The Secret Lives of Everyday Things* (Seattle: Northwest Environment Watch, 1997), 5.

5 Alan Durning, *How Much Is Enough?* (New York: W. W. Norton, 1992), 30, 130.

6 John de Graaf, David Wann, and Thomas Naylor, *Affluenza: The All-Consuming Epidemic* (San Francisco: Berrett-Koehler Publishers, 2001), 36.

7 Durning, *How Much Is Enough?* 27.

8 Ibid., 51.

9 Lester Brown, Christopher Flavin, Hilary French, and Linda Starke, eds., *The State of the World Report 1998* (New York: W. W. Norton, 1998), 115.

10 De Graaf et al., *Affluenza*, 91.

11 Quoted in Neva Goodwin, "Overview Essay," *The Consumer Society*, ed. Neva R. Goodwin, Frank Ackerman, and David Kiron (Washington, DC: Island Press, 1997), 3.

12 De Graaf et al., *Affluenza*, 57.

13 Ibid., 4.

14 Alan D. Kanner and Mary E. Gomes, "The All-Consuming Self," in *Ecopsychology*, ed. Theodore Roszak, Mary E. Gomes, and Allen D. Kanner (San Francisco: Sierra Club Books, 1995), 81; and de Graaf et al., *Affluenza*, 149.

15 De Graaf et al., *Affluenza*, 52.

16 David Loy, "The Religion of the Market," *Journal of the American Academy of Religion* 65, no. 2 (1997): 275–90.

17 De Graaf et al., *Affluenza*, 104–8, 2.

18 Michael Schudson, "Delectable Materialism: Second Thoughts on Consumer Culture," in *The Ethics of Consumption*, ed. David Crocker and Toby Linden (Lanham, MD: Rowman and Littlefield, 1998), 249–68.

19 Ibid., 258.

20 E. F. Schumacher, *Small Is Beautiful: Economics as if People Mattered* (New York: Harper and Row, 1975); and Gary Snyder, *The Practice of the Wild* (San Francisco: North Point Press, 1990).

21 Philip Kapleau, *To Cherish All Life: A Buddhist Case for Becoming Vegetarian* (San Francisco: Harper and Row, 1982); Robert Aitken, *The Practice of Perfection* (San Francisco: Pantheon Books, 1994); Thich Nhat Hanh, *For a Future to Be Possible: Commentaries on the Five Wonderful Precepts* (Berkeley: Parallax Press, 1993).

22 Rita Gross, "Buddhist Resources for Issues of Population, Consumption, and the Environment," in *Buddhism and Ecology: The Interconnectedness of Dharma and Deeds*, ed. Mary Evelyn Tucker and Duncan Ryūken Williams (Cambridge, MA: Harvard University Press, 1997), 291–312, and Rita Gross, "Toward a Buddhist Environmental Ethic," *Journal of the American Academy of Religion* 65, no. 2 (1997): 333–53.

23 Sulak Sivaraksa, *Seeds of Peace* (Berkeley: Parallax Press, 1992).

24 See David Loy, "Pave the Planet or Wear Shoes? A Buddhist Perspective on Globalization," in *Subverting Greed*, ed. Paul F. Knitter and Chandra Muzaffar (Maryknoll, NY: Orbis Books, 2002), 58–76, and *A Buddhist History of the West: Studies in Lack* (Albany: State University of New York Press, 2002).

25 Allan Hunt-Badiner, ed., *Mindfulness in the Marketplace: Compassionate Responses to Consumerism* (Berkeley: Parallax Press, 2002), and Stephanie Kaza, ed., *Hooked! Buddhist Writings on Greed, Desire, and the Urge to Consume* (Boston: Shambhala, 2005).

26 Watts, "Concocted Death," 144.

27 See Andrew Cockburn, "21st Century Slaves," *National Geographic* 204, no. 3: 2–25.

28 Watts, "Concocted Death," 141–42.

29 David A. Crocker, "Consumption, Well-Being, and Capability," in *The Ethics of Consumption*, ed. David Crocker and Toby Linden (Lanham, MD: Rowman and Littlefield, 1998), 366–90.

30 See Pibob Udomittipong, "Thailand's Ecology Monks," in *Dharma Rain: Sources of Buddhist Environmentalism*, ed. Stephanie Kaza and Kenneth Kraft (Boston: Shambhala, 2000), 191–97.

31 Kaz Tanahashi, ed., *Moon in a Dewdrop* (San Francisco: North Point, 1985), 70.

32 Shohaku Okamura, "To Study the Self," in *The Art of Just Sitting*, ed. John Daido Loori (Boston: Wisdom, 2002), 105.

33 Ibid., 107.

34 Ibid., 110.

35 For an environmental commentary on the precepts, see John Daido Loori, "The Precepts and the Environment," in *Buddhism and Ecology*, 177–84.

36 Hammalawa Saddhatissa, *Buddhist Ethics* (London: Wisdom, 1987), 73–74.

37 For analysis of the issues facing Buddhists and vegetarian eating, see Kate Lawrence, "Nourishing Ourselves, Nourishing Others: How Mindful Food Choices Reduce Suffering," in *Mindfulness in the Marketplace*.

38 See Watts, "Concocted Death," for further review and interpretation of the twelve links in relation to consumerism and construction of the false self.

39 For a description of this process in Tibetan Buddhist terms, see Pema Chodron, "How We Get Hooked, How We Get Unhooked," *Shambhala Sun* (March 2003): 30–35.

40 The Center for Media Literacy (Los Angeles) and others are taking the lead in raising these issues in relation to public education; see hrrp://www.medialit.org.

41 See Naomi Klein, *No Space, No Choice, No Jobs, No Logo: Taking Aim at the Brand Bullies* (Toronto: Knopf Canada, 2000), and Alissa Quart, *Branded: The Buying and Selling of Teenagers* (Cambridge, MA: Perseus, 2003).

42 See, for example, John Elkington, Julia Hailes, and Joel Makower, *The Green Consumer* (New York: Penguin Books, 1988).

43 Described in Christopher Queen, ed., *Engaged Buddhism in the West* (Boston: Wisdom, 2000).

44 As explained by Sulak Sivaraksa in *Seeds of Peace*.

45 Stephanie Kaza, "American Buddhist Response to the Land: Ecological Practice at Two West Coast Retreat Centers," in *Buddhism and Ecology*, 219–48.

46 Sulak Sivaraksa, "Alternatives to Consumerism," in *Mindfulness in the Marketplace*, 135–41.

Pure Land Buddhism and Its Perspective on the Environment

Mitsuya Dake

INTRODUCTION

Today's environmental crisis continues to grow in severity despite the ongoing efforts of those deeply aware of the problem. It is becoming obvious that science and technology alone cannot lead us to a resolution of this crisis, since the cause of the problem is deeply rooted in the very way that we live and our way of thinking.

The complexity of the environmental crisis is closely related not only to the economic, political, and social activity of human beings, but it is also conditioned by our moral and spiritual attitude toward the environment. What we choose to do about the environment is deeply connected to how we understand ourselves in relation to the environment. It follows that each of us needs to undergo a fundamental change in our style of life and way of thinking. Questions remain, however, as to what sort of alternative lifestyles and styles of thought might be adopted, and how we might go about finding them.

For many people in the West, Buddhist perspectives and approaches to the environment provide clues for the development of ecologically based lifestyles and ways of thinking. For instance, Buddhist ideas such as the early Buddhist teachings of morality, the concept of interdependence (*pratītyasamutpāda*), Chinese Huayan Buddhist notions of interconnectedness, the mandalic cosmology of tantric Buddhism, and the Zen state of mind have been offered as examples of Buddhist points of view that can provide useful approaches to our consideration of the problems of the environment.

Certainly, Buddhist thought may well provide an important and useful standpoint from which to understand the structure and causes of environmental problems. However, at the same time, we should be very careful about arriving at quick and easy conclusions about the link between Buddhism and the environment, since the tendency to regard Buddhist doctrines as identical with the ecological conception of the environment could potentially distort the original purpose of the Buddhist teachings. Moreover, as we try to resolve today's environmental problems, that tendency is often tied to a failure on our part to recognize that the essence of the problem lies in the structure of the modern age itself. As Lewis Lancaster has observed, "We may seek only to find expressions and practices in Buddhism that can be interpreted as supportive of ethical norms and values established in our modern and postmodern era."[1]

With these thoughts in mind, I shall present some aspects of Pure Land Buddhist spirituality, paying particular attention to the teachings of Shinran (1173–1262), who in thirteenth-century Japan forged a Buddhist path that is accessible to all in daily life. It is my hope that this approach will provide some useful perspectives for our consideration of today's environmental problems.

Pure Land Buddhism and the Environment

The set of beliefs and practices surrounding Amida Buddha and his Pure Land is usually broadly referred to as Pure Land Buddhism. In Buddhist history there are many sūtras and discourses that refer to the idea of Amida Buddha or the Pure Land, but the most important Indian textual sources for Pure Land Buddhism are the Larger Sūtra (the Larger Sukhāvatīvyūha Sūtra) and the Smaller Sūtra[2] (the Smaller Sukhāvatīvyūha Sūtra), which are said to have been compiled in Northwest India around 100 CE. Pure Land Buddhism was transmitted to China through Central Asia as early as the middle of the second century and then underwent further development until it reached its philosophical and cultural culmination in the seventh century.[3] In China, along with the Larger Sūtra and the Smaller Sūtra, the Contemplation Sūtra also became very popular. Appealing as it did to both ordinary lay people and clerics, Pure Land Buddhism spread widely throughout East Asia, including Japan.

However, in comparison with Zen Buddhism, which also grew up in the same region around the same period, Pure Land Buddhism has not received extensive attention in the West.[4] Moreover, since much of the Western literature on East Asian Buddhism has accepted Zen apologetics uncritically, a general perception that Pure Land Buddhism is somehow a less sophisticated, and perhaps even less authentic, form of Buddhism has been created. This does not, however, mean that Pure Land Buddhism had less cultural, societal, or philosophical influence in East Asia than did Zen Buddhism. In fact, it might be said that Pure Land Buddhism was more substantially influential upon the peoples and societies of East Asia.

Much, if not all, of the early Western interest in Buddhism was derived from books written by Westerners whose concerns lay in the doctrines of canonical Buddhist scriptures or the speculations of Buddhist thinkers and meditating yogis. A recent shift in focus among some groups toward the teachings of living Zen or Tibetan Buddhist teachers seems to have redirected that earlier tendency to a certain extent. Even then, however, people in the West tend to be drawn to those forms of Buddhism that emphasize self-cultivation and that are usually connected with some sort of cognitive, personal, and empowering experience. But for many Buddhists in East Asia, this image represents only a part of the Buddhist belief system, which as a whole comprises more than just meditation or mental cultivation.[5]

For instance, Pure Land Buddhists have valued Amida Buddha's vows as the source of their religious guidance and aspiration. Although closely connected with the self-cultivation of believers, Pure Land Buddhism shifts the focus of its teaching from self-cultivation to the realization of a self-transcendental relationship of practitioners with Amida Buddha's vows. The belief system of Zen Buddhism and Pure Land Buddhism seem to sharply contrast with one another. But what they hold in common is the Buddhist path of seeking to achieve nirvāṇa or enlightenment. The external differences between the two reflect the different kinds of people to whom the respective teachings are directed, that is, practitioners in the monastery or ordinary lay people, as well as differences in the method of attaining enlightenment.

What perspective might Pure Land Buddhism be able to contribute to the resolution of today's environmental problems? Although such discussions among Pure Land Buddhists have been increasing in recent years, they remain insufficient both in numbers and the range of their discussions. But, in considering Buddhist models for an ecological world, frequently attention is drawn to the concept of the Pure Land.

The Pure Land is often taken to be a place similar to the Christian God's Heaven or the land of Utopia. Nevertheless, the Pure Land is not the product of God's creation; nor is it the place of simple human imagination. Rather, as mentioned above, it represents the manifestation of the Buddha's enlightenment. Intrinsic reality and external appearances find inseparable expression in the Pure Land. Further, the intrinsic reality of the Pure Land has its foundation in the Mahāyāna concept of *śūnyatā* or emptiness. Although the Pure Land sūtras depict a variety of glorious forms of the Pure Land, it also explains over and over again that the Pure Land is established through practicing the dharma of emptiness, desirelessness, and signlessness by the Bodhisattava Dharmakara, who attains buddhahood and becomes Amida Buddha. It states:

> Holding the great ornament of virtue, possessed of all the practices, he made all living beings gain possession of merit and virtue. He [Bodhisattva Dharmakara] remained firm in his awareness of the reality of emptiness, firm in his detachment from distinctions and preferences, and free from desire. Not construction or giving rise to any conceptualizations, he had insight into the fact that all things are like a magical illusion.[6]

In other words, the essential meaning of the Pure Land does not lie in the physical existence of the land, but rather in the exhibition of the state of enlightenment or the reality of emptiness, desirelessness, and signlessness. In this context, the *Treatise on the Pure Land* attributed to Vasubandhu, a great Indian Mahāyāna master of the Yogācāra (Jpn. Yugagyō ha, also Skt. Cittamātra, "Consciousness Only") school, asserts that "The Pure Land is the realm of purity above various states of existence in the three worlds of saṃsāra."[7] And Tanluan, a Chinese master of the Pure Land school, explains in his *Commentary on the Treatise on the Pure Land* that "Because it is formless, it can take all forms,"[8] Further, Shandao, another Chinese master of the Pure Land school, declares, "The land of bliss is the realm of nirvana, the uncreated."[9] These descriptions and interpretations of the Pure Land are all based in Mahāyāna logic, and clearly point to the essential difference between the Pure Land and God's Heaven or the land of Utopia.

On the other hand, it is also true that the idea of the Pure Land is sometimes taught in a dichotomous manner, which portrays sharp contrasts between the Pure Land and this world. It is taught that this deluded world (*sahā*) is to be abandoned and the Pure Land as the land of bliss is to be sought after. There can be no doubt that this explanation became a useful vehicle for spreading the Pure Land teaching, especially among ordinary people.

In addition, when the idea of the Pure Land was introduced to countries in East Asia, the Pure Land was comprehended in ways conditioned by indigenous religious thinking. This sometimes makes it difficult to understand Pure Land Buddhism in the larger context of Mahāyāna logic.

In Sui and early Tang China, many Buddhist masters also suggested ways to resolve these inconsistencies. Some masters insisted that there were limitations to the Pure Land itself, while others emphasized the equality of enlightenment realized in the Pure Land. The former, including such masters as Huiyuan of Jingying, Jizang, and Kuiji, understood the Pure Land in more conceptual and philosophical schemes, whereas the latter, including such masters as Daozhuo and Shandao, viewed the Pure Land in more practical or soteriological schemes.

In the early stages of Japanese Buddhism, from the seventh through the eighth centuries, this contradiction was apparently acknowledged in a rather simplistic manner without understanding of Mahāyāna logic. Here the concept of the Pure Land was utilized to explicate indigenous religious notions such as unseen deities (Jpn. *kami*) and their world. By the ninth century, the Pure Land teachings were systematically introduced to Japan and flourished all over Japan after that. However, the Pure Land was basically comprehended as that place where one would be born after death. In any event, this approach did not pay heed to the contradictory aspects of the idea of the Pure Land, which has its basis in Mahāyāna logic. It rarely examined the significance of the tension between this world of delusion and the Pure Land, which is the manifestation of enlightenment. Nor did it explore the significance of the idea of a Pure Land in which even an evil person can be born.

On the other hand, as we shall see later, Shinran seems to have grasped the radical meaning of this tension with his deep insight into the Pure

Land. But before turning to his understanding of the Pure Land, let us examine a bit more the way in which the idea of the Pure Land is explicated in the Pure Land Sūtras, while adopting the notion of the environment as a central concern.

THE ECOLOGICAL PERSPECTIVES SEEN IN THE IDEA OF THE PURE LAND

According to the Smaller Sūtra, the Pure Land is the place where Amida Buddha presently resides and expounds the teaching. Amida's Pure Land is also called "the Land of Supreme Bliss," because "the living beings in that realm are free from all forms of suffering and they only experience all forms of happiness."[10] The Smaller Sūtra describes the sphere of Sukhāvatī, the "Land of Bliss," in the following way:

> Furthermore, Shariputra, all around this Land of Supreme Bliss, there are seven tiers of railings, seven rows of netting, and seven rows of trees. They are all made of four precious substances. . . . In the Land of Supreme Bliss there are bathing pools made of the seven precious substances. They are filled with the best water, endowed with eight good qualities: their water is always limpid, cool, sweet-tasting, light, soft, placid, healthy, and thirst-quenching. . . . Above, there are towered pavilions, adorned with gold, silver, lapis-lazuli, crystal, coral, red pearls, and agate.[11]

The sūtra mentions the inhabitants of the Pure Land in this way:

> Furthermore, Shariputra, in this buddha-field celestial music is constantly heard. And the ground is made of gold. Four times a day, exactly on the hour, day and night, mandara flowers rain down from heaven. Early every morning, each living being in this land picks some of those exquisite flowers, places them in the hem of his robe, and travels to worship with these flowers a hundred billion buddhas in other worlds in the regions of the universe. Immediately thereafter, each of these persons returns, in time for forenoon meal, to this, his meal and afternoon stroll.[12]

The sūtra depicts a splendid image of the Pure Land full of symbols of glory and happiness. The glorious form of the Pure Land, described with all kinds of detailed and figurative expressions—such as jeweled trees, jeweled nets, jeweled ponds, jeweled towered pavilions, heavenly music, and flowers—fascinates readers. The Pure Land is described as the ideal place in which to live and enjoy supreme bliss.

But these symbolic physical descriptions are not meant to gratify our sensuous desires. They are the manifestation of the Buddha's enlightenment or of the Dharma. The Smaller Sūtra states:

> Shariputra, in that Buddha-land, a subtle breeze blows, swaying the rows of jeweled trees and the jeweled nets, so that they emit an exquisite sound, like that of hundreds of thousands of diverse kinds of musical instruments playing together at the same time. All those who hear this sound enjoy spontaneously and immediately thoughts of Buddha, of the Dharma, and his Order, and keep these three in mind incessantly, bringing to mind the Buddha, bringing to mind his Dharma, bringing to mind his Order.[13]

We are impressed with the skillful imagination of the sūtra in the way that it connects the physical existence of the land with spiritual meaning. Every existence in the Pure Land represents the enlightenment of Amida Buddha and the inhabitants of the Pure Land naturally enjoy the Buddha-dharma and attain supreme enlightenment. Therefore, many Pure Land masters have explained that we cannot be born in the Pure Land for the purpose of satisfying our desires.

Furthermore, the image of the Pure Land fully embodies the ideas of interconnectivity and harmony in diversity. For example, the sutras explain that the Pure Land is covered by Indra's jeweled net, which also appears in the *Avataṃsaka Sūtra*.

> Nets studded with countless gems are stretched all over this Buddha-land. These ornaments (Indra's nets)[14] extend everywhere unto four corners of that land, with jeweled bells, perfumes, and bright colors shining splendidly, in the most charming way.[15]

Indra's jeweled nets have been hung by some cunning artificer in such a manner that it stretches out indefinitely in all directions of Indra's heaven. The artificer has hung a single glittering jewel at every node of the net, and since the net itself is infinite in dimension, the jewels are infinite in number. If we arbitrarily select one of these jewels for inspection and look closely at it, we will discover that in its polished surface there are reflected all the other jewels in the net, infinite in number. Not only that, but each of the jewels reflected in this one jewel is also reflecting all the other jewels, so that the process of reflection is infinite.[16] This idea of Indra's jeweled net symbolizes the dependent co-arising of all events and the interconnectedness of all existences in the universe. Therefore, it can be said that the Pure Land is also symbolized by these ideas of interconnectivity and harmony in diversity.

At the same time, the idea of interconnectivity and harmony in diversity of the Pure Land does not nullify the characteristics of each individual existence in that land. For instance, in the Smaller Sūtra, it states:

> On the surface of the pools, there are lotus blossoms as large as cart wheels. These are blue colored, with a blue sheen; yellow colored, with yellow sheen; red colored, with a red sheen; white colored, with a white sheen; they are delicate and fragrant.[17]

Each lotus flower in the Pure Land adorns the land with its own individual color. Strange as it may sound in repeating these simple refrains, this passage in fact points to the unique characteristics of each existence. On this point, the Larger Sūtra gives more glorious and detailed explanation:

> Moreover, many jewel lotuses fill this world system. Each jewel blossom has a hundred thousand million petals. The radiant light emanating from their petals is of countless different colors. . . . From every flower issue thirty-six hundred thousand million rays of light. From each one of these rays issue thirty-six hundred thousand million buddhas.[18]

The Pure Land is filled with lotuses of countless colors and millions of rays of light. And from each ray of light a buddha appears. The color of each flower petal and each ray of light is neither mixed with nor hindered by others, meaning that each buddha or bodhisattva in the Pure Land is completely unique, even as they all enjoy the same supreme enlightenment. This idea of harmony in diversity may suggest another ecological perspective of Pure Land Buddhism.

The ideas of interconnectivity and harmony in diversity, seen in the idea of the Pure Land, provide us with an alternative view that may help us to understand the global expansiveness of the world in which today's environmental problems arise. Having been born from individual causes, environmental problems now expand limitlessly. Although this perspective may seem quite natural, our understanding the situation in this way and our being able to solve those problems are really separate issues. The understanding of environmental problems from the viewpoint of interconnectivity and harmony in diversity and the resolution of those problems are not unrelated; yet they are still not the same thing. In order to solve the environmental problems we face, it will be necessary to develop a connection between that method of thought and concrete norms of behavior in this modern age.

The Tension between the Ideal and the Actual in Buddhism

Norms of behavior for Buddhist followers are based in the precepts. In that sense, it is possible that upholding the precepts would entail a basic attitude such that one would relate to the environment from the perspective of the Buddhist teachings. Of course, this is not to say that the Buddhist precepts, which were assigned to priests and lay followers, would be applicable just as they are to the issue of the environment. Precepts, for instance, were enacted in order to preserve the community. More specifically, the purpose was to accomplish the perfection of an individual's practice. The intent of the precepts was not to preserve the environment or nature per se. Rather, the goal was the preservation of the environment of practice so that practice might be perfected.

Still, the existence of Buddhist precepts clearly indicates that Buddhism is a religion that seeks to put the teachings into practice, since it bears great concern not just for the community of priests but also for the greater society that surrounds it. However, when it comes to practice, precepts often involve a tension between the ideal and the actual.

For example, Śākyamuni Buddha's instruction "not to take life" is expressed as:

> All are frightened of the rod.
> For all, life is dear.
> Having made oneself an example,
> One should not neither slay nor cause to slay.[19]

Here the Buddha perceived that each existence includes relationships of confrontation between the self and others. In reality there exists a symbiotic relationship between all living things in this world whereby they exist in solidarity and in mutual support of each other. At the same time, there are also confrontational relationships, which are essentially inescapable. Knowing this contradictory fact, the Buddha urged each Buddhist practitioner and follower "neither to slay nor cause to slay." In this sense, to interpret the Buddhist precept "not to take life" as simply teaching of a harmonious relationship between living beings would lose another important message of the Buddha.

Hence, the Buddha also taught, as the practical aspect of the rule, that it is important to control one's desires. For instance, he warned his followers against simply living in response to one's desires, being controlled by one's desires, or being submerged within delusion and defiled passions.

> Knowing fulfillment is (to know) wealth, happiness, and peace;
> one who does not know fulfillment might be wealthy, but he
> would (still be) poor.[20]

As long as a human being is alive, he or she will have many desires, both great and small. However, Śākyamuni Buddha realized, to be controlled only by one's desires or to live just in order to satisfy them would not match the image of what a human being should be. The Buddha described human desire as "thirst." He likened the mind of greed, in which desires increase without cease, to a state of terrible thirst. Thus, "lessening desires" and "knowing fulfillment" means that one becomes free of the state of being controlled by one's greedy heart and mind, and one turns one's deluded desires into an aspiration for enlightenment.

Buddhism does not simply teach that one should abandon one's desires.

Instead, one is to know deeply the basic essence of human desires and, making that the turning point, redirect one's desire (in this case it is referred to as bodhicitta or bodhi mind) based on wisdom and compassion. In the history of Buddhism, the control of desires has been sought through various methods of practice. In other words, it might be said that the viewpoint of maintaining the Buddhist precepts and the insight into the contradictory structure of the existence of the self, which becomes clear with the performance of practice, give rise to the development of a new and true mode of expression that is based on the Buddhist method of thought for Buddhist followers whose religious concern is to realize ultimate enlightenment.

Controlling desires in everyday life is a norm of behavior that cannot be lacking if we are to grapple with the problems of the environment. However, no matter how often one teaches of "lessening desires" and "knowing fulfillment," or about compassion, they would be completely meaningless if they were to simply end up being pleasing words or were used in a way that allows us to evade our responsibility.

Rather, we must look squarely at our own acts of taking life, and bear down deeply so as to penetrate into the root of our desires or defiled passions. For example, a feeling of gratitude for the food we eat does not eliminate the fact of taking life nor does it justify the act of killing. Rather, it gives expression to our insight into the basic contradiction inherent in our existence. Although we are considering the problem of the environment today, are we not also facing the same problems within ourselves?

The same question can be raised when we consider the Pure Land view on the environment. Needless to say, to understand the environment from the viewpoint of interconnectivity and harmony in diversity would be meaningless were we to fail to realize the tension between the ideal conception of living in accord with the Pure Land vision and the actual nature of our existence. In the history of Japanese Buddhism, Shinran grasped this tension, which underlies Pure Land thought, through his deep insight into Amida Buddha and the idea of the Pure Land.

SHINRAN'S RADICAL UNDERSTANDING OF THE PURE LAND AND THE ENVIRONMENT

The Pure Land teaching was introduced to Japan in the late sixth century, at the early stage of Buddhist history in Japan. Pure Land Buddhism was incorporated into other mainstream Buddhist schools, such as Sanronshū, Tendaishū, and Shingonshū, and practices focusing on Amida Buddha were performed as a part of their own programs of practice. However, the Pure Land teaching of nenbutsu attracted many ordinary lay people who were not able to pursue such monastic practices and who hoped to be born in the Pure Land. In the thirteenth century, Hōnen (1133–1212) declared the independence of the Pure Land school in his work *Senchaku-hongan-nenbutsu-shū*, based on the teaching of the exclusive practice of the nenbutsu. Hōnen insisted that Amida Buddha's vows made no distinction between people intelligent and ignorant, noble and lowly, or good and bad; they were all alike as ordinary human beings. According to Amida Buddha's compassionate vows, all who simply said the nenbutsu would attain birth in the Pure Land.

Inheriting Hōnen's nenbutsu teaching, Shinran made a radical paradigm shift in Pure Land teaching based upon Mahāyāna logic. Here I would like to examine why and how he did so. For example, Shinran states in his "Notes on Once-Calling and Many-Calling":

> From this treasure ocean of oneness form was manifested, taking the name of Bodhisattva Dharmākara, who, through establishing the unhindered Vow as the cause, became Amida Buddha. For this reason Amida is the "Tathagata of fulfilled body." Amida has been called "Buddha of unhindered light filling the ten quarters." This Tathagata is also known as *Namu-fukashigikō-butsu* (Namu-Buddha of inconceivable light) and is the dharma-body as compassionate means.[21]

Shinran says that oneness, which has neither color nor form and thus cannot be grasped by the mind or described by words, takes form as Bodhisattva Dharmakara, who has fulfilled the unhindered vow and becomes Amida Buddha. In other words, form, such as Bodhisattva Dharmakara or Amida Buddha, is founded upon the ultimate truth of reality or supreme Buddha, which is formless. Thus, he also states in his letter, "Amida Buddha fulfills the purpose of making us know the significance of *jinen*."[22] Shinran interprets the term *jinen* as "being made so from the very beginning," or "Supreme Buddha is formless, because being formless is called *jinen*."[23] In this sense, Shinran understands Amida Buddha and the Pure Land to be the dynamic working of ultimate truth.

Shinran explains another aspect of Amida Buddha and the Pure Land in the following passage:

> Reverently contemplating the true Buddha and the true land,
> I find that the Buddha is the Tathagata of inconceivable light
> and the land also is the land of immeasurable light. Because
> they have arisen through the fulfillment of Vows of great com-
> passion, they are called true fulfilled Buddha and land.[24]

Here we need to pay attention to the fact that Shinran describes Amida Buddha and the Pure Land as "true fulfilled Buddha and land." This means that both Amida Buddha and the Pure Land exist for the sake of all sentient beings. Shinran does not comprehend either Amida or the Pure Land as some kind of metaphysical reality or as having any actual, essential existence. He realizes that they are the ultimate point of reference that approaches this deluded world. In his "Hymns of the Pure Land," he states:

> Each feature and mark release, throughout the ten quarters,
> A hundred thousand beams of light;
> Thus the Buddhas (light) constantly reach and spread the
>   excellent dharma
> And lead beings into the Buddha's path.[25]

Shinran's reference to the innumerable beams of light of the Pure Land, which approach this world and lead all sentient beings to the Buddha's path, shows that he understands the existence of the Pure Land in connection with the working of true Dharma in this world of suffering. The Pure Land and this world are viewed as opposites, standing in contrast to each other; and yet, as the "Other Shore," the Pure Land transcends that opposition and is actively working on "this shore," the world of delusion. Shinran understands the Pure Land to be a world that illuminates this world of delusion, revealing it to be a world of delusion. In this sense, Shinran's radical understanding of the Pure Land transcends the traditional framework of Pure Land Buddhist faith, in which one desires to be born in that land in the life-to-come. The principle of his approach is one that is critical of both this world and this age.

Therefore, when Shinran states that "there is no need to wait in anticipation for the moment of death, no need to rely on Amida's coming."[26] he is describing the establishment of the practitioner of true *shinjin*[27] in the realization of enlightenment here and now.

How do we realize the working of Amida Buddha and the Pure Land in this present world? Shinran explains that we encounter Amida Buddha and the Pure Land through the nenbutsu. Through the nenbutsu, we come to deeply realize the true meaning of Amida Buddha and the Pure Land here and now. Through our experience of the tension between this deluded world and the Pure Land—the actual and the ideal—within the nenbutsu, we truly realize the real state of ourselves and the world. It is obvious that we cannot resolve environmental problems by saying nenbutsu or doing religious practices alone. But in Shinran's radical understanding of the Pure Land, we can find a Pure Land Buddhist spirituality that might provide some useful perspectives to our consideration of the environmental problems today.

POSTSCRIPT

Many years have passed since the deterioration and crisis of the global environment was first pointed out. In 1973, the Rome Club put together a report entitled *The Limits of Growth*. Already thirty years have passed since that report sounded an alarm to people who did not question the great amounts of production, consumption, and waste going on throughout the world. Forty years have passed since the publication of Rachel Carson's *Silent Spring*, which sent out a warning about the pollution of the planet. Needless to say, in comparison with that time, people's concerns about the environment have grown, as have our concerns for building a society that has the potential to survive. There are now signs that our ecological understanding is developing, so that, having taken another look at our close relationship with nature, we will consider the symbiosis between human beings and nature, and act accordingly.

In addition, policies for the protection of the environment are being affirmatively implemented, and there is progress in the development of technical solutions to the direct causes of environmental destruction. Furthermore, lively debates are occurring in the area of environmental ethics, which seeks a new ethical framework in order to resolve environmental problems and reexamines the norms of human behavior in the natural world.

There is a tendency to believe that, through this kind of consciousness-raising and many active discussions, countermeasures for the protection of the environment are progressing, and the environment is being preserved. However, in reality things have not progressed to that extent. The lifestyles of most people in industrially developed countries like the United States or Japan do not necessarily encourage them to take action to care for the environment.

People who have concerns about the state of society's ability to survive are certainly increasing in number. However, when it comes to changing our behavior, there are many who postpone any changes until some time in the future. The reason could be that the relationship between environmental problems and our normal, everyday lives is not apparent or obvious to us. Or we might actually feel optimistic that solutions to the problems of the environment, produced by contemporary science and technology, are likely to be realized.

If we take this into consideration, the jeweled net of Indra, Buddha's instruction of "lessening desires" and "knowing fulfillment," and the radical meaning of the Pure Land take on significance as environmental ideas. The problem is, however, that thinking about those ideas and attitudes is not connected to actions actually taken in order to protect the environment.

It would be meaningful for us to know about the need to deepen our understanding or change the norms of our behavior in order to protect the environment. In fact, it is absolutely necessary and increasingly important that we do so. Additionally, however, as we become more aware of the importance of this kind of knowledge and such new norms, it would be necessary to consider the problems of the environment from the point of view that we are incapable of performing actions based upon them. On this point, it seems to me that Shinran's deep insight into human existence is very suggestive in our efforts to examine the tension or dilemma of today's environmental movement.

Shinran's understanding of Buddhism arose out of despair as to this world and human beings. In "A Record in Lament of Differences," Shinran's words are recorded in this way:

> Concerning compassion, there is a difference between the Path of Sages and the Pure Land Path.
>
> Compassion in the Path of Sages is to pity, commiserate with, and care for beings. It is extremely difficult, however, to accomplish the saving of others just as one wishes.
>
> Compassion in the Pure Land Path should be understood as first attaining Buddhahood quickly through saying the nenbutsu and, with the mind of great love and compassion, freely benefiting sentient beings as one wishes.
>
> However much love and pity we may feel in our present lives, it is hard to save others as we wish; hence, such compassion remains unfulfilled. Only the saying of the nenbutsu, then, is the mind of great compassion that is thoroughgoing.[28]

For Shinran, the good that we perform and our acts of compassion are not thoroughgoing; we are not able to fulfill them as we might wish. Is this understanding of human beings a mere resignation to the "realities" of life? Not in the least. What it means is that Shinran was able to encounter the truth and reality of existence as he stood before the abyss of despair.

The following words of Shinran are also noted in the same text:

> In this impermanent world, which is like a burning house, all things are empty and vain, therefore, untrue. Only the nenbutsu is true, real, and sincere.[29]

It can be said that the essence of Shinran's understanding of human existence can be seen in the mutual identity of despair as to the self and one's awakening to truth and reality. Shinran also deeply examined the problem of the "self-powered mind of attachment," which represents human delusion. That is, the problem is one of human calculation, in which, even when one despairs of the world, one is still trying to justify oneself in some way. It is the problem of the self, which always attempts to rationalize and justify one's state of being, engaging in these behaviors as if they were some kind of true practice. This may sound like a negative way to tackle today's environmental problems, but in my opinion, it gives us the firm ground from which to solve the problems.

Today, we human beings seek to justify ourselves and rationalize our actions through the use of human values such as humanism or justice. The issue of the environment, however, harbors the potential that we will fall into the abyss if we take even one false step. In that sense as well, Shinran's understanding of human existence contributes a very important perspective to the manner of engagement toward the resolution of the problems of the environment.

Today's environmental problems arose when that environment was no longer able to support human civilization, which was a human product. The power of human beings arose when our state of comfort and the potential for self-perpetuation overcame the power of nature to recover from them. Accordingly, it is not a problem of the environment, but rather a problem of humanity. And that humanity refers to each and every one of us, who live here in today's civilized society.

Shinran's ideas about the Pure Land and the nature of human existence, which we have seen above, are not mere words. Rather, in a variety of ways they provide us with a useful perspective and can help us to develop constructive ways of thinking about our lives today. What is even more important, however, is that they also become manifest in our own way of life.

Notes

1 Lewis Lancaster, "Buddhism and Ecology: Collective Cultural Perceptions," in *Buddhism and Ecology: The Interconnection of Dharma and Deeds*, ed. Mary Evelyn Tucker and Duncan Ryūken Williams (Cambridge, MA: Harvard Center for World Religions, 1997), 4.

2 Luis O. Gómez uses the term "Shorter Sūtra," though traditionally it has been called the "Smaller Sūtra." He asserts that the term "shorter" is more idiomatic. Although I use Gómez's translation, I refer to it as the Smaller Sūtra in this paper, not because I am definitively against his position, but because the title of the Smaller Sutra is still used conventionally in many English books.

3 For an illuminating account of the development of Pure Land Buddhist thought, see Kenneth Tanaka, *The Dawn of Chinese Pure Land Buddhist Doctrine* (Albany: State University of New York Press, 1990), 1–19.

4 For an extensive discussion of the neglect of Pure Land Buddhism in modern accounts of Buddhism and Japan's cultural heritage in the West, see Galen Amstutz, *Interpreting Amida: History and Orientalism in the Study of Pure Land Buddhism* (Albany: State

University of New York Press, 1997). James C. Dobbins, a historian of medieval Japanese Buddhism, points out that, "Superficial comparisons to Christianity have not helped the attempt to present Pure Land Buddhism as part of Buddhism's mainstream" (*Jodo Shinshu: Shin Buddhism in Medieval Japan*, Preface [repr., Honolulu: University of Hawaii Press, 2002], ix).

5 Luis O. Gómez, *Land of Bliss—The Paradise of the Buddha of Measureless Light* (Honolulu: University of Hawaii Press, 1996), 11–12.

6 Gómez, *Land of Bliss*, 174.

7 Vasubandhu, *Jingtu lun* (The Treatise on the Pure Land; Jpn. *Jodoron*), Taisho-shinshu-daizokyo (Tokyo: Daizokyo-shuppankai, 1914–22), vol. 26, 230c.

8 Tan-luan, *Jingtu lunzhu* (Commentary on the Treatise on the Pure Land; Jpn. *Jodoronchu*), T. vol. 40, 826.

9 Shandao, *Wuhui fashi zan* (Jpn. *Goehojisan*), T. vol. 47, 481a–882a.

10 Gómez, *Land of Bliss*, 146.

11 Ibid., 146.

12 Ibid., 146–47.

13 Ibid., 147.

14 This parenthesis is an author's note. The Chinese version of the Larger Sūtra literally calls this net "Indra's nets."

15 Gómez, *Land of Bliss*, 185.

16 See Francis H. Cook, *Hua-Yen Buddhism: The Jewel Net of Indra* (University Park: Pennsylvania State Press, 1977), 197.

17 Gómez, *Land of Bliss*, 146.

18 Ibid., 186.

19 Dhammapada v. 130, "The Rod / *Daṇḍavaggo*," *The Dhammapada*, trans. John Ross Carter and Mahinda Palihawadana (Oxford: Oxford University Press, 1987), 25.

20 *Butsusu-nehanryakusetsukyokaikyo* (The Last Teaching Sūtra), T. vol. 12, no. 389, 1111c. Translation by author. [Ed. Cp. "Sutra of the Teachings Left by the Buddha, Translated from Kumārajīva's Chinese," trans. Philip Karl Eidmann, *Pacific World: Journal of the Institute of Buddhist Studies* 3, no. 6 (Fall 2004): §III.2, 113.]

21 Shinran, "Notes on Once-Calling and Many-Calling" (Ichinen tanen mon'i), *The Collected Works of Shinran* (CWS), 2 vols. (Kyoto: Jodo Shinshu Hongwanji-ha, 1997), I.486.

22 Shinran, "Lamp for the Latter Ages" (Mattōshō), CWS, I.530.

23 Ibid. The Japanese term *shizen*, which usually refers to "nature" today, did not exist prior to the importation of the concept of nature from the West during the process of the modernization of Japan in the nineteenth century. In addition, the term was originally not read as *shizen*, but as *jinen*. As a Buddhist term, *jinen* implies "naturally," which refers to "things-as-they-are" or "suchness." Shinran further understood it to be the "mode of non-dichotomous thinking," which arises as the working of Amida's vow that enables all sentient beings to realize the attainment of birth in the Pure Land. It would be interesting to consider why the Japanese began to use this term as a translation for the concept of nature in the nineteenth century. However, I would like to devote our present discussion on Shinran's thought to a search for the norms of our behavior.

24 Shinran, "The True Teaching, Practice and Realization of the Pure Land Way" (Ken jōdo shinjitsu kyōgyōshō monrui), CWS, I.177.

25 Shinran, "Hymns of the Pure Land" (Jōdo Wasan), CWS, I.335.

26 Shinran, "Lamp for the Latter Ages," 523.

27 [Ed. *Shinjin* is a term notoriously difficult to translate into English. Frequently rendered as "faith" this has often led to it being confused with Christian conceptions. It may perhaps be better rendered as "confidence," being both the confidence needed to begin practice (*śraddhā*) and the calm and peaceful confidence of one who is close to awakening (*cittaprasada*). For a much fuller explanation, see CWS, II.206–07.]

28 Shinran, "A Record in Lament of Divergences" (Tannishō), CWS, I.663.

29 Ibid., I.679.

Gary Snyder's Ecosocial Buddhism

— ∎ ∎ ∎ —

David Landis Barnhill

There is nothing in human nature or the requirements of
human social organization which intrinsically requires that a
culture be contradictory, repressive and productive of violent
and frustrated personalities. . . . One can prove it for oneself
by taking a good look at Original Nature through meditation.
Once a person has this much faith and insight, one will be
led to a deep concern for the need for radical social change
through a variety of non-violent means.[1]

Buddhist environmentalism in the United States can be said to begin
with Gary Snyder's early writings in the 1950s.[2] Since his writings became
popular in the late 1960s, he has been the most influential Western "eco-
Buddhist." But Snyder's approach is complex, an integrated part of a
broader social critique and radical political vision. Because of that, it is
more accurate to talk about Snyder's "ecosocial" views rather than his
environmentalism. In this he is similar to some Asian Buddhist leaders,
such as Sulak Sivaraksa and A. T. Ariyaratne, who combine social and
environmental concerns, radical political critique, and a vision of ideals
fundamentally different from current social systems.

In this essay I will analyze how Snyder fuses Buddhism, ecology, and
radical politics. These three are interdependent, each one mutually defining and reinforcing the others. In exploring Snyder's ecosocial Buddhism,
we need to ask several questions. What is his fundamental political orientation, and what are his political critique, his social ideal, and the types
of activism he espouses? What are his specific ecological views, and how
does his environmentalism fit into this radical political orientation? And

what is the significance of Buddhism to his ecosocial perspective? We will find that Snyder has throughout his career espoused anarchism, which has shaped and been shaped by both his Buddhism and his environmentalism. These three elements in his thought find their most complete and concrete expression in his bioregionalism. In addition, his approach to environmental and social issues manifests a multifaceted nondualism that is informed by but also extends Mahāyāna Buddhism.

Buddhism, Environmentalism, and Politics

Snyder's fusion of Buddhism, environmentalism, and political critique first appears in his early works, in particular his poetry collection *Myths & Texts*.[3] That work is divided into three sections: Logging, Hunting, and Burning. In the second verse of "Logging" we encounter the first of many passages that reflect a painful witness at the destruction of the natural world. It begins with a quotation from Exodus 34:13.

> But ye shall destroy their altars,
> break their images, and cut down their groves.[4]

This theme is picked up again in the fourteenth verse:

> The groves are down
> cut down
> . . . .
> Cut down by the prophets of Israel
> the fairies of Athens
> the thugs of Rome
> both ancient and modern;
> Cut down to make room for the suburbs
> Bulldozed by Luther and Weyerhaeuser
> Crosscut and chainsaw
> squareheads and finns
> high-lead and cat-skidding
> Trees down
> Creeks choked, trout killed, roads.[5]

Like Lynn White a decade later,[6] Snyder highlights the long-standing connection between environmental destruction and the Western religious traditions, from the Hebrew Bible to Protestantism's influence on capitalism (symbolized by Luther and Weyerhaeuser). But unlike White, he also impugns other societies, including Asian ones. Immediately following the quotation from *Exodus*, we read: "The ancient forest of China logged/and the hills slipped into the Yellow Sea." Western civilization has not held patent on ecological ruin.

However, Snyder does not confine himself to environmental degradation. Examples of social injustice appear throughout *Myths & Texts*. In the seventh verse he refers to a historical incident in which police killed labor activists in the radical organization International Workers of the World (I.W.W., or Wobblies). It took place in Snyder's home state of Washington, and he accentuates the personal dimension of the tragedy by listing the names.

> Felix Baran
> Hugo Gerlot
> Gustav Johnson
> John Looney
> Abraham Rabinowitz
> Shot down on the steamer Verona
> For the shingle-weavers of Everett
>   the Everett Massacre November 5 1916

The verse concludes with

> "Thousands of boys shot and beat up
> For wanting a good bed, good pay,
>   decent food, in the woods—"
> No one knew what it meant:
> "Soldiers of Discontent."[7]

In another verse, using logging now as a trope, he mentions Marx in a way that affirms the goal they share—ending an oppressive social order—but also his rejection of Marx's approach to it.

a big picture of K. Marx with an axe,
"Where I cut off one it will never grow again."
    O Karl would it were true
    I'd put my saw to work for you
& the wicked social tree would fall right down.[8]

This political concern is fused with Snyder's commitment to Buddhism. A wide variety of references to Buddhism run throughout all three sections of *Myths & Texts*, particularly in the final section, "Burning," which offers suggestions of personal and social transformation. In one verse, titled "Amitabha's Vow," Snyder fuses three different traditions: the bodhisattva ideal with its vow to save sentient beings; the social marginalization embodied by Joe Hill, Woody Guthrie, and the Beats; and imagistic nature poetry. Here are two stanzas:

"If, after obtaining Buddhahood, anyone in my land
gets tossed in jail on a vagrancy rap, may I
not attain highest perfect enlightenment.

wild geese in the orchard
frost on the new grass
. . . .
"If, after obtaining Buddhahood, anyone in my land
can't get a ride hitch-hiking in all directions, may I
not attain highest perfect enlightenment.

wet rocks buzzing
rain and thunder southwest
hair, beard, tingle
wind whips bare legs
we should go back
we don't[9]

THE ANARCHIST TRADITION

These references in *Myths & Texts* demonstrate that from the outset of his literary career Snyder was integrating Buddhism, environmentalism, and radical politics. He identifies the specific nature of his political orientation in the title of one of his first essays: "Buddhist Anarchism."[10] In fact, Snyder grew up in a milieu of radical politics. "Our family tradition was radical politics on both sides," he said in an interview, noting that his father was active in the I.W.W.[11] As Snyder began to study and practice Buddhism, he saw a direct link between the two traditions. In a 1990 interview concerning the search for a positive culture, he commented that

> If you keep in touch with the Buddhist or Taoist insight, you're constantly reminded that, no matter what your cultural regenerative exercises are, they're not in the direction of revalidating hierarchy, or revalidating structures of dominance, or reconstructing the state. We are anarchists; we must never forget that. And the proof of anarchism is self-government. Without hierarchy.[12]

Of course, anarchism is not a topic conventionally associated with Buddhism, so to understand Snyder's Buddhist environmentalism, we need to review—if all too briefly—the complex tradition of anarchism. This will seem to take us far from the sayings of the Buddha, but without at least a cursory understanding of anarchism, we will miss an essential component of Snyder's ecosocial Buddhism. In fact, anarchism has informed other American nature writers influenced by East Asian religion,[13] so knowledge of that tradition is important for our broader understanding of American Buddhism.

Anarchism as a political philosophy is over two hundred years old, and it includes a wide range of social philosophies. Ironically, one of the chief stumbling blocks in understanding anarchism is the term anarchy. In common parlance, the term suggests violent chaos stemming from the lack of any central authority. Without an imposed order, it is believed, nothing will keep people from acting in destructive ways. In this view, anarchists are seen as those who use violence to tear down the orderly structure of society.

The anarchist response to such a view is: "Liberty is not the Daughter but the Mother of Order."[14] We don't achieve our freedom because someone imposes order on society; the only true order comes when people are not oppressed by centralized, authoritarian rule. In Snyder's words, "it is the State itself which is inherently greedy, destabilizing, entropic, disorderly, and illegitimate."[15] Such a belief may go directly against the dominant ideology of our times, but a cursory review of the behavior of nation-states in the twentieth century makes this conclusion seem quite reasonable.

The first political philosopher to develop this line of thought was the Englishman William Godwin (1756–1836). In his *Enquiry Concerning the Principles of Political Justice* (1793), he took certain ideas of the European Enlightenment to their logical conclusion. He argued that people are rational individuals sovereign to themselves. The state, then, is an illegitimate and disruptive force that constrains our autonomy: "government even in its best state is an evil."[16] Human nature, on the other hand, is able to recognize justice and act rationally. As a result, appropriate education can turn individuals toward selfless justice, ultimately to establish a libertarian society devoid of any centralized state or even communal arrangements.

Godwin did not use the word anarchism to describe his view, but the French social theorist Pierre-Joseph Proudhon (1809–65) embraced that term. He continued Godwin's emphasis on the individual and on reason, but he also argued that each individual is a social being who "carries within himself the principles of a moral code that goes beyond the individual."[17] The state, on the other hand, is not a moral guardian but rather exists to protect the wealth and power of the elite; the only type of order it can create is repressive. It must be overthrown and replaced by a voluntary and egalitarian system of cooperation he termed "mutualism." Crucial to Proudhon's vision is federalism. Rather than top-down centralized government, he calls for worker associations that form federations from the bottom up, with greatest authority maintained at the local levels. Transformation to this free society cannot be accomplished by electoral politics—the parliamentary system inevitably serves the elite. Instead, workers need to emancipate themselves by direct action against the current hegemony and by working toward alternative economic structures. The ideal is thus to be reached through a peaceful, economic revolution. Because of the importance, complexity, and inconsistency of Proudhon's writings, they have been influential to both individualist anarchism associated with right-wing politics[18] and to trade union anarcho-syndicalism that influenced the I.W.W. of Snyder's upbringing.

While Proudhon added a social dimension to individualism, the Russian Mikhail Bakunin (1814–76) went further and developed a theory of "collectivism," which emphasized the priority of the social group. For him, we are social beings, inherently equal, with a natural drive for both solidarity and freedom. This form of communitarian anarchism is thus both descriptive and prescriptive: it reflects the inherent nature of the universe, and it is the only way to achieve human fulfillment. The goal must be "political, economic, and social equalization"[19] in which there is no government protecting an elite through domination and coercion. This can happen only if agricultural and industrial workers control the means of production by collective ownership. To ensure justice, the goods of society would be distributed according to the degree of productive work done: no person will profit off of the labor of others. Like Proudhon, Bakunin emphasized federalism, a "union of free associations, agricultural and industrial,"[20] which would coordinate the activities of a broader society while maintaining the primacy of local control. Bakunin's view was particularly influential among labor unions, including the I.W.W.

The trend away from individualism toward increasing communitarianism continued with the next great anarchist theorist, the Russian Peter Kropotkin (1842–1921). He began life as a wealthy young prince, but he came to believe that privilege was an injustice that led to the misery of peasants. As a young adult, he became an important geographer and student of evolution, training that enabled him to give anarchism a scientific basis. His book *Mutual Aid* argued that it is cooperation rather than competition that makes for successful evolutionary progress—as well as a healthy human society. Modern history itself, he believed, is leading in the direction of decentralized societies freed from the oppression of the state, the military, and the clergy. The ideal was a social order based on voluntary work that combined the physical and the mental, the agricultural and industrial. Not only would the means of production be owned and shared by the people; going beyond Bakunin, Kropotkin argued that the products of everyone's labor would be distributed freely according to need: a full communism of both production and consumption. He was the most prominent proponent of an anarchist form of communism, which was directly at odds with the authoritarian state socialism of Lenin. Kropotkin's perspective is similar to Snyder's in many ways, and it has been particularly influential in the writings of Ursula K. Le

Guin, science-fiction novelist who has drawn from Taoism, ecology, and feminism.[21]

Several themes are important in nineteenth-century anarchism. Individualism and communalism coexist in creative tension. The anarchist stress on liberty tends to emphasize the individual,[22] while a concern with equality and solidarity has led to a strong communitarian tradition. In addition, theories of human nature are also central. Human nature is usually presented as either naturally moral and cooperative or at the least capable of a selfless sense of justice. In either case, the coercive order of the state is unnecessary and repressive.

The most controversial and perhaps most misunderstood part of the anarchist tradition is violence. Anarchists have articulated a wide range of views on violence, from those who enthusiastically embrace violence as both effective and creative (such as Bakunin) to those who have hesitatingly affirmed that violence may be necessary (such as Kropotkin) to those who have renounced violence altogether (such as Leo Tolstoy).[23]

Another issue that anarchists have debated is spirituality. Most nineteenth-century anarchists were critical of and even highly antagonistic toward religion, associating it with hierarchical churches. However, for two anarchists, Leo Tolstoy (1828–1910) and Gustav Landauer (1870–1919), spirituality was a central component to creating a liberatory and egalitarian society. Tolstoy's spirituality was a radical version of Christianity, summarized in *The Kingdom of God Is Within*, while Landauer retained a deep suspicion of traditional religions but affirmed the importance of a communal spirituality.[24]

Nineteenth-century anarchist theorists also tended to be optimistic. They believed that reason and science can provide compelling arguments for a libertarian society; they believed that history is teleological, characterized by progress toward a free and egalitarian society; and they believed that radical social revolution was not only possible but likely. In part because of this optimism about social change, early anarchists usually argued against forming alternative communities where small groups could try to realize the ideal separate from mainstream society. Efforts needed to be directed toward a transformation of society as a whole.

After the horrors of the twentieth century, such optimism is far more difficult to uphold. Attempts to establish anarchist societies in the early twentieth century were crushed by the Bolsheviks soon after the Russian

Revolution and by the Fascists in Spain during the Civil War. Anarchists were persecuted in the United States, the most infamous example being the execution of Sacco and Vanzetti in 1927. In addition, U.S. trade unions have largely aimed at entry into the middle class rather than social transformation. Anarchist theory has continued, however, in thinkers such as art historian Herbert Read, poet and critic George Woodcock, and linguist-activist Noam Chomsky. It also has been influential in the upheavals of the late 1960s, the current resistance to corporate globalization, and the growing bioregional movement.

One of the most important contemporary embodiments of anarchism is social ecology. Social ecology's most basic point is that social and environmental issues are intertwined. Whether it is articulating a philosophy, analyzing current problems, or proposing concrete solutions, we need to consider both ecological and social dimensions. More specifically, social ecology asserts that our environmental and social problems are rooted in centralized, authoritarian government and a hierarchical society. The nation-state's system of domination and the exploitive economic system it supports, capitalism, inevitably create profound social and environmental problems. In addition, individuals in such a society lack personal liberty and responsibility and are alienated from other people and the natural world. The only true solution to both our environmental and social problems is found in a decentralized economy, a grassroots participatory democracy, and small-scale egalitarian societies in which our natural communitarian drive can flourish. Although Snyder is usually associated with deep ecology, his ecosocial Buddhism is in agreement with all of these points of social ecology.[25]

Social ecology was initially developed by Murray Bookchin. His libertarian municipalism provides a structure for direct democracy, human-scaled societies, and a deep sense of interdependence with the Earth. As Snyder has noted, Bookchin has been a powerful and perceptive proponent of social ecology, but he also has tended to be highly sectarian and irascible, disdaining and dismissing other approaches and eventually alienating some of his prominent followers. He has been antagonistic toward spiritual perspectives, in particular those based in Asian or Native American cultures. Recently, a broader and more nuanced social ecology has been articulated by others, in particular John Clark, who is appreciative of the anarchist values that can be found in spiritual traditions such as Buddhism and Taoism. He also is open to a rapprochement with other schools such as deep ecology. It is Clark's type of social ecology that is particularly relevant to Snyder's ecosocial Buddhism.[26]

There is another tradition related to anarchism that is also important in understanding Snyder's ecosocial Buddhism. This is the communalist tradition, primarily religious groups that have separated themselves from the dominant culture in order to pursue a communitarian society. Kenneth Rexroth (1905–82), the American Buddhist poet who influenced Snyder, chronicles this tradition in his book *Communalism*.[27] Two examples are particularly worth noting here. During the religious and political upheavals of seventeenth-century England, Gerrard Winstanley led a radical Christian group known as the Diggers to settle on unused land on St. George's Hill. They formed an egalitarian, anarchist, and communist community, based on the belief that nature was both the manifestation of God and a resource created for all to share. "In the beginning of time the great creator Reason made the earth to be a common treasury.... [N]ot one word was spoken in the beginning that one branch of mankind should rule over another."[28] Winstanley is generally credited with establishing the first anarchist community. It did not last long, however, as both the authorities and local landowners felt threatened and responded by raiding and harassing the community until it finally dispersed.

The next recorded alternative community based on anarchist principles was nearly two centuries later, established by the American Josiah Warren (1798–1874). In 1825 Warren joined Robert Owen's utopian community, New Harmony, but he disagreed with the communistic approach to property and he left after two years. In 1834 Warren formed his own experimental community, Village of Equity, in Ohio, and later founded a second colony, Utopia, and a third, Modern Times. These were similar to Winstanley's experiment in being alternative intentional communities outside the mainstream, but there were two major differences. First, Warren's political approach was closer to the continental nineteenth-century anarchists in being based in Enlightenment ideas of reason, justice, and the sovereignty of the individual, rather than in a radical reading of Christian communalism. And second, his societies were not communistic but rather were similar to Proudhon's mutualistic individualism (although Warren and Proudhon developed their ideas independently). None of

Warren's intentional communities lasted for an extended period of time, but they were serious experiments in taking anarchism in a direction that the continental anarchist thinkers did not support: establishing an alternative society that was largely independent of mainstream society. This goal has been revived in the twentieth century with the back-to-the-land movement, and it plays a role in the bioregional movement. We will examine Snyder's Buddho-anarchistic bioregionalism later in this essay.

THE NATURE OF REALITY

Anarchists usually ground their social views in a view of reality—ontology, human nature, and history—and Snyder is no exception. His ontology involves both metaphysics (primarily Buddhist) and physical science (primarily ecological science). His principal image for the metaphysical character of reality is Indra's net. Developed by the Huayan school of Buddhism (Kegon in Japanese), Indra's net suggests the radical interrelationship among all phenomena in the universe. In this image, the universe is considered to be like a vast web of many-sided and highly polished jewels, each one acting as a multiple mirror. In one sense each jewel is a distinct entity, different from all others. But when we look at a jewel, we see nothing but the reflections of other jewels, which themselves are reflections of other jewels, and so on in an endless system of mirroring. Thus in each jewel is the image of the entire net. The result is a single field of mutual interaction among distinct elements in the field (as in gravitational and electromagnetic fields). As Snyder notes, "Avatamsaka (Kegon) Buddhist philosophy sees the world as a vast interrelated network..." in which "the universe and all creatures in it are ... acting in natural response and mutual interdependence."[29]

This perspective involves a nondualistic view of the individual and the whole, the one and the many, which counters the extremes of atomism and monism. An atomistic view asserts that individuals are essentially autonomous. The individual is distinct, independent, and primary; relationships and wholes (species, ecosystem, social bodies) are secondary and accidental. A monist view holds that the whole is primary, and individual distinctions are secondary or even illusory. Snyder's Huayan view affirms the reality and primacy of both the individual and the whole. Indeed, as suggested by the image of Indra's net, the individual and the whole are "not two": "any single thing or complex of things *literally* [is] as great as the whole."[30] Thus Snyder says, "all is one and at the same time all is many."[31] An individual is distinct from others not in being independent from them but in being constituted by a unique set of those interrelationships with others and a unique position in the field (as with a niche in an ecosystem). This perspective can be called "relational holism," for it simultaneously affirms the primacy of relationships among particulars and also the primacy of the whole, which is a single field of all interrelationships.[32]

In its traditional presentation, Indra's net remains a rather abstract image of the metaphysical interpenetration of all things. Snyder, however, makes that image concrete by tying it to ecology, what Snyder has called the science of the "reciprocity of things."[33] For Snyder, Indra's net is embodied in the physical, ecological interrelationships of the natural world. Thus he has stated that "The web of relationships in an ecosystem makes one think of the Huayan Buddhist image of Indra's net."[34] Put differently, if you want to know Indra's net as manifested in the phenomenal world, study ecology; if you want to understand the subtle nature and full significance of ecological relationships, see it as Indra's net. Thus Snyder says, quoting a Buddhist text, "If you understand [one] blade of rice, you can understand the laws of interdependence . . . [and] you know the Buddha."[35] He presents this combination of Indra's net and ecology in another extended hyphenization: "The Avatamsaka ('Flower Wreath') jeweled-net-interpenetration-ecological-systems-emptiness-consciousness tells us, no self-realization without the Whole Self, and the whole self is the whole thing."[36]

Snyder's metaphysical and ecological perspective is relevant to axiology: the issue of value. Like most environmental philosophers, he affirms that nature has intrinsic value, but he does so in line with Huayan's insistence that each particular is essential and has unlimited value.

> In the course of coming to understand the interconnectedness of life and the remarkable ways that energy flows through living systems on the planet, we are possibly finally seeing that the time has come to put aside unexamined human assumptions of species superiority and all the destruction that goes with them. We humans might just learn to see ourselves as fully part of the transhuman realm. This means allowing the intrinsic *value*— soul, if you like—of the rest of the world. There is nothing in

our whole occidental tradition to prepare us for such an attitude, yet it is essential.[37]

This intrinsic value extends to all beings. "Every creature, even the little worms and insects, has value. Everything is valuable—that's the measure of the system."[38] Snyder put this inclusive axiology into a Buddhist framework with his "Smokey the Bear Sutra," a playful but serious statement of his key environmental ideas. Smokey the Bear appears as an American bodhisattva, "Wrathful but calm. Austere but Comic." "His left paw in the mudra of Comradely Display—indicating that all creatures have the full right to live to their limits and that deer, rabbits, chipmunks, snakes, dandelions, and lizards all grow in the realm of the Dharma."[39]

While all things are of value and are interrelated, Snyder emphasizes that the world is not an idyll in which the lion lies down with the lamb. A crucial aspect of the ecological embodiment of Indra's net is the food web. Mutual interaction involves death as well as life, and Snyder affirms the first Noble Truth: life is suffering. "To be truly free," he asserts, "one must take on the basic conditions as they are—painful, impermanent, open, imperfect—and then be grateful for impermanence and the freedom it grants us."[40] Snyder uses Huayan ecological metaphysics to take a middle path, or a nondualistic one, by affirming both that all beings share a condition of suffering death and also that life has unqualified beauty and value. "The larger view," he contends, "is one that can acknowledge the simultaneous pain and beauty of this complexly interrelated world. This is what the image of Indra's net is for."[41] In Snyder's own interconnected terminology, this is the "sacramental energy-exchange, evolutionary mutual-sharing aspect of life.... And that's what communion is."[42] This mutuality of death-and-life is a movement filled with love. "Looking close at this world of oneness," he says, "we see all these beings as of our flesh, as our children, our lovers. We see ourselves too as an offering to the continuation of life."[43] Turning the conventional attitude of survival of the fittest on its head—or turning it into Indra's net—Snyder can ask rhetorically, "if we eat each other, is it not a giant act of love we live within?"[44]

Snyder's relational holism is directly related to his anarchism in at least three ways. First, it provides a nuanced alternative to the debates in anarchism concerning the individual and society. Godwin, Proudhon, Bakunin, and Kropotkin form a continuum of theories: the strong individualism of

Godwin, the social individualism of Proudhon, the collectivist view of Bakunin, and the communist view of Kropotkin. Each perspective has certain potential dangers, from selfishness and lack of cooperation in an individualist view, to oppression of the individual for the sake of society in a completely socialist view. Snyder's relational holism is dialectical in that both the individual and the whole are upheld and any attempt to make one primary or fundamental is rejected.[45] Second, Snyder's relational holism is relevant to social value. The statement "Everything is valuable— that's the measure of the system" is true socially as well as ecologically. Any individual, social class, gender, ethnic group, or nationality is as valuable as any other, a view that undercuts assertions of hierarchy and justifications for domination. And third, relational holism offers an alternative image of a political ideal. When asked what kind of counterimages could motivate fundamental changes, Snyder replied, "The image of organism. The imagery of a marvelous complexity, working on many levels, in pathways too delicate to be grasped, and doing this in a totally uncentralized way. No center. No visible source of authority."[46]

Like most anarchists, Snyder claims that true order (as opposed to oppression and obedience) arises not from the external authority of the state but from the people themselves freely interacting. Snyder develops this idea most cogently in "The Etiquette of Freedom." In this examination of the word "wild," he seamlessly analyzes ecological and political systems in primarily Taoist terms. While our culture usually defines the term wild by what it is not (e.g., uncivilized, uncultivated), he proposes positive characterizations. Wild plants and animals are those "flourishing in accord with innate qualities," "each with its own endowment." The same holds with wild—anarchistic—societies, "whose order has grown from within." So too with wild individuals, who act spontaneously according to their nature and resist any oppression.[47] Snyder notes that his positive set of definitions "come very close to being how the Chinese define the term *Dao*, the *way* of Great Nature: ... self-organizing, self-informing, ... independent, complete, orderly, ... freely manifesting, self-authenticating. ... It is not far from the Buddhist term *Dharma* with its original senses of forming and firming."[48] The related term wilderness is a place where "a diversity of living and nonliving beings [are] flourishing according to their own sorts of order."[49] In an interview he summarized his notion of wild: "It means self-organizing. It means elegantly self-disciplined, self-regulating, self-maintained. That's what wilderness is. Nobody has to do the management plan for it."[50]

Similarly, in Snyder's ideal of a "civilization of the wild," people act with similarly emergent, anarchic order, responsive not only to other people but to the natural world as a whole. Snyder suggests this possibility metaphorically in the poem "Straight-Creek—Great Burn," where a flock of birds in flight displays self-organizing. "A whoosh of birds / swoops up and round / tilts back / almost always flying all apart / and yet hangs on! / together."[51] Murphy explicates the verse this way: "There is also a significant political theme developed in this poem, which does not come clear until almost the end: 'never a leader, / all of one swift / / empty / / dancing mind.'"[52] "Nature contains a high degree of complex organization and interaction. . . . [The birds] too are highly organized and complex, but their leadership consists of 'mind' rather than other trappings of the modern nation-state."[53]

Snyder uses two traditional Buddhist images to suggest his complex and creative merging of Buddhism and ecology. With his inclusive sense of the interpenetration of all things, the Buddhist sangha in the broadest sense comes to mean the entire natural world, the "great earth sangha,"[54] and in a narrower sense the local ecosystem people live in. Snyder frequently reminds us that this eco-Buddhist sense of community includes not just human society but the larger biological community. "Human beings who are planning on living together in the same place will wish to include the non-human in their sense of community. This also is new, to say our community does not end at the human boundaries; we are in a community with certain trees, plants, birds, animals. The conversation is with the whole thing. That's community political life."[55]

Another aspect of reality plays a crucial role in anarchist theory and Snyder's ecosocial Buddhism: human nature. Authoritarian, hierarchical societies are usually based on a view that humans are naturally contentious and selfish; thus we need a centralized state to control our disorderly nature. Snyder, however, takes a view that is traditional in anarchism: people are aggressive not by nature but as a result of living in an authoritarian society that stifles and frustrates our nature. He draws on Buddhism in presenting his view of human nature. "Buddhism holds that the universe and all creatures in it are intrinsically in a state of complete wisdom, love and compassion, acting in natural response and mutual interdependence."[56] It is true, he notes, that Buddhism teaches us that people fall victim to craving, aversion, and delusion. However, those characteristics are systematically exacerbated by an authoritarian society. "Organized society can inflame, pander to, or exploit these weaknesses, or it can encourage generosity, kindness, trust."[57] On the other hand, a free and communitarian society would assist in the task of diminishing or potentially eliminating craving, aversion, and delusion. Thus the need for a Buddhist anarchism.

Anarchists have supported their politics not only by tying them to the metaphysical and physical nature of reality and to human nature but also to earlier human cultures. These examples counter the establishment view that anarchism is bizarre and impossible. Anarchists traditionally point to medieval village society and the ancient Greek polis as examples of decentralized and largely libertarian human societies. Snyder also looks to history, but in a different and more ambitious way. His sense of history is deeper, going back to the Upper Paleolithic. "We have to develop a much larger perspective on the historical human experience. . . . This is the new, larger humanism."[58] Snyder's historical perspective is more ambitious than those of earlier anarchists also because he does not simply point to a few isolated examples but a continuous tradition. This is what he calls the Great Subculture, which has continued forty thousand years from the Upper Paleolithic to the contemporary period. "This is the tradition that runs without break from Paleo-Siberian Shamanism and Magdalenian cave-painting; through megaliths and Mysteries, astronomers, ritualists, alchemists and Albigensians; gnostics and vagantes, right down to Golden Gate Park."[59] The Great Subculture has been a continuous alternative to authoritarian states and their environmental ruin. "It seems evident that there are throughout the world certain social and religious forces that have worked through history toward an ecologically and culturally enlightened state of affairs."[60]

For Snyder, the Great Subculture is characterized by a communalism that links it to both early Buddhism and contemporary anarchist ideals. "As utopian and impractical as it might seem, [the Great Subculture] comes through history as a little dream of spiritual elegance and economic simplicity, and collaboration and cooperating communally. . . . Certainly it was one part of the early Buddhist vision."[61] Not only are simple, communal, anarchistic societies part of our past; they are the real mainstream of human history. "[T]he subculture is the main line and what we see around us is the anomaly."[62] Civilization, on the other hand, "stands outside of the mainstream."[63] Because the Great Subculture is, in fact, the mainstream, Snyder's analysis of it concerns not just the past but the present and future as well. As Murphy has noted, Snyder "has continued to excavate the heritage of . . . 'The Great Subculture' of mystics and visionaries. Recovering the past, imaginatively reconstructing gaps that remain, and envisioning the future have always been intertwined activities in Snyder's research and writing."[64]

SNYDER'S BUDDHIST ECOSOCIAL CRITIQUE

Snyder's view of metaphysics, ecology, and history also leads to a comprehensive critique of the political, social, and economic conditions of our times. It is comprehensive in part because of the holistic, systemic view of the problem. Environmental destruction has been taking place East and West, and it is a matter not only of needless human suffering and death but the devastation of whole watersheds and ecosystems.

> Even as the Buddhists were practicing vegetarianism and kindness to creatures, wild nature in China suffered significant species extinction and wholesale deforestation between the fifth and the fifteenth centuries A.D. India too was vastly deforested well before modern times. Now, with insights from the ecological sciences, we know that we must think on a scale of a whole watershed, a natural system, a habitat. To save the life of a single parrot or monkey is truly admirable. But unless the forest is saved, they will all die.[65]

In the poem "Front Lines," Snyder expresses his outrage at environmental ruin by using metaphors that have become common in environmental critiques, cancer and rape, as well as fascism ("Amerika") and a demonizing anthropomorphism of machinery. "The edge of the cancer / Swells against the hill—we feel / a foul breeze. . . . Realty Company brings in / Landseekers, lookers, they say / To the land / Spread your legs. . . . Every pulse of the rot at the heart / In the sick fat veins of Amerika / Pushes the edge up closer. . . . A bulldozer grinding and slobbering / Sideslipping and belching on top of / The skinned-up bodies of still-live bushes / In the pay of a man / From town."[66] In the "Smokey the Bear Sutra," Snyder compares our rapacious society in terms of the Buddhist image of a hungry ghost. We live in a "world of loveless knowledge that seeks with blind hunger: and mindless rage eating food that will not fill it."[67]

It is not merely the natural world that is being harmed. One of the social parallels to this environmental destruction is alienation. Snyder discusses our alienation from nature as a "loss of heart and soul." "This is serious!" he exclaims. "To lose our life in nature is to lose freshness, diversity, surprise, the Other—with all its tiny lessons and its huge spaces."[68] There is a deeper alienation as well, which he particularly associates with Western culture: "a culture that alienates itself from the very ground of its own being—from the wilderness outside . . . and from . . . the wilderness within—is doomed to a very destructive behavior, ultimately perhaps self-destructive behavior."[69] Snyder takes an anarchist view of this alienation when he complains of our European forebears who "got led down the garden path of centralized government, civilization, and alienation."[70]

In addition to psychological alienation, there is also massive social injustice. In fact, as social ecologists have done, Snyder has criticized environmentalists who seek to preserve nature while being indifferent to the consequences that might have to workers or the poor.[71] On the other hand, he faults those who merely focus on social problems. "Even if economic and social justice were achieved for all people, there would still be a drastic need for ecological justice, which means providing plenty of land and water for the lives of nonhuman beings."[72]

Snyder is similarly nondualistic in his analyses of the causes of these pervasive problems. As in social ecology, the environmental and social dimensions are interconnected. At times he has pointed out how social inequities aggravate the degradation of nature. "The unequal distribution of wealth in the world causes endless social turmoil and intensifies the destruction of nature."[73] At other times he has highlighted how our attitudes toward nature lead to social problems. "I suspect that many of the problems within the human community—racism and sexism, to name two—reflect back from confusion about our relations to nature. Ignorance and hostility toward wild nature set us up for objectifying and exploiting fellow humans."[74]

Thus Snyder's view of the cause of environmental and social problems diverges from traditional Buddhist teachings that emphasize psychological causes and cures. But in another sense, Snyder has extended the central Buddhist teaching of mutual co-arising: environmental and social problems are inextricably interrelated, and both social and psychological causes act together. We can see this co-arising even more clearly when we consider his critique of social structures. Much of the pain and loss among both people and nonhuman nature have not been simply an inescapable part of reality. They have been caused by certain economic, social, and political systems that supplanted earlier, healthier communal cultures. Sometimes Snyder focuses his condemnation on industrial, capitalist societies. "The whole planet groans under the massive disregard of the precept of *ahimsa* by the highly organized societies and corporate economies of the world."[75] At other times he points to "that relatively recent institution, the national state." "The state," he wrote in "Buddhist Anarchism," "is greed made legal, with a monopoly on violence."[76]

But Snyder recognizes that this problem has been endemic to all civilizations. "There are socially and politically entrenched attitudes and institutions that reinforce our misuse of nature and our cruelty toward each other. Our major civilizations objectify and commodify the natural world. They regard nature as a mere inanimate resource and a target of opportunity."[77] This has been supported by the fact that "[o]ur philosophies, world religions, and histories are biased toward uniformity, universality, and centralization—in a word, the ideology of monotheism."[78] As a result, the cause of the problem is broader than capitalism or the nation-state. It is "civilization [that] is ultimately the enemy. The very order of the society that we have lived in for the last 4,000 years has outlived its usefulness."[79] Snyder gives a Buddhist spin on this critique by associating civilization and the state with the ego. In an early essay he claimed that "Class-structured civilized society is a kind of mass ego. To transcend the ego is to go beyond society as well."[80] In a more recent essay, he presents a similar view: "Civilization itself is ego gone to seed and institutionalized in the form of the State, both Eastern and Western. It is not nature-as-chaos which threatens us, but the State's presumption that *it* has created order."[81] Given such a sweeping social critique, Snyder needs to articulate a radically different ideal.

THE IDEAL: ECO-BUDDHIST ANARCHISM

The ideal that Buddhism points to, Snyder asserts, is ecological and anarchist.[82] For him, the Huayan vision of reality calls for a "civilization of wildness," with humans interacting with nature in a harmonious and sustainable way, in tune with the character and limits of the local ecosystem. Similarly, Buddhism's stress on interrelatedness and inclusive value points to a libertarian, egalitarian, and communitarian society. "If we are lucky, we may eventually arrive at a world of relatively mutually tolerant small societies attuned to their local natural region and united overall by a profound respect and love for the mind and nature of the universe."[83]

The emphasis on the local ecosystem has become a central element in Snyder's ideal. Ever since the early 1970s, Snyder has couched his ideal in terms of bioregionalism.[84] Bioregionalism is a complex movement that centers on the distinctiveness of different local regions. Unlike the abstract and arbitrary political divisions of counties, states, and nations (think of the border between Montana and Canada or Wisconsin and Illinois), bioregionalism looks to natural divisions created by soil, climate, topography, river drainages, etc. Bioregions may be distinguished as watersheds (for example, the central valley of California) or biogeographically distinct territories. For instance, the biogeography of southeastern Wisconsin (unglaciated and characterized by native prairies and deciduous forests) is very different from that of northwestern Wisconsin (recently glaciated, characterized by coniferous forests). "Wisconsin" is an odd abstraction with very little relation to the real world. "The world is places,"[85] Snyder says with seeming simplicity, but his point is sophisticated: if we are to truly understand and live harmoniously with nature, we need to become intimate with the distinctive particularities of each place.

Bioregionalism develops this insight into a substantial philosophy and movement, with three basic elements. The first is biogeography—the study of the interaction of life with physical geography—both as it is used in natural-resource planning and as part of the personal development of intimate knowledge of the Earth. The second is the reformist programs that are currently being pursued, such as community-sustained agriculture, small-scale sustainable forestry, and green cities. And third is a radical view of a new society, characterized by the decentralization of politics, economics, and culture, as well as close harmony with the particularities of the local bioregion. "The aim of bioregionalism," Snyder has stated, "is to help our human cultural, political and social structures harmonize with natural systems. Human systems should be informed by, be aware of, be corrected by, natural systems."[86]

Part of the power of bioregionalism comes from its complexity, including various types of nondualism. It combines the "two cultures" of science and the humanities (philosophy, religious studies, aesthetics). It offers reformist activities immediately available, while also pointing to a radical, utopian ideal. It calls for both highly practical physical activities and also a "bioregional consciousness"—a highly refined sense of place and a deep feeling of identity with the land one inhabits. It has both individual and social dimensions: each person can pursue bioregional values or a community can work to create bioregional programs. And it involves both living in harmony with the land and also using it. As Charles Strain has said, "The practice of reinhabitation assumes that humans have a place, must find a place in the wild. Having a place means using its resources wisely; it entails transgressing the lines of division separating preservation and natural resource management."[87]

Snyder sees bioregionalism as related to Buddhism. The relational holism of his Huayan metaphysics leads one to a profound sense of interrelatedness with the local natural world in which one lives. The local bioregion or watershed then takes on his extended sense of a biogeographic mandala.[88] "An ecosystem is a kind of mandala in which there are multiple relations that are all-powerful and instructive. Each figure in the mandala—a little mouse or bird (or little god or demon figure)—has an important position and a role to play."[89] He adds that "The watershed is our only local Buddha mandala, one that gives us all, human and non-human, a territory to interact in. That is the beginning of dharma citizenship: not membership in a social or a national sphere, but in a larger community citizenship. In other words, a *sangha*; a local dharma community."[90] With this ecological notion of mandala as well as his extension of sangha to include all beings, Snyder is ecologizing the Buddhist notion of community and Buddhacizing the idea of ecological community.

The strong predilection toward decentralization and community makes bioregionalism's values intrinsically close to those of anarchism. In fact, Snyder has emphasized bioregionalism's link with both classical anarchist thought and contemporary social ecology. In an interview about bioregionalism, Snyder put it this way:

So this is an anarchist exercise, as foretold by Kropotkin in *Mutual Aid* and as described, in contemporary terms, by Murray Bookchin in *The Ecology of Freedom*, in which we try to realize the true meanings of being local, and having a culture, without letting it pull us back into centralized hierarchical forms.[91]

Snyder explicitly merges anarchist organizational principles with a biogeographic focus. "My own sympathies still lie," Snyder commented recently, "with a kind of anarcho-syndicalist organization of work groups blocked out in terms of bioregions."[92] However, he does not, like anarcho-syndicalists, make the industrial worker the principal focus. His bioregionalism is, nondualistically, inclusive of city and country. As he has put it, "The city is just as natural as the country, let's not forget it. . . . Got to get rid of those dualisms."[93] The key is, whatever the location, to have a deep sense of community in harmony with the land.

Although early in his career Snyder was associated with solitude in the mountains,[94] he has, as Michael Castro has emphasized, "remained steadfastly concerned in literature and life with the development of an alternative *community*."[95] This communitarianism puts Snyder more in line with Kropotkin than the more individualistic Proudhon and Godwin. But "alternative community" does not refer to the kind of communities Josiah Warren established, outside mainstream society. Some bioregionalists in fact have sought to establish separate, ideal communities,[96] but Snyder's bioregionalism is nondualistic here again: it works toward establishing alternative communities while remaining engaged in mainstream society. In any case, a bioregional community is virtually the opposite of the nation-state. Thus for Snyder, bioregionalism "destroys the national state's pretensions"[97] that it is the only or the best way to shape society. Snyder creates a neologism in order to suggest his communitarian anarchism: "Hope for the withering-away of the states / And finally arrive at True Communionism."[98]

THE PATH

Two crucial questions remain: how should we respond to the ongoing environmental ruin and social injustice, and how can an eco-Buddhist ideal be achieved? For Snyder, the fundamental element in the process is a state of mind. As John Whalen-Bridge has noted, "the first political act is to sit still long enough to see where we are, and then to see what and who we are."[99]

But cultivating a buddhistically based bioregional consciousness is just the beginning. Central to Snyder's approach to both questions is an insistence of personal engagement in the world. "[T]o be true to Mahayana, you have to act in the world. To act responsibly in the world doesn't mean that you always stand back and let things happen: you play an active part. . . . That's what the Bodhisattva idea is all about."[100] He told an interviewer that "there are several different strategies by which to live in the world. One is to withdraw from the world and to choose purity. To do that you could live in an ashram or a monastery or a nunnery or a utopian community." However, Snyder takes a different route. "In my case, my choice is what you might call from the Buddhist standpoint, the lay choice, the bodhisattva choice, the choice of engaging in it as it is—living in it as other people have to live in it, eating the same poisons and running the same karmic risks . . . and I have no apologies for that."[101]

Part of engagement is resistance to the ongoing and unnecessary pain and destruction. He portrays this vividly in "Front Lines," and he draws his readers into the struggle by using the pronoun "we." "Behind is a forest that goes to the Arctic / And a desert that still belongs to the Piute / And here we must draw / Our line."[102] The fact that he locates the forest by his home is important. "Think globally, act locally" is part of Snyder's approach.[103] An interviewer asked him, "How might people today say no to a wrong in a contemporary issue? How would you 'set yourself against it'?" He responded:

> Well, it depends on the nature of the wrong and it also depends on how close it is to you. Things that are dumped in your lap, things that come up to your front door, you are really karmically obligated to deal with, I do believe. Poverty, oppression, rank injustice right in front of you is yours. It's been given to you to take care of. The old Quaker concept of bearing witness and putting yourself out in front by civil and disobedient means is probably the best you can do. . . . Although, politically speaking, if you really want it to work, call the newspapers too. In other words, a civil disobedient or bearing witness move is

personally and morally satisfying if you simply do it, and it may do some good. But to make it really effective, we involve the rest of the society and let them know what we're doing, what's happening, and make it into an issue. If we go farther than that, we're into terrorism.[104]

The reference to terrorism points to Snyder's concern with violence as a tactic. Pacifism has long been part of Snyder's perspective, and that tendency has increased over time. Like other anarchists, he associates the nation-state with violence, whereas Buddhism is identified with nonviolence and *ahimsa*, which can be politically powerful. "The joyous and voluntary poverty of Buddhism becomes a positive force. The traditional harmlessness and refusal to take life in any form has nation-shaking implications."[105] However, Snyder has shown some hesitation about taking an absolute position supporting nonviolence. This can be seen in the different versions of the essay originally titled "Buddhist Anarchism" and comments he has made in interviews concerning them. In that original 1961 version, the issue of violence appears twice. Buddhist practice, he said, leads "to a deep concern with the need for radical social change and personal commitment to some form of *essentially non-violent* revolutionary action."[106] Later in the essay he approves various types of resistance: "Fighting back with civil obedience, pacifism, poetry, poverty—and violence, if it comes to a matter of clobbering some rampaging redneck or shoving a scab off the pier."[107] In the 1969 version in *Earth House Hold*, titled "Buddhism and the Coming Revolution," he limited this qualified approval of violence. In the case of the first passage, a Buddhist, he said, is lead to "a deep concern with the need for radical social change through a variety of *hopefully non-violent* means,"[108] and more importantly, in the second passage, he restricts the use of violence: ". . . even *gentle* violence if it comes to a matter of restraining some impetuous redneck."[109] In a third version published in 1988 and again in the fourth version published in 1999 (both titled "Buddhism and the Possibilities of a Planetary Culture"), he has dropped the word "hopefully" and stated unequivocally "a variety of non-violent means."[110] However, Snyder has kept the term "gentle violence" in these versions. Yet in interviews he has expressed a disquiet about even such tempered violence. In a 1977 interview, he declared that "If I were to write [the essay] now, I would use far greater caution. I probably wouldn't use the world 'violence' at all. I would say now that the time comes when you set yourself against something, rather than flow with it; that's also called for."[111] Still, he retained the phrase "gentle violence" in the two versions he revised later. This ambivalence, I believe, arises from his insistence on seeing honestly the complexity of the situation in which Buddhists find themselves. In a 1988 interview, Catherine Ingram brought up the issue of nonviolence.

CI: "Do you think nonviolence is always the way?"

Gary Snyder: "Yes. Nonviolence is always the way, but you can't always do it. This is the compassionate and practical paradox of the first precept, the precept of nonviolence. In an ultimate sense, there is no evasion of the precept."

CI: "What do you mean by that?"

Gary Snyder: "That there are no excuses, there are no justifying circumstances for violence. However, in our contingent and organic being in this karmic realm, the very law of impermanence is a law that is often enacted by processes that are violent. And we sometimes have clear choices before us that are of a very paradoxical nature which throw us between responding with violence or choosing that violence be done to ourselves or to someone else. So with no further ado, we respond. The response of the being who chooses not to be a victim is a fair response, and in some of these contexts it's hard to know who is being violent to whom."[112]

However, overall Snyder is more concerned about articulating the "real work" of trying to embody the ideal than resisting evil. Not surprisingly, as a Buddhist, Snyder emphasizes the need for a change of consciousness in working toward the ideal. When asked in an interview how people can work toward a "jujitsu flip" of modern civilization, Snyder replied, "It cannot even be begun without the first of the steps of the Eightfold Path, namely Right View."[113] This involves a "revolution of consciousness," which, he says, "will be won not by guns but by seizing the key images, myths, archetypes, eschatologies, and ecstasies so that life won't seem worth living unless one's on the side of the transforming energy."[114] Snyder's poetry, essays, and interviews are his attempt to seize these components of a new consciousness.[115]

Cultivating Buddhist insight through meditation and Dharma study is one of the ways to foster that revolution of consciousness. But the subtleties of Buddhist wisdom must be combined with other forms of learning. One type is bioregional, which unites ecological and cultural knowledge. "One project is to learn our natural system, learn our region, to such a degree that we can be sensitive across the centuries and boundaries of cultures. We should know what the life-cycle of salmon is, or what grows well here, but also become sensitive to what kinds of songs you might sing if you thought like a salmon. That's the learning that brings the place visibly into culture."[116] Another necessary form of learning is social scientific, though it too must be combined with the ecological. Our young people, Snyder says, "must become well informed about the workings of governments, banking, and economics—those despised but essential mysteries. We need an education that places them firmly within biology but that also gives them a picture of human cultural affairs and accomplishments over the millennia."[117] Such topics are clearly not part of the traditional Buddhist Dharma, but they are essential, Snyder believes, to making Buddhism an effective force in creating ecosocial change.

In addition, as the three treasures of Buddhism suggest, wisdom concerning Buddhist Dharma is not enough. Community is crucial both to the ideal and to the path toward it. "Nobody can move from Right View to Right Occupation in a vacuum as a solitary individual with any ease at all. The three treasures are Buddha, Dharma, and Sangha. In a way the one that we pay least attention to and have least understanding of is Sangha—community." Snyder adds that community can take various forms. "What have to be built are community networks—not necessarily communes or anything fancy."[118]

As is common in bioregionalism, a key ingredient to developing community and working toward the ideal is to "commit to one's place for the long term."[119] "For those who can do it, one of the things to do is not to move. To stay put. Now staying put doesn't mean don't travel. But it means have a place and get involved in what can be done in that place." Whalen-Bridge rightly points out that such an act is political: "Whether in city or country, the first political act is to sit still long enough to see where we are, and then to see what and who we are."[120] It is political in part because it undercuts the political establishment and promotes real democracy. "We're in an oligarchy right now," Snyder asserts, "not a democracy. Part of the reason that it slid into oligarchy is that nobody stays anywhere long enough to take responsibility for a local community and for a place."[121] True democracy is not simply voting every four years; far more important is being an active and informed citizen caring for the local community, both human and nonhuman.

Consciousness-raising, community, and commitment to place are all characteristics of the nonduality of bioregional practice. They are aspects of both the utopian ideal that bioregionalism points to and reformist changes that can be made in the short run. In other words, they are both the goal and the process. What is missing in Snyder's writings is the detailed proposals found in many anarchist theories. This fact might make his writings seem less significant: we are given no details of how society ought to be organized or how we should confront the current hegemony. Much of anarchist theory has, in fact, been debates about such details, whether it is Kropotkin disagreeing with Bakunin's collectivism and insisting on complete communism ("from each according to his ability; to each according to his needs"), or contemporary social ecologist John Clark disagreeing with the details of Murray Bookchin's libertarian municipalism.[122] Why the absence of such specifics in Snyder? One reason, no doubt, is that Snyder is a poet, not a political theorist. Even in his essays where he analyzes environmental and social issues, he has chosen to work primarily on the level of fundamental cognitive structures ("images, myths, archetypes, eschatologies, and ecstasies") rather than political specifics, which he leaves up to others. As he put it in an interview, "The work I see for myself remains on the mythopoetic level of understanding the interface of society, ecology and language, and I think it is valuable to keep doing that."[123]

In addition, Snyder is a pluralist in terms of both the process and the goal. As contemporary anarchist Noam Chomsky has argued,[124] to propose in the abstract the details of an anarchist society runs contrary to the anarchist spirit. Such questions must be addressed contextually by the people involved, and answers will differ depending on the circumstances. Snyder displays his pluralism concerning the process when he says he supports "any cultural and economic revolution that moves clearly toward a truly free world"[125]—an attitude that is certainly in line with the Buddhist notion of skillful means. But Snyder's perspective is not simply pluralism; the key points are diversity of different contexts and the creative change of social and ecological situations. Murphy puts it this way: "In the universal process of co-creation an individual's vantage point is not a fixed, static position but a momentary node in the ongoing transformation of energy. As a result, determining the proper forms of right practice requires attention to localized specifics . . . because diversity is a crucial feature of any healthy ecosystem."[126]

And finally, I would argue that Snyder advocates the social equivalent of virtue ethics. The task is not to rationally figure out ahead of time what is right and wrong in any or all situations. Rather, it is to develop certain basic virtues in people and in a community as a whole so they will be able to respond morally, wisely, and effectively to life's shifting complexities. Snyder finds those virtues in Buddhism, anarchism, and bioregionalism.

One of those virtues, as we saw at the beginning of this section, is active engagement in a morally messy world. In a sense this is like a Buddhist version of the nineteenth-century anarchist view against establishing utopian communities separate from the fallen world. But Snyder's bioregional practice is really nondualistic here as well. He participates in the world—flies to conferences and drives to meetings, cashes his checks and pays his taxes—but he also is cultivating bioregional community that is—in a partial way—the ideal he opposes to contemporary society. The path is "to be right in the middle of whatever is happening right here, rather than waiting for a theoretical alternative government to come along."[127] This means working on reformist activities—"to go to supervisors' meetings and deal with the establishment"—while also cultivating an ideal community as much as possible. Once again, Snyder draws on the bodhisattva ideal to support engagement: "the Bodhisattva view does *not* imply that first, you perfect your self-realization and second, enter the world to 'cure illnesses and loosen bonds.' The waterwheel swings deep into the water and spills it off the top in the same turning."[128]

Snyder's approach is nondualistic in yet another way, combining East and West.

> The mercy of the West has been social revolution; the mercy of the East has been individual insight into the basic self/void.

We need both. They are both contained in the traditional three aspects of the Dharma path: wisdom (*prajna*), meditation (*dhyana*), and morality (*shila*).[129] Wisdom is intuitive knowledge of the mind of love and clarity that lies beneath one's ego-driven anxieties and aggressions. Meditation is going into the mind to see this for yourself—over and over again, until it becomes the mind you live in. Morality is bringing it back out in the way you live, through personal example and responsible action, ultimately toward the true community (*sangha*) of "all beings."[130]

For Snyder, Buddhism is actually a way to combine Eastern insight and Western revolution.

Conclusion

There is probably no literary figure or American Buddhist more acutely concerned with environmental problems than Snyder. And there may be no one whose response to those problems is as complex and nuanced. Part of that richness comes from the bringing together of Buddhism, environmentalism, and politics. In the interconnection of these three, each is extended. Environmental concerns are placed in a context of Buddhist philosophies of nature and mind, linked with a radical vision of social problems and possibilities. Political issues are extended beyond the human to include nature, and political critique, ideal, and path are informed by nondualistic Buddhism. Buddhist philosophy of nature is grounded in the empirical world of ecosystems and food webs, and the Buddhist notions of suffering and liberation are broadened to include the social and political context. All of these come together in Snyder's distinctive version of bioregionalism.

One of the elements of Snyder's perspective, Buddhist nondualism, has become the focus of criticism, at least as it is applied to environmental and social issues. Ian Harris, for instance, has written several articles in which he argues, among other things, that a nondualistic view of reality such as found in Huayan Buddhism cannot support an environmental ethic: a truly nondualistic view would undercut any moral distinctions or ethical judgments. True, if Buddhism or Snyder were attempting simply to offer a logically coherent and philosophically complete portrait of the world in a totally nondualistic way, the argument would have merit. But Snyder, in true Buddhist fashion, integrates metaphysics and spiritual psychology, Indra's net and the bodhisattva vow, wisdom and compassion. In fact, Snyder in effect answered this criticism back in the original version of "Buddhist Anarchism."

> Avatamsaka (*Kegon* or *Hua-yen*) Buddhist philosophy sees the world as a vast interrelated network in which all objects and creatures are necessary and illuminated. From one standpoint, governments, wars, or all that we consider "evil" are uncompromisingly contained in this totalistic realm. The hawk, the swoop and the hare are one. From the "human" standpoint we cannot live in those terms unless all beings see with the same enlightened eye. The Bodhisattva lives by the sufferer's standard, and he must be effective in aiding those who suffer.[131]

In line with the bodhisattva tradition, Snyder has always combined spiritual contemplation of nondual reality with compassion for suffering.

The result is that, despite his Mahāyāna drive to "get rid of those dualisms," there *are* dualisms in Snyder's approach. One of the dualisms is crucial to all forms of Buddhism: the distinction between suffering and enlightenment.[132] In addition, for Snyder, as for many engaged Buddhists, there is a distinction between the suffering and destruction that are part of the natural process of the "great system,"[133] and the unnecessary pain and loss caused by craving, aversion, and delusion and the social structures that manifest and exacerbate those poisons. These imply another dualism: between a bioregional way of life that is egalitarian, libertarian, and in harmony with nature, and a culture of consumption and destruction, hierarchy and domination. In all these cases, the dualistic view is affirmed as a way to take the sufferer's standard and to work against that suffering.

These dualisms, particularly the third one, make Snyder's writings quite political. Those writings critique power structures, promote an alternative ideal, and offer a path toward that goal. In addition, his writings are, as Katsunori Yamazato has stressed, didactic, in the sense of "directing poet and reader to answers for the question 'how to be.'"[134] The answer to that question, for Snyder, is informed by Buddhism, bioregionalism, and anarchism.

So what are the possibilities for a better future? Snyder is realistic about the problems we face. We might say that he takes a middle path between naive optimism about revolution and a resignation that denies any possibility of real change. "The fact is that the dynamics of industrial capitalism are still so enormous that until it slows down of its own glut there isn't much we can do except holding actions, and to try to keep our heads clear about what can be and should be. But I have no illusions about the difficulty." As he often is, Snyder is practically minded here, focusing on what tasks we need to work on to prepare for the possibility of an ecoanarchist society. "[W]e would be well advised to have in mind what kinds of skills we really need and what it means to be self-governing, and to increasingly take responsibility for our own lives, our own neighborhoods, and our own communities."[135] When we do that, he says from his own experience, meaningful change is possible, however small.

> [W]hat Allen [Ginsberg] and I and the rest of us can say realistically, with absolute surety and with great pride, is we have moved the world a millionth of an inch. But it's a real millionth of an inch. That much happened. Not nearly as much as people think, perhaps, or would like to ascribe to it, but what it was, was real, and so, like, that much is possible, and the fact that that much was possible is what gives us a certain amount of confidence. If you can move it a millionth of an inch, you've got a chance.[136]

Snyder also expresses a cautious, ambivalent optimism about our future in "For the Children."[137] The poem begins with our problematic and paradoxical times: "The rising hills, the slopes, / of statistics / lie before us. / the steep climb / of everything, going up, / up, as we all / go down." The next stanza imagines the ideal: "In the next century / or the one beyond that, / they say, / are valleys, pastures, / we can meet there in peace / if we make it." The poem concludes with a depiction of the path, including an italicized triple imperative that is a brilliant metonymy for bioregionalism: community, bioregional consciousness, and ecological lifestyle.

> To climb these coming crests
> one word to you, to

you and your children:
stay together
learn the flowers
go light

Murphy reads the poem as expressing "an optimistic and virtually utopian mood."[138] However, the phrases "they say" and "if we make it," as well as uncertainty about time—"or the [century] beyond that"—weakens the optimism. What *is* certain are the current social and ecological decline and the difficult climbs ahead. Yet Murphy is right to point to a utopian mood, which is most strongly expressed not in predictions of an ideal perfect future but in the very real possibility of a true communionism of right practice—which may be the only utopia we can, or should, aim for.

Notes

1 Gary Snyder, *The Gary Snyder Reader: Prose, Poetry, and Translations* (Washington, DC: Counterpoint, 1999), 42.
2 Kenneth Rexroth (1905–82) preceded Snyder in his combined interest in nature, Buddhism, and radical politics. However, Rexroth is a "pre-environmentalist" writer, whose perspective was developed before the science of ecology or environmental concerns became culturally prominent. He did express concerns about environmental degradation before the 1950s, but it was not a central or developed part of his writings.
3 *Myths & Texts* was the first collection of poetry Snyder completed (New York: Totem Press, 1960; repr., New York: New Directions, 1978). However, the poetry collection *Riprap* (Kyoto: Origin Press, 1959) was published in 1959, one year before *Myths & Texts*. See Patrick D. Murphy, *A Place for Wayfaring: The Poetry and Prose of Gary Snyder* (Corvallis: Oregon State University Press, 2000), 20. Murphy's book is the best general introduction to Snyder's writings.
4 Snyder, *Myths & Texts*, 4.
5 Ibid., 14.
6 In "Historical Roots of our Ecologic Crisis" (*Science* 155, no. 3767 [March 10, 1967]: 1203–7), Lynn White argued that the environmental degradation of the planet is not simply a matter of policy or technology. It is rooted in a religious worldview, and unless we change that worldview, we will not really deal with the pressing issues at hand. He particularly impugned Christianity and its theology of devaluation and domination of nature. He suggested that we need either to find a religious view in another tradition, and he specifically noted Buddhism as a possibility, or reinterpret the Christian tradition according to a more earth-friendly theology, such as that of St. Francis. The article set in motion the field of religion and ecology.
7 Snyder, *Myths & Texts*, 9.
8 Ibid., 7.
9 Ibid., 40–41.

10 The title of this article has been revised over time along with changes in the text. It was published as "Buddhism and the Coming Revolution" in Gary Snyder, *Earth House Hold: Technical Notes and Queries to Fellow Dharma Revolutionaries* (New York: New Directions Press, 1969), 90–93, and as "Buddhism and the Possibilities of Planetary Culture" in *Gary Snyder Reader*, 41–43. But the basic perspective of Buddhist anarchism remains throughout.

11 Julia Martin, "Coyote-Mind: An Interview with Gary Snyder," *Triquarterly* 79 (Fall 1990): 148.

12 "Regenerate Culture!" in *Turtle Talk: Voices for a Sustainable Future*, ed. Christopher Plant and Judith Plant (Philadelphia: New Society Publishers, 1990), 16.

13 In particular Henry David Thoreau, Kenneth Rexroth, and Ursula Le Guin.

14 This statement by Pierre-Joseph Proudhon has been used by a wide range of anarchists, from the American individualist anarchist Benjamin Tucker (who used the phrase on the masthead of his journal *Liberty*) to the Buddhist communitarian anarchist Kenneth Rexroth, *The Complete Poems of Kenneth Rexroth*, ed. Sam Hamill and Bradford Morrow (Port Townsend, WA: Copper Canyon Press, 2003), 161.

15 Gary Snyder, *The Practice of the Wild* (San Francisco: North Point Press, 1990), 41.

16 William Godwin, *The Political and Philosophical Works of William Godwin*, 7 vols., ed. Mark Philp (London, Pickering and Chatto, 1993), 3:48.

17 Quoted in Peter Marshall, *Demanding the Impossible: A History of Anarchism* (London: Fontana, 1993), 249.

18 For a brief overview of anarcho-capitalism, see Marshall, *Demanding the Impossible*, 559–65.

19 Quoted in George Woodcock, *Anarchism: A History of Libertarian Ideas and Movements* (Cleveland: Meridian, 1962), 166

20 Quoted in Woodcock, *Anarchism*, 166.

21 Ursula K. Le Guin's most famous and most explicit evocation of anarchism is the novel *The Dispossessed: An Ambiguous Utopia* (New York: Harper and Row, 1974).

22 Not surprisingly, individualist anarchism is particularly strong in the United States, found, for instance, in an anarchist form of capitalism and the current Libertarian Party. However, an early and extreme form of individualistic anarchism was articulated by the German Max Stirner (1806–56), as detailed in his book *The Ego and His Own: The Case of the Individual Against Authority* (1845; repr., New York: Libertarian Book Club, 1963).

23 The issue of violence has been particularly relevant to Edward Abbey (1927–89), nature writer, novelist, wilderness advocate, and anarchist. His master's thesis in philosophy was entitled "Anarchism and the Morality of Violence," and his novel *The Monkey Wrench Gang* (Philadelphia: Lippincott, 1975) inspired the ecological sabotage of the Earth First! movement.

24 For Landauer on "spirit," see Gustav Landauer, *For Socialism* (St. Louis: Telos Press, 1978).

25 For an analysis of Snyder's social ecology, see my article "The Social Ecology of Gary Snyder," *Indian Journal of Ecocriticism* 1, no. 1 (August 2008): 21–28. That article is an earlier and much shorter version of this article.

26 For Bookchin's social ecology, see Murray Bookchin, *Toward an Ecological Society* (Montreal: Black Rose Books, 1980). See also John Clark, *The Anarchist Moment: Reflections on Culture, Nature, and Power* (Montreal: Black Rose Books, 1984).

27 Kenneth Rexroth, *Communalism: From Its Origins to the Twentieth Century* (New

York: Seabury, 1974). Rexroth was a major influence on Snyder and the Beats in the San Francisco literary renaissance of the 1950s. According to Snyder, the view that anarchism is "a credible and viable position was one of Rexroth's greatest contributions for us, intellectually. Also, linking that to Kenneth's sense of biology and nature . . . [and] his interest in Chinese and Japanese poetry" (James McKenzie, "Moving the World a Millionth of an Inch," in *The Beat Vision: A Primary Sourcebook*, ed. Arthur and Kit Knight [New York: Paragon House Publishers, 1987], 5).

28 Quoted in Rexroth, *Communalism*, 142.

29 Snyder, *Earth House Hold*, 91–92, 90.

30 Snyder, *Earth House Hold*, 31. Emphasis original.

31 Gary Snyder, *The Old Ways* (San Francisco: City Lights Books, 1977), 9.

32 For a detailed exposition of relational holism and the nondualistic affirmation of individual and whole, see my "Relational Holism" in *Deep Ecology and World Religions: New Essays on Sacred Ground*, ed. David Landis Barnhill and Roger S. Gottlieb (Albany: State University of New York Press, 2001).

33 Gary Snyder, *The Real Work: Interviews and Talks 1964–1979* (New York: New Directions, 1980), 130.

34 Gary Snyder, *A Place in Space: Ethics, Aesthetics, and Watersheds* (Washington, DC: Counterpoint: 1995), 67.

35 Snyder, *Real Work*, 35. Snyder does not identify the text.

36 Snyder, *Old Ways*, 64.

37 Snyder, *Place in Space*, 209. Emphasis original.

38 Trevor Carolan, "The Wild Mind of Gary Snyder," *Shambhala Sun* 4, no. 5 (May 1996): 23.

39 Snyder, *Gary Snyder Reader*, 242.

40 Snyder, *Practice of the Wild*, 5.

41 Snyder, *Place in Space*, 70.

42 Snyder, *Real Work*, 89. For an extensive analysis of the place of the food chain in Snyder's writings, see the chapter "Food Chain Poetics" in James W. Kraus, "Gary Snyder's Biopoetics: A Study of the Poet as Ecologist" (PhD diss., University of Hawaii, 1986), 73–110.

43 Gary Snyder, "Grace," *CoEvolution Quarterly* 43 (Fall 1984): 1.

44 Ibid. For an analysis of Snyder's application of Indra's net to ecology, the food chain, and hunting, see my "Indra's Net as Food Chain," *Ten Directions* 11, no. 2 (Spring–Summer 1990): 20–28.

45 Charles Molesworth has noted Snyder's affirmation of both the social whole and the individual. "In this sense Snyder is a quintessential American artist, torn by an idealizing vision between opposing hungers for both a new sense of community and a new sense of radical individuality" (Charles Molesworth, *Gary Snyder's Vision: Poetry and the Real Work* [Columbia: University of Missouri Press, 1983], 126). However, I do not see Snyder as "torn" between the two; his nondualism comfortably incorporates an affirmation of both. For a general discussion of how Buddhist nondualism can be applied to the social issue of the individual and the community, see my "Relational Holism." For an interpretation of Snyder's Buddhist sense of community, see my "Great Earth *Sangha*: Gary Snyder's View of Nature as Community" in *Buddhism and Ecology: The Interconnection of Dharma and Deeds*, ed. Mary Evelyn Tucker and Duncan Ryūken Williams (Cambridge, MA: Harvard Center for World Religions, 1997).

46 Snyder, "Regenerate Culture!" 17. For an analysis of Snyder's "acentric" Buddhist perspective, see Julia Martin, "Practising Emptiness: Gary Snyder's Playful Ecological Work" *Western American Literature* 27.1 (1992), especially pages 10, 12, and 16.

47 Snyder, *Practice of the Wild*, 9–10.

48 Ibid., 10. For a discussion of "anarchic" and "emergent" order in Taoism, see Roger Ames, "Putting the Te Back in Taoism," in *Nature in Asian Traditions of Thought*, ed. J. Baird Callicott and Roger Ames (Albany: State University of New York Press, 1989), 113–45.

49 Snyder, *Practice of the Wild*, 12.

50 Carolan, "Wild Mind," 24.

51 Gary Snyder, *Turtle Island* (New York: New Directions, 1974), 52–53.

52 Murphy, *Place for Wayfaring*, 53.

53 Ibid., 114–15.

54 Snyder, *Turtle Island*, 73.

55 Snyder, "Regenerate Culture!" 18.

56 Snyder, *Gary Snyder Reader*, 41.

57 Snyder, *Practice of the Wild*, 91.

58 Snyder, *Real Work*, 113.

59 Snyder, *Earth House Hold*, 114–15.

60 Carolan, "The Wild Mind," 23.

61 Ibid.

62 Snyder, *Real Work*, 68.

63 Ibid., 114–15.

64 Murphy, *Place for Wayfaring*, 3.

65 Snyder, *Place in Space*, 73.

66 Snyder, *Turtle Island*, 18.

67 Snyder, *Gary Snyder Reader*, 241.

68 Snyder, *Place in Space*, 59.

69 Snyder, *Turtle Island*, 106.

70 Snyder, *Real Work*, 155–56.

71 Snyder, *Practice of the Wild*, 119; and *Place in Space*, 237–38.

72 Snyder, *Place in Space*, 60.

73 Ibid.

74 Ibid., 211.

75 Ibid., 73.

76 Snyder, *Gary Snyder Reader*, 43.

77 Snyder, *Place in Space*, 61.

78 Snyder, *Practice of the Wild*, 41.

79 D. Kozlovsky, "Interview," *Modine Grunch* 3 (January 1970): 22.

80 Snyder, *Earth House Hold*, 122.

81 Snyder, *Practice of the Wild*, 92. Emphasis original.

82 Snyder's social critique extends to Buddhism. In his early essay "Buddhist Anarchism" (and its subsequent revisions), Snyder argues, in the mode of a social ecologist, that Buddhism has lacked political concern and analysis. "Historically, Buddhist philosophers have failed to analyze out the degree to which ignorance and suffering are caused or encouraged by social factors, considering fear-and-desire to be given facts of the human condition. Consequently the major concern of Buddhist philosophy

is epistemology and 'psychology' with no attention paid to historical or sociological problems. . . . Institutional Buddhism has been conspicuously ready to accept or ignore the inequalities and tyrannies of whatever political system it found itself under. This can be death to Buddhism, because it is death to any meaningful function of compassion. Wisdom without compassion feels no pain" (Snyder, *Gary Snyder Reader*, 41). But note that he specifies "institutional" Buddhism as part of the problem. For Snyder, true Buddhism leads to radical social critique and an anarchistic ideal.

83 Snyder, *Gary Snyder Reader*, 43.

84 While Snyder did not speak in terms of bioregionalism until the 1970s, he expressed bioregional views as early as 1955 in a letter to the State Department concerning his application for a passport. Murphy notes that in the letter, Snyder spoke of his "opposition to large, centralized modern nation states," and instead supported "decentralized land-based social organizations. These would be communities based on more ancient models of traditional societies, with territories defined by the lines of the natural boundaries and regions of a particular place" (Murphy, *Place for Wayfaring*, 6).

85 Snyder, *Practice of the Wild*, 25.

86 Snyder, "Regenerate Culture!" 13.

87 Charles R. Strain, "The Pacific Buddha's Wild Practice: Gary Snyder's Environmental Ethic," in *American Buddhism: Methods and Findings in Recent Scholarship*, ed. Duncan Ryūken Williams and Christopher S. Queen (Abingdon, England: RoutledgeCurzon, 1999), 153.

88 In Japan, some mountains have been treated as vast, three-dimensional mandalas, with walking through the mountains treated as a ritualized spiritual journey. This is particularly true of the *yamabushi*, mountain ascetics. While in Japan, Snyder practiced with *yamabushi* and he was initiated into the sect as a novice. For a discussion of some of his experiences, see "Walking the Great Ridge Ōmine on the Womb-Diamond Trail," in Snyder, *Gary Snyder Reader*, 371–82.

89 Snyder, *Place in Space*, 76.

90 Carolan, "Wild Mind," 24.

91 Snyder, "Regenerate Culture!" 16.

92 Snyder, *Place in Space*, 208.

93 Snyder, *Real Work*, 91. John Whalen-Bridge has emphasized that Snyder's writings have become increasingly nondualistic. "The relationship between part and whole, between culture and nature, between back country and city, has shifted in the later poem away from the dualistic conception of this relationship in the earlier poems" ("Spirit of Place and Wild Poetics in Two Recent Snyder Poems," *Northwest Review* 29, no.3 [1991]: 124).

94 The image of Snyder as hermit was particularly strong in *Riprap & Cold Mountain Poems*, and in Jack Kerouac's depiction of Snyder as Japhy Ryder in *The Dharma Bums*.

95 Michael Castro, *Interpreting the Indian: Twentieth-Century Poets and the American Indian* (Norman: University of Oklahoma Press, 1991), 140. Emphasis original.

96 For a narrative account of one such group, see Mike Carr, *Bioregionalism and Civil Society: Democratic Challenges to Corporate Globalism* (Vancouver: UBC Press, 2004), 185–96.

97 Snyder, *Real Work*, 23.

98 Ibid., 39. See Julia Martin's "True Communionism: Gary Snyder's Transvaluation of Some Christian Terminology," *Journal for the Study of Religion* 1, no. 1 (1988): 63–75, for an analysis of this term.

99 Whalen-Bridge, "Spirit of Place and Wild Politics in Recent Snyder Poems," *Northwest Review* 29 (1991): 130.

100 Snyder, *Real Work*, 106–7.

101 Catherine Ingram, *In the Footsteps of Gandhi: Conversations with Spiritual Social Activists* (Berkeley: Parallax Press, 1990), 240.

102 Snyder, *Turtle Island*, 18.

103 Snyder's emphasis on the local is rooted in an ethical view of greater obligation for problems at your doorstep (see the following quote) as well as his bioregional perspective. But his eco-Buddhism is also nondualistic concerning local and global. He has noted that "through my involvement on the local level, I'm working on and involved in issues that go all the way to the tropical rain forest. That's the way ecological activism works, since everything is connected. What you learn from working on, say, a soil or water or forest or wildlife or pollution issue in any one spot on the globe is very informative about what's going on everywhere and how it works everywhere" (Ingram, *In the Footsteps of Gandhi*, 230). For a discussion of "cosmopolitan bioregionalism" that integrates a local focus and a global view, see Mitchell Thomashow, "Toward a Cosmopolitan Bioregionalism," in *Bioregionalism*, ed. Michael Vincent McGinnis (London and New York: Routledge, 1999), 121–32.

104 Ingram, *In the Footsteps of Gandhi*, 242–43.

105 Snyder, *Gary Snyder Reader*, 42.

106 Snyder, "Buddhist Anarchism," *Journal for the Protection of All Beings*, 1 (San Francisco: City Lights Books, 1961), 11. Emphasis added. [Ed. One version available online: http://www.bopsecrets.org/CF/garysnyder.htm, accessed October 24, 2009.]

107 Ibid., 12.

108 Snyder, "Buddhism and the Coming Revolution," in *Earth House Hold*, 91. Emphasis added.

109 Ibid., 93. Emphasis added.

110 The third version, titled "Buddhism and the Possibilities of a Planetary Culture," was published in *The Path of Compassion: Writings on Socially Engaged Buddhism*, ed. Fred Eppsteiner (Berkeley: Parallax Press, 1988). There is a fourth version in *The Gary Snyder Reader*. While there are some minor differences between these last two versions, the two passages concerning violence are the same in both versions.

111 Snyder, *Real Work*, 106.

112 Ingram, *In the Footsteps of Gandhi*, 244–45.

113 Snyder, *Real Work*, 108.

114 Snyder, *Place in Space*, 43.

115 For a sophisticated analysis of Snyder's cognitive rhetoric in *The Practice of the Wild*, see Sharon Ann Jaeger, "Toward a Poetics of Embodiment: The Cognitive Rhetoric of Gary Snyder's *The Practice of the Wild*" (PhD diss., University of Pennsylvania, 1995).

116 Snyder, "Regenerate Culture!" 13–14.

117 Snyder, *Place in Space*, 80.

118 Snyder, *Real Work*, 110.

119 Ibid.

120 Whalen-Bridge, "Spirit of Place," 130.

121 Eliot Weinberger, "The Art of Poetry LXXIV," *The Paris Review* 38, no. 141 (Winter 1966): 116.

122 See John Clark, "Municipal Dreams: A Social Ecological Critique of Bookchin's Politics," in *Social Ecology after Bookchin*, ed. Andrew Light (New York: Guilford Press, 1998), 137–91.

123 Weinberger, "Art of Poetry," 92.

124 In an interview with Tom Lane, Chomsky responded to questions about how an anarchy would be structured and how it would function, by saying, "How one should react . . . depends on circumstances and conditions: there are no formulas. . . . These are matters about which we have to learn, by struggle and experiment" (Tom Lane, "Noam Chomsky on Anarchism," June 13, 2006, http://www.zmag.org/chomsky/interviews/9612-anarchism.html). [Ed. Access to this site is restricted to members only, free membership available. Accessed October 24, 2009.] Snyder would likely agree, except to assert that some general principles (such as no hierarchy) and some virtues (such as humility) are essential.

125 Snyder, *Gary Snyder Reader*, 43.

126 Murphy, *Place for Wayfaring*, 106.

127 Snyder, *Real Work*, 117.

128 Snyder, *Old Ways*, 51. Emphasis original.

129 This statement confirms and expands on what Charles Molesworth has noted, that for Snyder "the reigning value is neither exclusively Western nor Eastern, but a master term—compassion or love—that surmounts the ethical system of both world views" (Molesworth, *Gary Snyder's Vision*, 37). In the Snyder quotation given here, the "master term" is actually three Buddhist terms—wisdom, meditation, and morality—which, if interpreted in his ecosocially engaged way, can encompass both world views. However, I think Molesworth is correct in saying that compassion also can serve as such a master term, as long as it is understood as Buddhist compassion linked to *prajñā* and *śīla* as well as compassion arising from a deep ecosocial concern for suffering caused by hierarchy, centralization, and domination.

130 Snyder, "Buddhism and the Possibilities of Planetary Culture," *Gary Snyder Reader*, 42–43.

131 Ibid., 42.

132 This dualism is nuanced by the Mahāyāna doctrine of original enlightenment: all beings are inherently buddhas, they just don't realize it or manifest it. However, this simply refines the dualism: between manifesting and not manifesting one's original enlightenment.

133 Snyder, *Place in Space*, 66.

134 Katsunori Yamazato, "How to Be in This Crisis: Gary Snyder's Cross-Cultural Vision in *Turtle Island*," in *Critical Essays on Gary Snyder*, ed. Patrick Murphy (Boston: G. K. Hall, 1990), 245.

135 Snyder, *Real Work*, 143.

136 McKenzie, "Moving the World," 12–13.

137 Snyder, *Turtle Island*, 86.

138 Murphy, *Place for Wayfaring*, 119.

A Buddhist Economics to Save the Earth

Shinichi Inoue
(Translated by Duncan Ryūken Williams[1])

BORROWING FROM THE COSMOS

Although natural resources are usually considered in terms of their use-fulness to human society, they must be considered in the context of the planet as a whole according to a Buddhist approach to economics. This is especially true in the case of nonrenewable resources: rather than trying to exploit them, a new economics must recognize that we are only bor-rowing them from the cosmos. Indeed, we need to persuade companies to avoid taking the quick path to short-term profits, and must help them make better long-term choices that assist in the preservation of our natu-ral environment.

The Buddha taught nonviolence and the avoidance of destruction, not only as regards our fellow human beings but also as regards plants, trees, and even inanimate objects. He taught that all things are endowed with buddha nature. From this perspective, resources are not simply inanimate objects. They have their own existence and serve a purpose in this cosmos. Recently, a Buddhist monk led a campaign in Tokyo to save an ancient urban stand of trees from being destroyed so that an apartment block could be built. He erected a large sign near the grove stating that these trees have buddha nature. In other words, they are sacred.

Thinking that we own these resources leads us to believe that we can do with them what we please. However, if we're to become better stewards of those resources, we should regard them as part of a universe that is only on loan to us. The passage in the Bible that says "Be fruitful and multiply, and replenish the earth and subdue it" seems to be the philosophical basis for this kind of feeling toward land ownership. We may buy or sell property through real estate agents, or take out mortgages on land, but the land, like air and water, is actually a blessing from Mother Earth. At present, the Earth is experiencing a tremendous ecological crisis because we have been treating land as an object that can be freely bought and sold for development into golf courses, theme parks, and the like. We need to shift to a new cosmology, one that is based on ideas such as the one expressed in the old Japanese saying, "Everyone returns to the earth after death." Various philosophers and ecologists have noted that a society's level of civilization can be measured by how well it treats land. By regarding land as a mere commodity, we will sooner or later destroy the very thing that sustains human life.

ENVIRONMENTAL EDUCATION

At the end of each year, *Time* magazine publishes a special edition that features a "Man of the Year." In 1989, the magazine broke with tradition and selected Earth as the "Planet of the Year." One of the articles featured schoolchildren in Nagano Prefecture, central Japan, who were participating in a school project to collect recyclable items. This type of environmental education would be another component of a new Buddhist approach to economics.

Unfortunately, the education system in Japan is centered around harsh examinations, with students undergoing fierce competition to enter the nation's prestigious universities so they can subsequently land good jobs. This places the educational focus on money rather than on building an individual's character. After all, developing a well-balanced, "complete" human being and responsible citizen of the Earth is a far loftier goal than simply passing exams. At long last, the Japanese government seems to have recognized this, and in 1997, discussions were being carried out between the Ministry of Education and the Environment Agency on the topic of how to improve environmental education in all schools, from elementary to high school levels.

Teaching values in our school system is something we should embrace, not shy away from. For example, the Buddhist idea of "benefiting others as well as oneself" could be an important part of a curriculum oriented toward producing young people who are able to live in a socially and environmentally responsible way. There are approximately five thousand kindergartens run by Buddhist denominations or temples in Japan. These teach children such values as to avoid waste and to show respect for the food nature provides by saying grace before each meal. In Zen Buddhist temples, monks not only say grace but also leave a small portion of their food to be offered to birds and other animals. Saying a few words before eating may seem insignificant, but such sentiments will ensure the future survival of the Earth.

Regrettably, very little of this sort of education is available today for most elementary, junior high, or high school students. One notable exception to this can be found in the efforts of Hisaaki Saga, a social studies teacher at a junior high school located in Tokushima Prefecture, on the island of Shikoku. Regarded as a pioneer of environmental education in Japan, Saga draws inspiration from the Buddhist principles of Shōtoku Taishi, as well as from the humanistic values of the Montessori educational system, which stresses each child's creative ability. In his book *Chikyū jidai no kyōiku* (Education for the Earth Era), he outlines why a new philosophical basis for the improved coexistence of human beings and nature is necessary. He also makes concrete suggestions about how to incorporate environmental issues into textbooks and about interesting and practical ways to talk about environmental values in the classroom. In 1997, the Japanese Ministry of Education finally implemented plans to support environmental education through the development of teachers' manuals on ecology and the funding of ecology clubs for children.

We should start asking governments all over the world to direct more funding toward education of this kind. While we should be wary of too much state involvement in education, which would be undesirable, surely we could support a type of education that would lay down solid foundations for the future by cutting the discretionary accounts of defense budgets and politicians.

THE ENVIRONMENTAL AND SOCIAL ASSESSMENT OF INDUSTRIES

Buddhist economics must start by proposing new ways of thinking about the economy that emphasize saving rather than destroying the Earth. In the past, economic models emphasized profits and production levels as the only criteria for measuring the value of industries. A consideration of the amount of natural resources consumed, or their methods of production, was very much secondary in the equation, if present at all.

If we are truly to take the concept of protecting the Earth seriously, we must examine individual industries to see whether they are friendly or harmful to the environment. Variables such as how natural resources are extracted, the production methods used, and the levels of pollution caused by the production of various goods must all be carefully examined. I hope the criteria for evaluating industries in this manner can be determined on a global scale in conjunction with scientists and with sensitivity toward the needs of the so-called developing nations, which may still require industries that are considered harmful to the Earth.

There are obviously many issues to be thought through in tackling such a complex project, but one important model has been developed by Mitsuru Tanaka of the Environment Agency in Kawasaki, south of Tokyo. Tanaka suggests that two variables, production (P) and consumption (C), must be examined when assessing various products and industries. He ranks production according to four levels: P_1 for production that has a negligible negative impact on the environment; P_2 for a minimal negative impact; P_3 for some negative impact; and P_4 for a large negative impact.

Likewise, consumption is ranked according to four levels: C_1 for the consumption of goods that are vital for human subsistence; C_2 for the consumption of goods that, while not absolutely necessary, make living more tolerable; C_3 for the consumption of goods that are not very necessary; and C_4 for the consumption of goods that are frivolous or even harmful.

At the risk of oversimplification, the table below combines these two variables so that we can immediately determine whether the production of any given product is relatively Earth-friendly, and whether its consumption is truly necessary.

	P_1	P_2	P_3	P_4
C_1	1	2	3	4
C_2	2	4	6	8
C_3	3	6	9	12
C_4	4	8	12	16

Here we can see that the lower the number, the better is it for our environment, while the higher numbers such as 12 or 16 indicate an environmentally destructive and unnecessary product. For example, depending on how it is grown, rice can be classified as a P1 production process because it does not negatively affect the environment, and at the same time it is a basic food staple, thus earning a C1 classification with an overall mark of 1. On the other hand, there are numerous products on the market today whose production has a negative environmental impact, such as pollution, and that are at the same time not essential for human subsistence. Such products would earn a high number, such as a 12 or 16. The citizens of Kawasaki are now discussing the idea of levying a "green tax" on products that incur such high numbers.

This kind of policymaking is becoming increasingly important as we begin to understand that environmental destruction carries with it an economic price that may not become evident until much later. A Buddhist approach to economics must lead in this direction.

AGRICULTURE AS AN EARTH-FRIENDLY INDUSTRY

Commerce and industry are considered key economic areas by most people and nations, but land and agriculture are also relevant factors according to the new Buddhist economics. Agriculture in particular reveals to us our dependence on the Earth, since it is ultimately dependent on nature's blessings of adequate rain and sunshine. People who live in urban areas are the farthest removed from this direct connection with nature's rhythms. According to the author Schumacher, when people are cut off from nature, their societies become increasingly characterized by violence toward nature as well as violence toward other human beings.

Every year, during a special religious ceremony, the Japanese emperor descends onto the paddy-fields to plant the year's first rice. He does this not for himself, but as a representative of the people praying for a good harvest. This act, though symbolic, suggests the significance of agriculture, and particularly rice, for the Japanese people. In recent years, we have seen the part played by rice in the ongoing trade dispute between Japan and the United States. While, on the one hand, the cheaper American rice has had limited access to the Japanese market, on the other hand, according to Hisashi Inoue's book *Kome no hanashi* (The Book of Rice), American rice would not necessarily be cheaper once Japan's higher standards on pesticides were met and the extra cost of shipping the rice over long distances was factored in. More importantly, however, Inoue points out the tremendous ecological function that agriculture, particularly the paddy-field system, plays in Japan.

Rice paddies, especially those located high on Japan's mountain terraces, function as natural dams and are a key to water control in the country. Building artificial dams to perform this function would cost the Japanese taxpayers approximately 4 trillion yen (roughly $40 billion).

Monetary costs aside, if we take into account Japan's ecology, it would not make sense for the Japanese to subscribe to an international trade policy that lumps agriculture together with all other industries. Fortunately, other European nations in addition to Japan have given higher priority to long-term sustainable agriculture rather than focusing on short-sighted and short-term monetary gains.

Another industry that exemplifies the principle of "not wasting" and the need for a context-driven economics is mountain dairy farming. Dairy farming, which does not require a lot of capital, is attractive to small businessmen because it can survive on limited natural resources. It is also Earth-friendly: everything, including animal waste, is recycled.

Introduced during the Meiji period to promote the drinking of milk, dairy farming on Japan's mountain slopes clearly suits the ecological terrain of this mountainous country, just as it is ideal for New Zealand and Switzerland. Some farms have adopted the American style of plains dairy farming, where farms are on flat terrain, cattle are given expensive feed, and the land is often bulldozed to create more space. However, this has proven to be "inefficient" as well as inappropriate for Japan. Specialists like Kyōji Naohara (1908–87) have developed a more sustainable model for dairy farming through mountain dairy methods, which use native natural grasses for feed and allow the byproducts of feces and urine to be recycled naturally.

Although the milk produced by cows in the mountains does not have as high a fat content as milk produced by plains dairy farming, even this can be regarded as a potential additional benefit in our health-conscious age. The most striking advantage to this method of farming is the way it exemplifies how humans can live and work with greater sensitivity and respect for nature, thus proceeding toward what the United Nations

University terms a state of "zero-emissions"—in other words, a pollution-free society. This example also reminds us that economics is a culturally and environmentally contingent phenomenon. What works in the West does not necessarily work in Asia, and vice versa, so we must be sensitive to regional ecologies and cultures.

UNRESTRAINED CONSUMPTION

From the Buddhist point of view, consumption is based on human desire or greed. Although Buddhism is sometimes understood as a religion that shuns desires, if we recall the story of the Buddha accepting milk from the young maiden rather than continuing to indulge in ascetic practices, Buddhism can be viewed as a tradition that takes a moderate stance toward desire. In other words, certain basic desires are accepted because they affirm life. What Buddhism warns against is self-centered desires that do not affirm life but rather work against it.

It is an undisputed fact that the world's natural resources will be depleted if the ever-increasing population growth and the mismanagement of desire are not immediately addressed. Stemming the population explosion has been a theme from the age of Malthus down to the U.N. Cairo Conference of 1994, but the problem of desire needs to be addressed, especially as regards people in the so-called advanced nations.

A poem carved into a stone at Ryoanji, the Buddhist temple in Kyoto famous for its stone and sand garden, reads as follows: "Know what one really needs." This is no simple injunction: to know what one really needs requires great wisdom. Moreover, to have the strength to say no to unessential products leads to freedom from the chains of consumption. Wanting only what is really essential reflects the Buddhist view of consumption: happiness is not achieved by consuming more and more products, but by being able to enjoy the simple, beautiful things in life.

COMPETITION

Although many people in business talk of the necessity of competition, they rarely talk about the ultimate purpose of competition.

The Buddhist way of thinking teaches that the ultimate purpose of competition is to benefit the consumer. One contemporary example of this can be found in the activities of the well-known detergent manufacturer, Kao Soap Co., Ltd. The president of Kao Soap, Yoshirō Maruta, takes two historical figures, Prince Shōtoku and Zen Master Dōgen, as his inspiration. According to Maruta's management philosophy, both management and employees are "students of the way (Ch. dao)" who share the same company cafeteria, learn together, and use the workplace as a *dojo* (lit. "hall of the way"), in other words, as a place for martial arts and spiritual training. Maruta felt that people could develop "wisdom" in the workplace just as well as at some remote monastery: wisdom here involves thinking about and developing types of products that would benefit consumers. The company's soaps, detergents, and toiletries have become very successful everyday items only because the company invested in and made great advances in improving the quality of its products. Consumers have directly benefited from this better quality, and the investments have given Kao Soap an edge over other products on the market. Maruta has even shared his quality-improvement methods with his competitors because he believes that this will benefit the public as a whole.

The belief that the consumer, rather than the manufacturer, should be the main beneficiary of competition should underlie Buddhist economics. Putting the customer first was also a characteristic of Matsutarō Shōriki (1885–1969), the president of Japan's largest newspaper, *Yomiuri Shinbun*, and founder of Nippon Television Network Corporation (NTV). In his youth, Shōriki had been a keen student of the martial arts, and he studied and practiced Zen Buddhism from an early age. This Buddhist training propelled him to introduce innovations in his newspaper long before his competitors. For example, the *Yomiuri Shinbun* was the first paper to put news on the front page rather than following the prevailing practice of having advertisements there. Shōriki was also one of the first business leaders to channel his profits into charitable causes and philanthropic works. He founded the Butsugan Kyōkai (Association of the Buddha's Eyes) to support research for the prevention of blindness and to assist blind members of society.

This example shows that one can be fiercely competitive and succeed in business while placing the customer first, thus becoming a positive and helpful member of society. One's competitors should be seen as old buddies in a long chess game. There is no need to make the chess game, or business, less competitive, but at the end of the day, all the competition engaged by the players should be for the benefit of society.

THE BUDDHIST APPROACH TO MONEY

Historically, the Buddhist attitude toward economics in general and to money in particular has been one of moderation. Early Buddhist communities regarded money as a symbol of materialism and even rejected donations of money. However, Buddhism eventually came to view money in more neutral terms. In East Asian Buddhism in particular, money was seen in a very positive light. Scriptures such as the *Avataṃsaka Sūtra* (known in English as the "Flower Garland" sūtra) advocate moneylending and the use of the accrued interest for social and religious purposes. In China and Japan, temples served as moneylenders and often used the interest to build new temples or annexes to existing ones. Buddhist temples and fraternal associations from the early modern period also operated what we would now call "mutual fund" banking. Buddhist attitudes toward money have been relatively tolerant when compared to the Christian view, which tended to look down on moneylenders and wealth. In general, the Buddhist orientation is to not be afraid to make money, but to spend it wisely using our greater wisdom, or buddha-mind.

Zennojō Tani (1899–1976), the Buddhist founder of Mikasa Kaikan, a major restaurant/catering business, has said that a businessman is like a pipeline for money. One should not fear making oneself a pipeline for the flow of large sums of money, but at the same time, one needs to have the courage to give it away. Tani was a great advocate of Zen Buddhism, believing that Zen meditation was an essential human discipline that provided a good basis for living as well as for conducting business. In this way, making money as a businessman and living a spiritual life are not contradictory and need not be considered two separate and conflicting activities.

The Buddhist banker mentioned earlier, Zenjirō Yasuda of Fuji Bank, has also noted that making money is not antithetical to living a spiritual life. If we look at his five principles for making money, we can see how moneymaking is tempered by the buddha-mind:

1. Proceed toward your goals slowly, cautiously, and surely. Don't overstretch yourself in the beginning.

2. Know your weaknesses and correct them.
3. Be sincere in all things.
4. Avoid superficiality and always try to penetrate to the core of things.
5. Do not overspend, and be prepared for unexpected expenses.

With this cautious approach, Yasuda became a very wealthy man. We might say that he became a millionaire disciple of the Buddha.

AVOIDING WASTE BY RECYCLING

While the modern economic principle of lowering costs and increasing profits seems like a model for economic efficiency, once we factor in the additional costs of environmental pollution, the model no longer works on a macro-economic or societal level. This economic principle only seems attractive when efficiency is measured in sheer monetary terms, with the result that the private sector is perceived as being much more efficient than the public, or government, sector.

On the other hand, a Buddhist approach to economics recognizes that any economic enterprise is located in the context of the entire natural universe. Therefore, not taking into account such factors as environmental and social costs appears quite absurd. Economic efficiency must be based on a different principle, namely, that of "not wasting," which carries with it the goal of living happily in a simple way rather than always concentrating on making more money. For instance, although recycling paper and other items costs time and money and may seem "inefficient" and troublesome, we are ultimately being more efficient by not wasting such products. This is because we recognize that any given product exists in relationship to the Earth and human society as a whole.

One Buddhist entrepreneur in Japan who actualized this principle is Shūzō Nishihara (1883–1965), whose company recycles raw sewage from major urban centers and turns it into fertilizers for farmers. What seems worthless in one context may well be precious in another, and this multi-faceted nature of all things is a key concept based on the Buddhist notion of emptiness and interrelatedness. As all things are ultimately "empty" of a set value, everything, including what is usually considered garbage, can be seen as a precious resource, depending on one's point of view. Not wasting things is simply an extension of this way of seeing the world. We need to promote a recycling culture that is economically sound instead of a throw-away culture that is neither economically nor environmentally sound.

NOTES

1   [Ed. Excerpted from Inoue's *Chikyū o sukū keizaigaku: Bukkyō kara no teigen* (Economics for Preserving the Global Environment: Proposals Based on Buddhist Thought) (Tokyo: Suzuki Shuppan Kabushiki Kaisha, 1994). For Inoue's work in English, see Shinichi Inoue, *Putting Buddhism to Work*, trans. Duncan Ryūken Williams (Tokyo: Kodansha International, 1997).]

The Noble Eightfold Path as a Prescription for Sustainable Living

Tetsunori Koizumi

INTRODUCTION

The Noble Eightfold Path is presented by the Buddha in his first sermon known as "the Setting-in-Motion of the Wheel of Dharma," which he delivered to a group of five bhikshus in the Deer Park at Isipatana near Benares. This sermon carries a special meaning in the history of Buddhism because it marks the start of the Buddha's life as a teacher for humanity, for he was now speaking to the five bhikshus, not as a young ascetic who had earlier trained together with them, but as an awakened one who had attained full enlightenment.[1]

While the Noble Eightfold Path, presented as the last of the Four Noble Truths, is generally regarded as the Buddha's prescription for salvation from the condition of pain that permeates individual life, it can also be construed as a prescription for conducting social life for a community of individuals who share the goal of attaining enlightenment.[2] As a matter of fact, the Noble Eightfold Path can be construed as a prescription for sustainable living, based as it is on an environmental ethic that is implied in the Buddha's view of the world as represented by his idea of "dependent origination."

The purpose of the present discussion is to develop an interpretation of the Noble Eightfold Path as a prescription for sustainable living, as a practical guide for conducting social life that maintains harmony with the natural environment. This is done by rephrasing the Buddha's view of the world, including the Noble Eightfold Path, in the language of modern systems science. By doing so, it is shown that the Noble Eightfold Path, as a prescription for sustainable living, combines many insights of such academic disciplines as ecology, economics, and ethics that have gone into the recent debate about sustainable development.

THE MANIFEST VERSUS THE LATENT WORLD

That the Buddha prescribed the Noble Eightfold Path as a practical guide for liberating ourselves from the pain of life suggests that the Buddha saw two worlds—the world in which *dukkha*, or suffering, is the basic condition of life and the world in which suffering is no longer binding. Thus we begin our discussion by introducing two terms—the "manifest world" and the "latent world"—to refer to these two worlds. The manifest world is the world of all manifest phenomena around us. It is the world of our normal existence, that is, the world into which we are born, in which we conduct our affairs of life, and from which we exit at our death. This is the world that the Buddha calls the world of "name and form" (*nāmarūpa*), and which is governed by dukkha, that is, "suffering" or "dissatisfaction."

There is another world beyond the manifest world where there is "the unborn, unoriginated, unmade and unconditioned."[3] This is the world from which name and form are projected, which we shall call the latent world. It is the ground for all the manifest phenomena in the world around us. It is not the world of material things, as the Buddha reminds us: "There is no material that exists for the production of Name and Form; and when Name and Form cease, they do not go anywhere in space. After Name and Form have ceased, they do not exist anywhere in the shape of heaped-up music material."[4]

For analytical purposes, it is convenient to think of all name and form in the manifest world as existing as potentialities in the latent world. The Buddha himself hints at such an interpretation when he says, "In the beginning there is existence blind and without knowledge; and in this sea of ignorance there are stirrings formative and organizing."[5] From a formal point of view, the latent world can be interpreted as the domain set for mappings that project name and form into the manifest world.[6] (See Figure 1.)

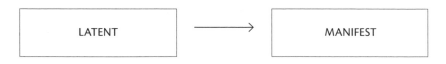

FIGURE 1. LATENT VERSUS MANIFEST WORLD

The Manifest World as a Space for Interdependent Systems

While many ideas are ascribed to him, arguably the single most important idea that captures the Buddha's view of the world is that of *pratītyasamutpāda*, or "dependent origination." Dependent origination expresses the idea that nothing in the manifest world around us exists as an independent and separate entity.[7] Something exists, if at all, because it is enveloped in a network of causes and conditions that has given rise to it. Thus, when something exists in the manifest world, it is always as a part of some aggregate entity.

But where do that something and that aggregate entity of which it is a part come from? They come, according to the Buddha, from the latent world by a concurrence of causes and conditions. In general, we do not have access to a specific configuration of causes and conditions that gives rise to a specific aggregate entity. For one thing, it is our perception that recognizes something as a part of a specific aggregate entity. For another, our very existence, including our perception, is an outcome of such concurrence of causes and conditions.

Modern systems science treats this problem of isolating and identifying a specific aggregate entity by bringing in the role of the observer. It is up to the observer to perceive something as a part of an aggregate entity, that is to say, a system with its own boundary from other systems. The idea of "systems" in modern systems science is quite similar to the Buddha's idea of dependent origination, for something exists in the manifest world as a part of a system, where a system is defined by a set of component elements and a relationship among them.

The principle of dependent origination, carried to its logical end, means that everything in the manifest world depends on everything else. The manifest world can thus be seen as consisting of a whole collection of interdependent systems in which every system exists in the context of connections and linkages with other systems. The corresponding idea in modern systems science would be that of open systems, where an open system is defined as a system that exchanges matter, energy, and information with other systems.[8]

From a systems perspective, the manifest world, which is the space of evolution, can be viewed as consisting of the biosphere, the sociosphere, and the psychosphere.[9] By the biosphere is meant the space of interaction among natural systems such as plants, animals, rivers, and oceans. By the sociosphere is meant the space of interaction among social systems such as families, groups, organizations, and nations. And by the psychosphere is meant the space of interaction among psychic systems such as languages, symbols, artifacts, and other cultural systems that are projections of the human psyche. (See Figure 2.)

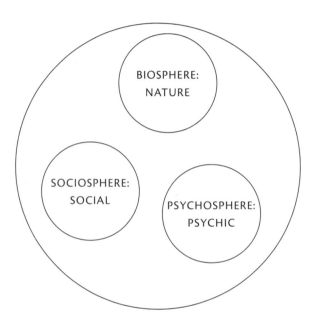

FIGURE 2. THE SPACE OF HUMAN EVOLUTION

In each of the three spheres of the space of evolution, every entity, or system, is subject to another principle in the Buddha's view of the world, that is, the idea of *anitya*, or "impermanence": "All compound things are transitory: they grow and they decay."[10] The manifest world, thus defined as the unified space of evolution consisting of the biosphere, the sociosphere, and the psychosphere, can be regarded as a space in which every system stands in interdependent relationships with other systems and is subject to systems evolution involving the three phases of creation, preservation, and decay.

THE NOBLE EIGHTFOLD PATH AS A SET OF COMPLEMENTARY PRINCIPLES

The Noble Eightfold Path (*ārya aṣṭāṅgika mārga*), as first delivered by the Buddha in the Deer Park at Isipatana, is presented as the Middle Path: "The Tathagata . . . does not seek salvation in austerities, but neither does he for that reason indulge in worldly pleasures, nor live in abundance. The Tathagata has found the middle path. . . . A middle path, O bhikkhus, avoiding the two extremes, has been discovered by the Tathagata, a path which opens the eyes, and bestows understanding, which leads to peace of mind, to the higher wisdom, to full enlightenment, to Nirvana!"[11]

The Buddha goes on, explaining why the Middle Path is indeed the right path, the Noble Eightfold Path, to salvation: "He who recognizes the existence of suffering, its cause, its remedy, and its cessation has fathomed the four noble truths. He will walk in the right path. Right views will be the torch to light his way. Right aspirations will be his guide. Right speech will be his dwelling-place on the road. His gait will be straight, for it is right behavior. His refreshments will be the right way of earning his livelihood. Right efforts will be his steps: right thoughts his breath; and right contemplation will give him the peace that follows in his footprints."[12]

Why is it that the path the Buddha recommended for termination of suffering consists of eight factors, and not five or seven factors? As it turns out, there is a simple explanation for this: the eight factors divide themselves into two complementary sets, each with four factors.[13] To be more specific, the four factors of right view, right thought, right aspiration, and right mindfulness form one set, and the four factors of right speech, right conduct, right effort, and right livelihood form the other set.

As a group, the four factors in the first set all refer to mental states. They can be interpreted as corresponding to four types of mental activities: understanding, thinking, aspiring, and being mindful. These four factors as a group can therefore be interpreted as stating the importance of maintaining the right frame of mind. On the other hand, the four factors in the second set all refer to physical activities—speaking, acting, exerting, and earning (one's livelihood)—and can therefore be interpreted as stating the importance of observing the right use of body. (See Figure 3.)

The Noble Eightfold Path, as a practical guide for conducting one's life, thus draws our attention to the importance of keeping proper balance

MENTAL ACTIVITIES	PHYSICAL ACTIVITIES
Right View	Right Speech
Right Thought	Right Conduct
Right Aspiration	Right Effort
Right Mindfulness	Right Livelihood

FIGURE 3. NOBLE EIGHTFOLD PATH AS COMPLEMENTARY SETS OF MENTAL AND PHYSICAL ACTIVITIES

between mind and body, between mental and physical activities. This does not mean that the Buddha had a dualistic view of mind and body. On the contrary, mind and body, like other things in his thought, arise only in the context of dependent origination, that is, as a result of a concurrence of causes and conditions.

By dividing the eight factors in the Noble Eightfold Path into two complementary sets, we are also suggesting a correspondence, factor by factor, between these two sets. Thus, right view in the first set is matched by right speech in the second set, right thought in the first set by right conduct in the second set, and so on. This way, each pair of two factors is also subject to the principle of dependent origination. It is not that right speech is caused by right view, or that right view is caused by right speech. One practices right speech because one holds right view, and one holds right view because one practices right speech. Indeed, the eight factors in the Noble Eightfold Path are complementary principles that mutually reinforce one another, for following the Path requires keeping balance between mind and body, between reflection and action, between mental and physical activities.

THE NOBLE EIGHTFOLD PATH AS A STATE OF SYSTEMIC BALANCE

We are now in a position to examine the implications of the Noble Eightfold Path in terms of the language of modern systems science. Let us first look at what the Noble Eightfold Path as the Middle Path means. The central idea behind the Middle Path is, of course, the idea of balance between two extremes of austerity and indulgence. The Buddha was talking primarily about the importance of maintaining balance for the individual who seeks enlightenment. But the individual human being is a system that exists in the aggregate space of all systems called the universe. Thus we can interpret "the Noble Eightfold Path" as "the Middle Path," meaning a state of balance for the individual human being as an open system in the universe. That state of balance applies, at the micro level, to the individual human being as well as, at the macro level, to the universe as a whole.

At the micro level, the Middle Path can be interpreted as a state of "systemic balance" in the individual human being as a composite system of mental and physical activities. As the Buddha reminded the five bhikshus: "To keep the body in good health is a duty, for otherwise we shall not be able to trim the lamp of wisdom, keep our mind strong and clear."[14] Recall that the Buddha indeed had a systems view of the human being in that he saw the human as an organism of many aggregates, consisting of the material form (the body) and the mental states as represented by perception, thought, will, and consciousness. Needless to say, we can expand on the Buddha's conception of the human being by talking about the human body as an aggregate of cells, tissues, muscles, bones, organs, and so on, and the human mind as an aggregate of emotions, feelings, sensations, and thoughts. What is important here is that, in order to pursue the path of enlightenment, both mind and body, both the mental and physical aspects of our existence, must be kept in systemic balance.

At the macro level, the Middle Path can be interpreted as a state of systemic balance between humans and the natural environment. This interpretation is suggested by the Buddha's view of the world, which is systemic and evolutionary. As he saw it quite clearly, individual human beings are open systems in that they are in constant interaction with their environment, engaging in physical interaction with the use of their five senses and spiritual interaction with the use of their consciousness. The environment influences humans in many ways: light, gravity, physical stress such as temperature and noise, and psychological stress such as fear, tension, and uncertainty. In turn, humans influence the natural environment through consumption of food and other materials and production of goods and services with the use of raw materials. Humans can cause "stress" on the natural environment in the form of pollution, ozone depletion, and other types of environmental degradation. In view of such mutual influence between humans and the natural environment, it is clear that the Noble Eightfold Path as the Middle Path, the path that maintains the health of the individual human being, is also the path that maintains the health of the natural environment. Indeed, the idea of maintaining the health of the natural environment is the environmental ethic implied by the Noble Eightfold Path, which calls for systemic balance between humans and the natural environment.[15]

THE NOBLE EIGHTFOLD PATH AS A LAW OF CONSERVATION OF MATTER-ENERGY

Our interpretation of the Noble Eightfold Path as calling for a state of systemic balance between humans and the natural environment can be rephrased in terms of the law of conservation of matter-energy by treating humans as living systems.[16] As living systems, humans operate both as mechanical systems and thermodynamic systems.

In the first place, we humans are mechanical systems in the sense that we move about in this world and engage in our daily activities.[17] Appealing to the Hamiltonian representation of dynamic systems[18] and borrowing the terminology from classical mechanics, the total energy of humans as mechanical systems can be interpreted as consisting of potential energy associated with the state of reflection and kinetic energy associated with the state of action.[19] In the case of the Noble Eightfold Path, potential energy is expressed in terms of the four factors of right view, right thought, right aspiration, and right mindfulness, associated with four mental activities of understanding, thinking, aspiring, and being mindful. On the other hand, kinetic energy is expressed in terms of the four factors of right speech, right conduct, right effort, and right livelihood, associated with four physical activities of speaking, behaving, exerting, and earning one's livelihood. (See Figure 4.)

The Hamiltonian representation of humans lends itself to an interpretation of the Noble Eightfold Path as a law of conservation of matter-energy. While going about the affairs of life as mechanical systems, we humans are not in the state of stable equilibrium in which the total energy is minimized. As a matter of fact, as we engage in our activities as living systems, we exchange matter, energy, and information with other systems in the environment. This means that, from the point of view of

POTENTIAL ENERGY	KINETIC ENERGY
Understanding	Speaking
Thinking	Behaving
Aspiring	Exerting
Being mindful	Earning

FIGURE 4. NOBLE EIGHTFOLD PATH AS THE SUM
OF POTENTIAL AND KINETIC ENERGY

thermodynamics, we humans are not isolated, closed systems. As open systems, we humans cannot maintain the law of conservation of energy in the strict sense in which this law is formulated in thermodynamics. However, we all operate in the universe, which is a closed system subject to the first as well as the second law of thermodynamics.

It is in relation to this global system called the universe, in which we humans exist, that we can interpret the Noble Eightfold Path as a law of conservation of matter energy. We first note that we need not talk about matter (or mass) and energy as separate entities in view of Einstein's special theory of relativity. As thermodynamic systems, we exploit matter-energy as we engage in our daily activities. Following the Noble Eightfold Path, as it is the Middle Path between the path of ascetic life and the path of indulgent life, means that our use of matter-energy is kept at the "right level," that is, in a state of balance vis-à-vis the carrying capacity of the closed universe we live in. To put it more technically, to the extent that we follow the Noble Eightfold Path, we behave as "conservative systems" in the use of matter-energy.

The Noble Eightfold Path, according to this interpretation, becomes practical advice on how we can keep the fire, that is, desires, within us under control by maintaining the "right level" of energy associated with our mental and physical activities. What is more important from a social systems perspective is that a community of individuals, living as members of a sangha who adhere to the Noble Eightfold Path, follows a path of sustainable development, for individuals who maintain balance between reflection and action, between mental and physical activities, do not try to exploit matter-energy in the environment to maximize their material well-being. This does not mean that the accumulation of wealth is to be condemned altogether; what is to be condemned is "cleaving" to wealth, as the Buddha explains to Sudatta: "He that cleaveth to wealth had better cast it away than allow his heart to be poisoned by it; but he who does not cleave to wealth, and possessing riches, uses them rightly, will be a blessing unto others."[20]

CONCLUSION

Interpreting the Noble Eightfold Path as a law of conservation of matter-energy, as we have attempted to do in this discussion, offers an insight into what might be termed the "thermoeconomics" of living systems. All living systems operate within the universe subject to the laws of thermodynamics, and we humans are no exception to this. As such, we humans must "economize" our use of matter-energy if we are to be viable in the global evolutionary environment, which is subject to the principles of "dependent origination" and "impermanence." Indeed, with the Noble Eightfold Path, the Buddha may well have been suggesting a "sustainable living," namely, a "conservative" way of life from the point of view of the thermodynamics of living systems which Schumacher expressed with his catchy phrase: "Small is beautiful."[21]

Ecology, economics, and ethics, as these academic disciplines are practiced today, are not linked in a way that would provide unified intellectual support for promoting sustainable living. However, many researchers have pointed out in recent years that the broken circle among these three disciplines is very much at the root of the current ecological crisis.[22] This is so because economics, despite its privileged status as a science that has direct impact on social policy, has not incorporated important insights obtained in ecology in recent years into the main body of its theoretical foundation. Nor, for that matter, have economists, especially those working in the mainstream tradition, admitted the need to incorporate ethical considerations in formulating social policy. In fact, they continue to prescribe the universal pursuit of higher standards of living as measured by per capita GNP, neglecting the finite carrying capacity of the natural environment.

While ecology, economics, and ethics have come to be separated in the scientific tradition of the West, there is no such separation in the philosophical tradition of the East as exemplified by the Buddha's Noble Eightfold Path. Economics, as a prescription for conducting right livelihood, is founded on an ecological view of the world and a nonanthropocentric environmental ethic as embodied in the fundamental principles of the Buddha's thought: the principles of "dependent origination" and "impermanence." Figure 2 introduced earlier shows the unity of ecology, economics, and ethics by interpreting them as disciplines dealing, respectively, with the biosphere, the sociosphere, and the psychosphere.

Needless to say, it is one thing to state that the Noble Eightfold Path offers a practical guide for sustainable living but quite another to translate it into a daily practice for individuals and into a social policy for social systems. This step of translating the Buddha's insight into an agenda for individual action and social policy is the challenge that confronts us today.

NOTES

1 [Ed. See "II. Setting in Motion the Wheel of the Dhamma; Saccasaṃyutta: Connected Discourses on the Truths," in Bhikkhu Bodhi, trans., *The Connected Discourses of the Buddha: A Translation of the Saṃyutta Nikaya* (Boston: Wisdom, 2000), no. 56, § 11–20, 1843–52. For an introductory discussion, see Donald W. Mitchell, *Buddhism: Introducing the Buddhist Experience* (New York and Oxford: Oxford University Press, 2002), 46–52.]

2 [Ed. There are many discussions of the Noble Eightfold Path in the suttas. For one extended discussion, see the "I. Ignorance; Maggasaṃyutta: Connected Discourses on the Path," in Bodhi, trans., *Connected Discourses*, no. 45, § 8, 1528–29.]

3 Udana, VIII.3, as quoted in John Snelling, *The Buddhist Handbook: A Complete Guide to Buddhist Schools, Teaching, Practice, and History* (New York: Barnes and Noble, 1991), 45.

4 Paul Carus, *The Gospel of Buddha* (repr. Oxford: Oneworld, 1994), 114.

5 Ibid., 40.

6 The manifest world is the world of manifest phenomena around us and, for analytical purposes, may be called M-space. The latent world, on the other hand, is the ground for all manifest phenomena in the manifest world, and may be called L-space. That the latent world is the ground for all manifest phenomena in the manifest world implies that there are mappings between L-space and M-space such that all manifest phenomena in the manifest world are the projections of potentialities in the latent world. Formally speaking, this means that every set in M-space is a projection from L-space:
$$(LM) \ \forall \ X \subset M, \ \exists \ F: L \rightarrow M \ni F^{-1}(X) \subset L.$$

7 The idea of *pratītyasamutpāda*, or interdependence, can be expressed by referring to a
   mapping between L-space and M-space as:
   (PS) $x_i \in M \Rightarrow \exists F: L \rightarrow M \ni x_i \in X \subset M$,
   where $F = (f_1, f_2, ..., f_m)$ and $X = \{x_1, x_2, ..., x_n\}$.
   The formalism above says that something (x_i) exists in the manifest world only because
   there exists some configuration of causes and conditions $(f_1, f_2, ..., f_m)$ which brings into
   the manifest world some aggregate entity $X = \{x_1, x_2, ..., x_n\}$ of which x_i is a part.
8 See, for example, Ludwig von Bertalanffy, *General System Theory* (New York: George
   Braziller, 1968), and James Miller, *Living Systems* (New York: McGraw-Hill, 1978).
9 For a view of human evolution involving three processes taking place in three spheres see
   Tetsunori Koizumi, *Interdependence and Change in the Global System* (Lanham, MD:
   University Press of America, 1993).
10 Carus, *Gospel of Buddha*, 158.
11 Ibid., 49–50.
12 Ibid., 51.
13 For a more detailed discussion of this and other interpretations of the Noble Eightfold
   Path, see Tetsunori Koizumi, "Reinventing the Wheel of Dharma: The Noble Eightfold
   Path as Comprehensive Program for Individual and Societal Transformation," *Kokusai
   Bunka Kenshu* (Journal of Intercultural Studies) (1996).
14 Carus, *Gospel of Buddha*, 51.
15 For a more comprehensive review of many discussions of the Buddha's worldview as an
   environmental ethic, see Allan Badiner, ed., *Dharma Gaia: A Harvest of Essays in Buddhism and Ecology* (Berkeley: Parallax Press, 1990); Stephanie Kaza and Kenneth Kraft,
   eds., *Dharma Rain: Sources of Buddhist Environmentalism* (Boston: Shambhala, 2000);
   and Joanna Macy, *World as Lover, World as Self* (Berkeley: Parallax Press, 1991).
16 For a comprehensive discussion of living systems, see Miller, *Living Systems*. [Ed. For a
   more recent discussion of both the background of systems theory as applied to living
   systems and its extension into the analysis of society and politics as systems, see Robert
   Jervis, *System Effects: Complexity in Political and Social Life* (Princeton, NJ: Princeton
   University Press, 1997).]
17 Formally, humans as mechanical systems can be represented as:
   (HM) $H(x, dx/dt) = P(x) + K(dx/dt)$
   This is the Hamiltonian representation of humans as mechanical systems and expresses
   the total energy, $H(x, dx/dt)$, as the sum of potential energy, $P(x)$, and kinetic energy,
   $K(dx/dt)$. Here, potential energy, $P(x)$, is associated with a vector x of four mental activities of "understanding," "thinking," "aspiring," and "being mindful," and kinetic energy,
   $K(dx/dt)$, is associated with a vector dx/dt of four physical activities of "speaking,"
   "behaving," "exerting," and "earning (one's livelihood)." The Noble Eightfold Path as a
   law of conservation of matter-energy and therefore as a prescription for sustainable living
   can be stated as: (SL) $\Box H = \Box P + \Box K = 0$
18 [Ed. A "Hamiltonian representation of dynamic systems" refers to the equation named after
   the Irish mathematician William Rowan Hamilton (1805–65). Hamilton proposed a brilliant reformulation of Newtonian dynamics by combining potential energy (energy associated with "position") and kinetic energy (energy associated with "motion") into a single
   equation. The Hamiltonian has proved to be quite useful in the subsequent development of
   physics, and it still plays an important role in modern physics, including Prigogine's work on
   chaotic behavior. See http://en.wikipedia.org/wiki/Sir_William_Rowan_Hamilton, and

http://en.wikipedia.org/wiki/Hamiltonian_%28quantum_mechanics%29, sites accessed September 18, 2006.]

19 See, for example, Ilya Prigogine, *The End of Certainty: Time, Chaos and the New Law of Nature* (New York: Free Press, 1997).

20 Carus, *Gospel of Buddha*, 74.

21 See E. F. Schumacher, *Small Is Beautiful: Economics As If People Mattered* (New York: Harper and Row, 1973).

22 See, for example, F. H. Bormann and S. R. Kellert, *Ecology, Economics, Ethics: The Broken Circle* (New Haven: Yale University Press, 1991); H. E. Daly and K. N. Townsend, *Valuing the Earth: Economics, Ecology, Ethics* (Cambridge, MA: MIT Press, 1992); and G. Hardin, *Living Within Means: Ecology, Economics, and Population Taboos* (New York: Oxford University Press, 1993).

The Debate on Taking Life and Eating Meat in the Edo-Period Jōdo Shin Tradition

Ikuo Nakamura
(Translated by LeRon Harrison)

Taking Life and the Idea of the Karmic Wheel

Acceptance of the ethical precept of "not taking life" by the Japanese can be tracked through a number of sources. For example, the second chapter of the *Brahmajāla Sūtra* includes the following passage:

> Disciple of the Buddha, out of compassion, you should gener-ate good karma by freeing animals. All men are your father and all women your mother. You should obey this [fact] and accept life. Thus the various living beings on the six paths are all your parents. That being the case, when you kill and eat meat, you are in fact killing your parents, which is killing your former body.[1]

This theme of animals—or "living beings on the six paths"—is also pre-sented in a poem attributed to Gyōki (668–749), which reads:

yamadori no	When I hear
horohoro to naku	the mountain pheasant
koe kikeba	crying out "horohoro"
chichi ka to zo omou	How I wonder if it could
haha to zo omou	be my father or mother.

This argument that wild creatures should not be killed as they might be the reincarnation of one's parents appears to have been influential. Tales of parents turned into animals due to bad karma, then released from their suffering by prayers offered on their behalf, are a recurring motif in texts such as the *Nihon ryōiki* (Miraculous Stories of Karmic Retribution in Japan).[2]

Nonetheless, it is unclear exactly what impact the more general Indian Buddhist concept of the wheel of karma had on the boundary between the human and the animal worlds during the mythic, ancient, and medieval periods of Japan. One suggestive instance is found, for example, in the courtship story of the deity on Mount Miwa. In this story we can see the motif that traces clan ancestry back to interspecies marriages with animals. Such stories show how even in pre-Buddhist Japan, deities, people, and animals were viewed as being loosely connected and capable of mutual intermingling.

This kind of connection between people and animals is not limited to the realm of storytelling or faith, but extends its influence (either directly or indirectly) into the real world as well. The more conscious one becomes of the connections between people and animals, of the mutually interactive relationship between the two, the stronger the awareness of the significance of killing animals and eating meat becomes. As a result, the indigenous Japanese view of animals and the Buddhist concept of not taking life mutually influenced each other and brought about the creation of a unique understanding of the relation between humans and animals.

Awareness of such a connection between people and animals is rooted in a view of the equality of all things as expressed in Buddhist notions like "There is buddha nature within all living things" and "Trees and grasses can become a buddha." But these ideas have a flipside; on a practical level, the same idea of original buddha nature creates a context that makes it possible for people to accept the doctrine of "the nonduality of good and evil" and inverts the original concept of not taking life, allowing its polar opposite to emerge. As I will discuss, assertions such as "the evil man is the proper vessel," as argued by Shinran's followers, makes it possible to view the practice of "eating meat and taking a wife" positively. This, in turn, is directly related to reliance on Amida's "original vow" as giving permission to commit "evil actions." Through this kind of antinomian interpretation, mainstream concepts and ideologies give rise to oppositional concepts and groups that depend on these oppositional concepts.

THE CONVERSION OF THE HUMAN-ANIMAL RELATION

If the space between human and animals is minimized, then hunting and fishing become comparable with taking human life, since both humans and animals have the same source. As a result, there is no choice but to condemn taking the lives of animals.

In nomadic and livestock-raising societies, where animals were killed and consumed for survival, such feelings of remorse were dissipated by the practice of sacrifices. An especially precious animal would be selected from among the livestock, the source of mutual prosperity, sacrificed, bled, and ceremonially offered up to the gods. The everyday killing of animals was thus regarded as having been sanctioned by the gods. These kinds of practices exist in the various sacrificial rituals of primitive religions throughout the world, such as in ancient Judaism, Brahmanism, and so on.

In Japan a different approach to resolving this problem was taken. "Memorial services for animals" were introduced as a religious apparatus to lessen feelings of remorse for having killed animals. Animals caught through hunting and fishing became objects of memorials similar to those offered for humans, especially from the Edo period onward. Thus, in my view, it might be better to call Japan "a culture of memorial services," unlike the other "sacrificial cultures."

Reexamining this tradition of memorial services for animals and the concepts bound up with it is crucial to ascertaining the development of the principle of not taking lives found in Japanese Buddhism. The "culture of memorialization" seems to have reached its final mode as the objects of memorial services expanded from humans to animals to even nonliving "things." What can be described as the "quasi-religious" feeling that results from such practices combines well with the "holistically minded" or "nature boom" trends these days and might even be a sign that these attitudes will gain greater acceptance.

However, while the concept of "a memorial service for animals" might change the reality of the human-animal relationship by giving definition to the feeling of connection between humans and animals, it does not bring about peaceful coexistence between the two parties. Rather, the opposite could be said to occur: memorializing and mourning animals to the same extent as humans further justifies the use of every kind of animal while eliminating any sense of guilt that may have originally accompanied taking life.

Among Japanese hunters from the Kamakura period onward, the belief that the divine benevolence of the Suwa deity would pardon them for the taking of life received strong support.[3] Here we see a skillful syncretization of both Shintō and Buddhist deities and beliefs. The first example of this idea that animal sacrifices were like buddhas being offered up to native deities can be seen in Pure Land Buddhism from the late Heian period. For example, even if a person "takes life and consumes meat," thus violating Buddhist principles, if that person intones the nenbutsu, the Amida Buddha will honor his vow and grant the person passage into the Pure Land. This tenet of Pure Land Buddhism won support from various people, including the nonagricultural population of the time. Medieval collections of Buddhist didactic tales such as the *Shasekishū* and *Kokonchomonjū* acknowledge the potential to escape the mortal world through stories of clams and carp offered up as sacrifices at the Kamo and Ise Shrines. Taking as a premise this kind of Pure Land, nenbutsu-centered law of avoiding Buddhist punishment and gaining salvation for wrongdoers, the religious world of the medieval period formulated the connection between Buddhist and Shintō deities that is central to syncretization. This syncretization helped reinforce the position of the buddhas and bodhisattvas, with their vast powers of salvation, while the native, marginal deities were reborn and activated as new subjects of salvation. As seen in the example of the Suwa sect, the theory of salvation that developed based on the fate of offerings foresaw a very particular kind of human-animal relationship.

In contrast, the idea of animals achieving buddhahood hypothesized a clearly different human-animal relationship, one in which animals themselves are potential subjects for enlightenment. The influence of reincarnation described earlier is clearly not small. While humans and animals were loosely connected and imagined as occupying a mutually interchangeable space in Japan from the legendary age onward, the human-animal relationship was fundamentally reshaped in medieval times, for example, with the Suwa sect: humans and animals alike were capable of leaving behind the "dusty world" of suffering and going to the Pure Land.

THE JŌDO SHINSHŪ DISCUSSION OF "TAKING LIFE AND EATING MEAT"

The view that humans and animals are interconnected clearly existed as a native concept before Buddhism's arrival. However, by utilizing the Buddhist concepts of reincarnation and "not taking life," the professions involved in ending the life of living beings were placed under the religious label of "evil" and as such were condemned. To put that another way, the concept of the crime of taking life permeated into all facets of society, even bolstering religious and social discrimination against those who could not avoid these professions. That being said, it is important to recognize that the actual situation was never that simple. In the Jōdo Shinshū tradition, as a rhetorical stance against the mainline exoteric and esoteric schools, the themes of the "rebirth of the evil man" became its main way of reaching out to the laity. An example of this is the following passage from Shinran's *Tannishō*:

> Those who cross the world to cast their nets and lines into the rivers and seas, those who spend their lives hunting game and fowl in the wild, they are the same as people who spend their days conducting commerce and cultivating fields.[4]

In this passage, the daily practices of farmers and merchants are held to be ethically equal to, just as sinful as, the activities of hunters and fishermen. This can be taken as an example illustrating that only the salvation of Amida Buddha is directed toward all wrongdoers. Again, a person must be accountable for making the crime of taking life one's "livelihood"; Shinran himself called this *toko no gerui*. He explains the meaning of this phrase in the passage below.

> The *to* refers to the butchering of myriad creatures; it is a term for hunters. The *ko* refers to the selling and buying of myriad items; it is a term for merchants. These people are placed in the lowest rank (*gerui*). Hunters, fishermen, and other members of this rank are us, we are them, we are all like stones, tiles, and pebbles.[5]

What Shinran makes clear in this passage is that no matter who you are, there is no other place for you but the lowest rank—*toko no gerui*—comparable to "stone, tiles, and pebbles."

In this way, Shinran positively affirms his own peripherality and wrongdoing by taking the stance that his own ethical status is in no way different from those who follow professions such as hunting and fishing that involve the taking of life. If discussed from the standpoint of exoteric and esoteric Buddhist sects, this is fundamentally a statement of heresy. This kind of heretical rule that Shinran and his successors established went unchanged over the course of the medieval period. Rennyo was the patriarch of the Honganji temple who dramatically expanded the Jōdo Shinshū organization during the fifteenth century. When clarifying his sect's social position, he reiterated almost word for word Shinran's statement in the following lines:

> Just conduct your commerce, serve your master, do your hunting and fishing. Firmly believe in the vow of Amida Nyorai, who pledges to rescue useless creatures like ourselves who wander dawn to dusk in shallow sin-filled professions like these.[6]

In Rennyo, we can discern three important aspects of later medieval Jōdo Shinshū. First, that the Jōdo Shin sect's social basis centered on those persons whose indispensable nature was to take life by "hunting and fishing." Second, we can perceive in this assertion of a peripheral, heretical nature for all Shin adherents a strengthening of the close cohesiveness of the sect's organization. And third, we can see the sect's unique theory of salvation and definition of human existence. However, this peripheral, heretical nature would be fundamentally changed by a series of events. These included Honganji's surrender to the Oda-Toyotomi forces at the end of the battle of Ishiyama, the division of the Honganji temple in two (one part known as Eastern, that is, Higashi Honganji, and the other known as Western, that is, Nishi Honganji) in the aftermath of that battle, and Honganji's entry into the "regulatory system of shrines and temples" in the Tokugawa era.

The detailed documenting of this process is not the goal of this essay. We can note, however, that in opposition to the doctrines of other Buddhist sects until the Edo period, Jōdo Shinshū viewed consuming meat and taking a wife positively. As stated earlier, during Rennyo's time, the taking of life inherent to fishing and hunting was presented positively as a symbol of the sect's heretical nature. However, by the Edo (or Tokugawa) period, having been included in the Tokugawa shogunate's regulatory policies on religion and the government-backed parish system, this heterodox doctrine that might disrupt the newly established socioreligious order came to be considered potentially dangerous.[7]

The *Orthodox Record of the Life of the Holy Priest Shinran* includes a countermainstream view of meat eating and clerical marriage.

> "Consuming meat and taking a wife" are prohibitions of the prior Buddhas and are doctrines established by Shakyamuni. India and China have yet to hear the words of our sect. Only our founder's [i.e. Shinran's] disciples spread the opposite doctrine throughout the realm. The princes received these and their sons and grandsons enter the gates of our temples.[8]

Despite this, by the Edo period, the sect had to accommodate itself to the state. The sect's understanding of "taking a wife" was connected with a scene in Shinran's life that disciples and believers are very familiar with—the dream vision Shinran had in 1201 when, at the age of 29, he confined himself in the Rokkakudō, the so-called "Song Praising the Prior Life Merit of the Practitioner." This has been interpreted by post-Meiji period commentators as indicating some kind of anguish on Shinran's part regarding his "sexual desire." However, the orientation toward clerical marriage actually came from Shinran's acceptance of the premonition of his teacher, Hōnen, of a wedding between Shinran and Kanezane's daughter Tamahi, which Kanezane had proposed to Hōnen. In Hōnen's teaching of the nenbutsu, if a person intones the nenbutsu, regardless of whether he or she had taken the tonsure or not, that person could be reborn into the Pure Land of Amida. Kanezane, a follower of Hōnen, inquired into this teaching, asking, "if that is true, then how about a priest who all his life commits no violations but takes a wife and returns to the patterns of non-tonsured life?" Hōnen, upon receiving this question, commanded Shinran to take a wife. From the standpoint of the *Orthodox Record of the Life of the Holy Priest Shinran*, which states "from this moment, the founder [i.e. Shinran] took a woman as his wife," we can see that Shinran's taking a wife was not at all the result of a wrongdoing, heretical nature but, rather, an action based on a self-sacrificing and highly religious spirit.

As can be imagined from this story, the Jōdo Shinshū positions on "having a wife and consuming meat" continued to be harshly criticized by other sects as they had in the medieval period. However, justification in response to these criticisms and the subsequent countercriticisms grew more creative from the beginning of the Edo period. For example, *The Confused Debates on the Teachings of the Shinran Sect*, written by an unknown author in 1626, claimed on the basis of texts like the *Nirvāṇa Sūtra* that there was a tradition of allowing meat consumption based on the concept of "the three types of clean meat." The author also argued that various non–Jōdo Shinshū religious institutions, such as Angoin, Kiyomizu, Yoshino, Gion, and Nakayama, had histories of monks "taking a wife" and that at various Tendai and Shingon temples, the practice of homosexuality was rampant.[9]

Another defense of this practice can be found in Chiku's *Discussion on Consuming Meat and Taking a Wife*. Argued in three sections—"analogies," "proofs," and "reasoning"—Chiku offers a passionate defense of clerical marriage as a form of religious devotion. Shinran's consuming of meat and taking a wife, for Chiku, was an act for the salvation of all living things based on Kanezane's request to Hōnen that one of his disciples "become a non-tonsured person and the path setter for rebirth." The unique aspect of salvation found in the Jōdo Shinshū is asserted by identifying the wife with the bodhisattva of compassion: "Kannon, by her own accord, becomes a mate and instructs all living things." Thus, Shinran's "consuming meat and taking a wife" was considered by Chiku as totally different from ordinary motives. Chiku saw Shinran's marriage as a pact from a prior life between Shinran, a manifestation of Amida Nyorai, and Hōnen, a manifestation of the bodhisattva Seishi. Further, rather than simply an agreement between Hōnen as master and Shinran as disciple, the event was interpreted as originating in the heavenly realm of buddhas and bodhisattvas. Chiku concluded that eating meat was based on a deep acceptance of sinful acts as part of human life by claiming that the meat being consumed was "clean meat."

Over the course of the entire Edo Period, the sect continued to develop three rhetorical strategies. First, it utilized the language used by various exoteric and esoteric sects to comment upon the image that Jōdo Shinshū had a misguided and heretical teaching of "consuming meat and taking a wife." Second, an effort was made to reconstruct the context of Shinran's marriage and confer a religious meaning to it. Last, a strategy of stressing that their position was precisely what allowed the sect to guarantee salvation was developed. This course of argumentation allowed the sect to steer clear of questioning those followers who continued taking life through fishing and hunting for their livelihood. During the Edo period sect leaders distanced themselves from medieval justifications for these practices, focusing instead on ways to align Jōdo Shinshū with the mainline religious order that the shogunate established. The Honganji priest Gyōsei's *The Compilation of Debates on Taking a Wife and Consuming Meat* focuses on Shinran's teaching as an expedient means that was suitable to its time, namely, the era of the degenerate Dharma that was so closely associated with his times. The emphasis is on Shinran's response to his situation, where regardless of the fact that people may slander him, he appeared as stupid, dressed like a country bumpkin, and taught easy salvation through the great compassion of Amida as a method to win over converts in a degenerate age. But by the Kyōhō period (1716–35), the shogunate had issued the "Eleven Articles" that warned clerics of encounters with hunting and fishing parties even if it were to invite people to sermons. Those at the center of Jōdo Shinshū authority at Honganji acquiesced to these governmental norms for religion and transformed the context for this debate.

While the orientation of the Edo government fundamentally erased Jōdo Shinshū self-identification as a sect that embraced heterodoxies, it is not the case that the traditional concepts and customs were completely wiped out. In the next section, I would like to examine an example of this, the *manaita-biraki* (presenting of the cutting board) ceremony that is still performed to this day at the Hōonji Temple in the Asakusa district of Tokyo and the characteristics of the human-animal relationship that appears within it.

HŌONJI TEMPLE'S *MANAITA-BIRAKI*

manaita e	At the cutting board
sennin hodo no	a gathering of people
hito dakari	one thousand strong

From poems such as the one above, it would seem that for the residents of Edo the *manaita-biraki* ceremony performed at Hōonji Temple was a fairly well-known event. It was normal that many people visited temples at New Year's. However, the uniqueness of this temple's ritual of slicing a carp on a cutting board, preparing it, and passing it around to the participants on temple grounds—where the public stance is in opposition to the taking of life—made Edoites curious.

This ceremony, even today, is held every year on the twelfth day of January. It is famous for being performed before the wooden statue of Shōshin, the founder of the temple, in a Shijō-ryū carving knife ceremony. The temple formally calls this ceremony "The Practice of Preparing Carp Cuisine." In the pamphlet "The Origins of Carp Cuisine," which is handed out to the participants, after a simple explanation of the connection between Shinran and his disciple Shōshin and an introduction of the intriguing legend involving Shōshin and Tenjin, the text reads:

> As it was written in the legend, every year on the eleventh day of January, the carp received from the Tenjin Shrine of Iinuma is offered before the image of the founder at Hōonji Temple in Shimōsa Province and then is sent to Hōonji Temple in East Ueno. At the Hōonji Temple in Tokyo, from about 10 a.m. on the twelfth, before the image of the founder, the practice of preparing carp cuisine is performed solemnly and in accordance to ancient customs. *This practice is originally a rite for Shinto deities* and that such a practice is performed in the precincts of a temple can be seen as unusual. In the *Saijiki* (A Record of Seasonal Terms) of the Edo period, this practice was famous from ancient times as one of the annual events shrines and temples performed. What we call the *manaita-biraki* is the same practice.

As can be seen from the above explanation, while the legend draws on an important episode concerning Shōshin, the founder of Hōonji, there exists some "confusion" in the fact that the content of the practice is not suitable for a Buddhist temple. This is because from the Edo period onward, even though it is only fish, the fact remains that what is being offered before the founder's image is violating the prohibition on taking life.

It is worth noting that this ritual of sacrificing a living being is found at one of the oldest Jōdo Shinshū temples in eastern Japan. An Edo-period document, the 1698 *Sōrinshū* (A Collection of Buddhist Groves), highlights the close relation between Shōshin, Hōonji's founder, and Shinran. After becoming Shinran's disciple, Shōshin follows his master into exile. In 1232, Shōshin has a spiritual revelation from the Tenjin deity of Oono Shrine—an oracle that two carps from the Mitarai River would be presented to him as a testament of the Shintō deity's faith in Shōshin and his new form of Buddhism. Upon receiving this message, Shōshin, as repayment, offered up two *kagami-mochi* to Tenjin and this exchange of carp and *kagami-mochi* was the legendary beginning of the *manaita-biraki* ceremony.

Another text, Genchi's *Annals of the Ōtani Honganji Temple*, diverges slightly in its retelling of the origins of the ceremony. In this text, Shōshin built a small shrine at the side of his Hōonji Temple and named it the Itoku Tenjin. The Shintō deity Tenjin takes the form of an old man and listens to Shōshin's sermons. Upon hearing the Dharma, the deity is overcome with joy, and promises to become his disciple. Further, in order to show his gratitude, on the tenth of January the deity possessed one of the shrine maidens and presented to Shōshin the carp in the pond of the Tenjin Shrine. As in the first version, upon hearing this, Shōshin sent two *kagami-mochi* to the Tenjin Shrine as a token of his gratitude.

Finally, in an Edo period guidebook to the sacred places of the Jōdo Shinshū sect, *The Circuit Map of the 24 Temples*, a more elaborate narrative can be found. Bearing the name Akugorō, the young Shōshin, then with a wild and reckless heart, heads for Higashiyama and Yoshimizu on his way back from a pilgrimage to Kumano. The young man hears the teachings of Hōnen that one can gain rebirth in the Pure Land in accordance with Amida's vow, and requests to become Hōnen's disciple. But Hōnen, an elderly priest, decides Shōshin should be Shinran's disciple; thus Shōshin receives his name from Shinran. Shōshin earnestly follows Shinran; from his exile in Echigo, he accompanies Shinran to Bantō; at Yokosone he establishes a temple and struggles to spread the Jōdo Shinshū teachings. Finally, when his master Shinran returns to Kyoto, Shōshin sees Shinran off as far as Mount Hakone. There Shinran tells Shōshin that he entrusts him with the duty of spreading the teachings in eastern Japan. Pleased at Shōshin's success, Shinran helps name his temple, Hōonji, in

1214. This is followed by a recounting of an event in the summer of 1232. While Shōshin was spending day and night spreading the teachings on the nenbutsu, among the crowd of Buddhists and non-Buddhist listeners, there was an old man in a beautiful cap and robes, who came up to Shōshin after the crowd dispersed and said the following:

> I am the Tenjin deity of the Ikuno Shrine residing beside this pond. I received the good fortune of hearing your sermons on Amida's original vow day and night and have decided to become your disciple. I took this guise to let you know, but hereafter I wish to visit without taking on a guise. Thus to show my gratitude and that I am your disciple, every year in January, I shall unfailingly present to you two carp for a thousand generations.[10]

After saying this, the old man disappeared.

Shōshin told no one what happened and waited for a response for several months. On the night of January 10 of the following year, priests from the Tenjin Shrine visited Shōshin and told him of the strange oracle they had received. It seems that in the dream, Tenjin had said that because Shōshin was a sage capable of saving and benefiting sentient beings, Tenjin had agreed to become Shōshin's disciple and as agreed upon, would present two carps every year. Tomorrow the carp would be caught in the Mitarai Pond and presented to the temple. Five or six people in addition to the shrine priests had the same dream and, in exact accord with the dream, they caught two large carp and presented them to Shōshin. Shōshin subsequently received a written agreement from Tenjin and took the gift as a sign that Shinran's teachings would spread even in this degenerate age. Accepting the token symbolizing the master-disciple relationship as divine will, Shōshin offered up *kagami-mochi* as a token of gratitude.

Over six hundred years have gone by with carp from Mitarai Pond being sent annually to Hōonji Temple—only a single year having been missed. After the carp are offered before the wooden image of Shōshin, they are finely sliced and presented to the participants. At the same time, the *kagami-mochi* showing Shōshin's gratitude is presented to Tenjin's altar in Ikuno and remains there for seven days.

In conclusion, the Jōdo Shinshū rhetoric of not worshipping deities other than Amida, I believe, masks the pre-Buddhist animal worship and offerings found in the Japanese religious landscape. The *manaita-naoshi* ceremony—in which both East and West Honganji temples slice carp on a cutting board, offer it before Amida, and then prepare and distribute the fish among attendees—and the *manaita-biraki* can both be seen as a rupture into Buddhist orthodoxy of the Japanese festive ritualization that includes—apparently as a necessary part—the offering of animal sacrifices. I regard this as evidence that the memory of ancient sacrificial festivals is lodged within these Jōdo Shinshū ceremonies. The memory of the animals of the wild being deeply connected with human life—whether as daily catches for livelihood or sacrifices for festivals—is inherent within Jōdo Shinshū Buddhism. This complex relationship reveals something about both the nature of this sect as well as the nature of the sacred relationship between the human and animal worlds.

NOTES

1   *T.* vol. 24, no. 1484. [Ed. Not to be confused with the Pāli Brahmajāla sutta. Translated into English as *The Buddha Speaks the Brahma Net Sutra, With Commentary by Hui Seng*, trans. Buddhist Text Translation Society, 2 vols. (Talmage, CA: Dharma Realm Buddhist University, Buddhist Text Translation Society, 1981). Another English translation of the Mahāyāna text is "Brahma Net Sutra: Moral Code of the Bodhisattvas," trans. Sutra Translation Committee of the United States and Canada (New York, San Francisco, Niagara Falls, and Toronto: Sutra Translation Committee of the United States and Canada, 2000), http://www.ymba.org/bns/bnsframe.htm (accessed September 3, 2009). Also, "The Brahma Net Sutra," trans. Buddhist Text Translation Society in USA (publication details not provided), http://www.purifymind.com/BrahmaNetSutra.htm (accessed September 3, 2009).]

2   [Ed. English translation published as *Miraculous Stories from the Japanese Buddhist Tradition: The Nihon Ryoiki of the Monk Kyokai*, trans. Kyoko Nakamura (Surrey, England: RoutledgeCurzon, 1997).]

3   [Ed. For a study of the Suwa sect, see Lisa Grumbach, "Sacrifice and Salvation in Medieval Japan: Hunting and Meat in Religious Practice at Suwa Jinja" (PhD diss., Stanford University, 2005).]

4   [Ed. See Shinran, "A Record in Lament of Divergences" (Tannishō), *The Collected Works of Shinran* (CWS), 2 vols. (Kyoto: Jodo Shinshu Hongwanji-ha, 1997). See also, Taitetsu Unno, trans., *Tannisho: A Shin Buddhist Classic* (Honolulu: Buddhist Study Center, 1996), complete text available online at http://www.livingdharma.org/Tannisho/TannishoContents.html (accessed September 3, 2009).]

5   [Ed. This is from Shinran's "Notes on 'Essentials of Faith Alone.'" Cf. CWS, I: 459.]

6   [Ed. Rennyo, considered the second founder of Shin Buddhism, recorded his understanding of Shin thought in a series of letters. See Minor L. Rogers and Ann Rogers,

Rennyo: The Second Founder of Shin Buddhism, With a Translation of His Letters (Berkeley: Asian Humanities Press, 1991).]

7 [Ed. For a discussion of these issues and why they were interrelated, see Richard Jaffe, *Neither Monk nor Layman: Clerical Marriage in Modern Japanese Buddhism* (Princeton, NJ: Princeton University Press, 2001).]

8 [Ed. See James Dobbins, *Jōdo Shinshū: Shin Buddhism in Medieval Japan* (1989. Reprint. Honolulu: University of Hawai'i Press, 2002).]

9 [Ed. See Bernard Faure, *The Red Thread: Buddhist Approaches to Sexuality* (Princeton, NJ: Princeton University Press, 1998), and idem., *The Power of Denial: Buddhism, Purity and Gender* (Princeton, NJ: Princeton University Press, 2003).]

10 [Ed. Source unidentified.]

Is "Buddhist Environmentalism" a Contradiction in Terms?

Malcolm David Eckel

Several years ago I wrote an essay for a conference on "Buddhism and Ecology" at Harvard Divinity School.[1] The title of that essay posed a question like the question I have posed in this paper. There I asked whether it makes sense to say that there is a Buddhist philosophy of nature. Here I am asking whether the terms "Buddhism" and "environmentalism" can occupy the same intellectual space: Can one word be used to modify the other without falling into a morass of contradiction?

An honest observer would have to admit that the evidence is mixed. On one side there is the oft-repeated stereotype of Buddhism as an environmentally friendly tradition. Roderick Nash expressed this stereotype as a simple contrast between West and East. "Ancient Eastern cultures," he said, "are the source of respect for and religious veneration of the natural world." He goes on to say, "In the Far East the man-nature relationship was marked by respect, bordering on love, absent in the West."[2] Y. Murota draws the same contrast from a Japanese point of view when he says, "the Japanese view of nature is quite different from that of Westerners. . . . For the Japanese nature is an all-pervasive force. Nature is at once a blessing and a friend to the Japanese people. . . . People in Western cultures, on the other hand, view nature as an object and, often, as an entity set in opposition to mankind."[3] Other voices have pointed out that the reality of Buddhist cultures often falls short of this attractive ideal. Stephen R. Kellert points out what many of us know all too well when he says, "modern Japan and China have been cited for their poor conservation record—including widespread temperate and tropical deforestation, excessive exploitation of wildlife products, indiscriminate and damaging fishing practices, and widespread pollution."[4] In a statistical study about Japanese and

American attitudes toward wildlife, Kellert found that the most common approach in both cultures was the one that he called "humanistic": both cultures showed "primary interest and strong affection for individual animals such as pets or large wild animals with strong anthropomorphic associations." More than 50 percent of Kellert's Japanese respondents feared or disliked animals or were primarily concerned with their mastery or control. In later discussions, Kellert found that his respondents stressed the cultural transformation of nature: they preferred an experience of nature in which the wild aspects of the natural world were refined and abstracted so that they could serve as symbols of harmony, order, and balance. Donald Richie distills this point in his characteristically lapidary way when he says, "The Japanese attitude toward nature is essentially possessive. . . . Nature is not natural . . . until the hand of man . . . has properly shaped it."[5]

My own inclination is to rely less on statistics than on the small rhetorical gestures that reveal deeper attitudes about human beings and the natural world. One of these moments occurred in 1990 in Middlebury, Vermont, when the Dalai Lama was invited to speak at a conference on "Spirit and Nature." The audience expected to hear the Dalai Lama respect the natural world. The Dalai Lama began instead by saying that he had nothing to offer those who came to hear about ecology and the environment.[6] He interpreted the word "nature" as a reference to "the fundamental nature of all reality" and entered into a discourse about the concept of emptiness. It was not that he was hostile toward the natural world. He simply found it natural (if that is the right word) to shift attention away from nature toward the development of the human mind.

To see whether the Dalai Lama's ambivalence was widely shared, I recently put myself in my students' shoes and did a Google search for the words "Buddhism" and "environment." The search yielded two attractive websites: one from the Friends of the Western Buddhist Order in Great Britain, and one from the Earth Sangha, an organization that appears to be centered in Washington DC. Both acknowledge that Buddhist values appear to have little explicit connection with the environment. The Earth Sangha site begins: "Buddhism and environmentalism might appear to address two very different types of problems. You could say that the point of environmental work is to repair our relationship with the natural world. And the point of Buddhism, in a sense, is to repair our relationship with ourselves." It then goes on to assert that "these two fields overlap in all kinds of ways."[7] On the site of the FWBO, Nick Wallis is quoted as saying, "When we look at the traditional Buddhist texts there seems to be very little direct reference to what would these days be called environmental or ecological ideas."[8] Then he too elaborates a more positive image of the environment in Buddhist sources.

In my essay on the Buddhist philosophy of nature, I asked why there seems to be such a disconnection between Buddhist values and the natural world. In my view, the answer lies in ancient India, in what you might call the "yogic" worldview. Indian Buddhists do not accept the classic doctrinal assertions of Indian yoga, with its view of the eternal soul (*puruṣa*), but they do acknowledge the importance of distinguishing between things that are merely "natural" and those that involve the cultivation of the mind. One of the most telling expressions of this distinction is the story of Prince Siddhārtha's "going forth" as told by the Buddhist poet Aśvaghoṣa. Before he leaves the palace, the prince surveys a room full of sleeping women, in various postures of disarray. The poet compares them to *prakṛti*, the "material nature" of the Samkhya and Yoga systems. In a metaphorical sense, Siddhārtha is the soul. He sees the insentient, unconscious *prakṛti* for what it is, and he is no longer bound by it. It once had charmed him; now it fills him with disgust, and he leaves the palace for the ascetical life. Here the key idea is difference (*viveka*), combined with a sense of opposition. The interests of the soul are not the interests of nature, and the soul has to recognize this distinction to be free. For Buddhists in India the concept of the soul was problematic, but the sense of difference remained in the practice of renunciation and in the distrust of the "natural" habits of the saṃsāric world.[9]

In an article in *Tricycle* magazine, John Elder poses a question that should challenge any easy or uncritical attempt to link Buddhist values and the environmental movement.[10] He describes an afternoon of skiing with his friend Peter Forbes in the hills of Vermont. As they looked across the snowy landscape, Peter asked him whether the concept of conservation might be another form of attachment. Peter's question forced John to look at "conservation" in a new way: "It certainly involves a powerful effort of clinging to something precious, he pointed out, with all the personal and social suffering implied by such attempts in a world of transience." Peter's critique of the concept of conservation is familiar to anyone who has worked through the tradition of Buddhist philosophy. The key point is to identify points of improper reification, or sources of intellectual grasping, and to let them go. To think of elements in the natural world as entities to be "conserved" falls easily into this error. The practice of Buddhism is meant to challenge these instinctive modes of reification, not to encourage them.

Peter's critique also corresponds to a common analytical process in the environmental movement itself. John Elder points out that many of its most important intellectual icons are open to the same critique. The environmental historian William Cronon has argued that the concept of "wilderness" is the product of a particular moment in European and American cultural history.[11] It does not name an objective reality: it is simply a cultural construct. Wendell Berry has made a similar point about the word "environment": by separating human beings from their "environs," the word perpetuates the dualism that spawns environmental destruction.

When the words "conservation," "wilderness," and "environment" have become such targets of scrutiny, it was no small challenge for the staff at the Marsh-Billings-Rockefeller National Historic Site to give a name to the park's mission. The park is located in Woodstock, Vermont, and is meant to commemorate a tradition of conservation that goes back to George Perkins Marsh, author of *Man in Nature*, one of this country's first environmental classics. Marsh's family farm in Woodstock came into the hands of another Vermonter named Frederick Billings, who had made his fortune in the California Gold Rush. Billings turned the farm into a showcase of proper conservation practices. In the process, he put an indelible stamp on the landscape and on the agricultural practices of Vermont. The property then passed into the hands of Billings' granddaughter Mary French, who with her husband, Laurance Rockefeller, offered it to the U.S. government. After a series of learned conferences, the park leadership decided that this would be "the only national park to focus on conservation history and the evolving nature of land stewardship in America." As you can see, the formula is meant to be a compromise. "Conservation" is mentioned, but only as part of history; for the present and future, the operative word is "stewardship." The chief virtue of this word seems to be its vagueness: it does not decide whether the environment should be protected for human use or as a reality in its own right. The irony is that the word gains much of its moral force from the parable of the steward in the Christian Bible. It seems that the Christian echo is now so attenuated that it never became part of the discussion.

If the words "Buddhism" and "environmentalism" make an awkward combination, the problem now seems to come from both sides of the line. There are aspects of the Buddhist tradition that do not fit easily with a movement to respect the natural world, and there are problems with the definition of the movement itself. Perhaps this is why one of most radical and inspiring of Buddhist environmental movements has had such difficulty formulating a practice that protects the environment and also wins the acceptance of mainstream Buddhist organizations. The Thai Buddhist group known as Santi Asoke has tried to create something like a utopian community based on ideals of simplicity and harmony with nature. For a visitor, especially someone who has just escaped the noise and the congestion of Bangkok, the feeling of the community is astonishingly quiet and harmonious. The members of Santi Asoke observe a strict vegetarian diet, work in natural agriculture, eat natural food, use utensils made from coconut shells, and live in houses built from natural materials.[12] They walk barefoot and seem to exude an aura of modesty and serenity. And yet the rigor of their practices and the forcefulness of their teaching have brought them into a series of bitter conflicts with the hierarchy of the Thai sangha, so much so that they were formally expelled from the sangha and many of their members were jailed for presuming to function as legitimate monks. The conflict between Santi Asoke and the Thai authorities came from many factors, including the sense of political crisis and uncertainty in Bangkok in the late 1980s, but one important factor must be the ambiguity that surrounds the notion of the environment in classic Thai Buddhism. What constitutes a legitimate environmental program? In what sense is an environmental program "Buddhist"? In what way can it challenge or lay claim to the support of the religious hierarchy? "Buddhism" and "environmentalism" may not be contradictory in the strict sense of the word, but they make an uneasy combination, and each raises awkward and difficult questions about the other.

If the concept of Buddhist environmentalism is so problematic, where can we go from here? Is it possible to redeem these words so that they can address an environmental crisis that may not be easy to name, but that certainly deserves our attention and even our action? I would like to respond to these questions in two ways: first by making some formal observations about the critical process that leads us to question these important words, then by suggesting some ways to develop models of Buddhist environmental action.

Ten or fifteen years ago the Dalai Lama visited Harvard and spoke to a large group of students about the Buddhist concept of the self. He began by saying, "If you want to know who you are, be compassionate to your neighbor." Then he said that the question of the self is a bit more complicated than mere compassion, and he gave an elaborate account of the reason why the self and everything else are empty of identity. Then he paused, smiled, and asked, "If everything is empty, who told you this?" His answer was *bdag tsam*, the Tibetan words for "the mere I" or "just me." Whether you adhere to Dalai Lama's analysis of emptiness or not, you probably are familiar with this three-part pattern of thought. It begins by asserting or accepting the reality of something, it goes on to deny its reality, then it cycles back on itself and reappropriates the reality it has just rejected. The difference in the third stage is that this reality is appropriated in full awareness of its emptiness. This three-part pattern of thought is an expression of the Middle Path, where the word "path" (*pratipad*) means not merely a way of acting but a way of knowing. The first two stages represent the stages of affirmation and denial; the third represents the combination of the first two. In other words, the third stage *is* the Middle Path: it somehow balances the extremes of the first two and holds them together in a single form of awareness.

There are parallels for this three-part pattern in Western philosophy; some, such as the Hegelian dialectic, are too obvious to mention. A parallel that is particularly useful for the study of religion is Paul Ricoeur's analysis of the intellectual condition of modernity. The traditional understanding of myth has been stripped away by the process of critical thought initiated by the Enlightenment, but the myth cannot be discarded altogether. The challenge for the religious imagination is to hold the traditional myths together with their criticism in what Ricoeur calls a moment of second naiveté.

> Does this mean that we could go back to a primitive naiveté? Not at all. In every way, something has been lost, irremediably lost: immediacy of belief. But if we can no longer live the great symbolisms of the sacred in accordance with the original belief

in them, we can, we modern men, aim at a second naiveté in and through criticism. In short, it is by interpreting that we can hear again. Thus it is in hermeneutics that the symbol's gift of meaning and the endeavor to understand by deciphering are knotted together.[13]

The challenge of Ricoeur's third stage is not unlike the challenge we face when we want to give a critical and thoughtful account of Buddhism and the environment. From the unreflective point of view, the point is obvious: of course Buddhism respects the environment. When the tradition is scrutinized and the key terms are given careful examination, the answer is not so clear. There are Buddhist values that lead just as easily in another direction. In fact, there are Buddhist values that put concepts like "nature" and "conservation" in doubt. But the original problem remains: What to do about the environment, and what to do about the environment from a Buddhist point of view? The answer, as Ricoeur would have it, is to become enchanted once again by the symbols and "let the symbols give rise to thought."[14] The challenge is to appropriate the symbolic resources of the tradition while acknowledging that this appropriation has no inevitability. It is simply an act of imaginative reconstruction, as if one were shaping a new landscape out of the mixed and contradictory residue of Buddhist tradition.

For many Buddhist environmentalists, the most promising invitation to reflection is the doctrine of dependent co-arising (*pratītyasamutpāda*). This was certainly true in the volume on *Buddhism and Ecology*, edited by Mary Evelyn Tucker and Duncan Ryūken Williams. Whether this is articulated in the austere form of the Theravāda tradition or in the more elaborate form of the Mahāyāna, it provides immense possibilities not just for reflection, but for action. As John Daido Loori said at the beginning of his essay "The Precepts and the Environment": "Imagine, if you will, a universe in which all things have a mutual identity. They all have a codependent origination: when one thing arises, all things arise simultaneously. And everything has a mutual causality; what happens to one thing happens to the entire universe."[15] This image of an interconnected cosmos is immensely rich. In an aesthetic sense and in a purely practical sense, there is nothing to match it in any other religious tradition. And it plugs directly into the scientific, ecological vision of an interconnected world. It is no wonder that so many popular statements of Buddhist environmental ethics begin as Nick Wallis does on the website of the Friends of the Western Buddhist Order:

> In seeking to apply the Dharma to the area of the environment, we have to look for underlying principles that are appropriate to the very different world that we ourselves inhabit. We don't have to look very far. In the vision of universal interpenetration, one of the Mahāyāna flowers of the Buddha's teaching of Conditioned Co-production (pratitya samutpada), we have a basic insight into our relationship with nature.

One of the most useful features of the doctrine of dependent co-arising is that it undermines the idea that there is a *center* around which other things need to revolve. Some of the most important environmental explorations in the last few years have been cast as critiques of theocentric and anthropocentric views of the world. About this Buddhists would agree. But there is another way to read the tradition that recognizes the existence of a center and from it builds a concept of the holiness of the natural world. In my essay for the volume on *Buddhism and Ecology*, I explored the significance of Buddhist pilgrimage traditions, especially the tradition that the tree at Bodh Gaya, the pilgrimage site that marks the site of the Buddha's awakening, sits at the center of the cosmos. Some Mahāyāna texts pass on a tradition that every buddha, of every era, is enlightened at exactly the same site, and beneath the spot where the buddhas are enlightened sits a throne that is anchored at the center of the Earth. If there is to be a "center" in Buddhist ethical thinking about the environment, perhaps this is where it should be located, at the site where buddhas attain their awakening.

But where is this site? Northern India is one possibility. Another might be the mind itself. It is in the mind, after all, that one understands the nature of emptiness. But the mind still has to be located in a particular body, and the body is located in a particular place. While emptiness, in a sense, is everywhere, it is realized only in *this* moment, *this* place, and *this* body. In a fine meditation entitled "Zen Practice and a Sense of Place," Doug Cochida quotes a reference by the Zen master Dōgen to the Earth as the "true human body":

> The meaning of "true" in "the entire Earth is the true human body" is the actual body. You should know that the entire Earth is not our temporary appearance, but our genuine human body.[16]

The Earth is not, as it were, a mere illusion. It is the body of an enlightened sage, and it is as much worthy of reverence as the throne of the Buddha. In his essays in *The Practice of the Wild*, Gary Snyder said, "In some cases we might call [nature] sacred." To say only "in some cases" shows an appropriate Buddhist reticence toward attributing sacrality to nature in and of itself. But it is not completely implausible to use the language of "holiness" in speaking of the natural order. In his essay "Buddhism, Global Ethics, and the Earth Charter," Steven C. Rockefeller challenged Buddhists to find an appropriate way to say that all life is sacred.[17] We could pose the same challenge about the whole environment. The throne of the Buddha's awakening may take us in this direction. The natural world functions as a teacher when it exhibits the lesson of impermanence. In some strands of the Buddhist tradition it can be thought of as possessing buddha nature. But most importantly, it is the place made holy by the quest for awakening. Enlightenment is made present in this body and this Earth.

Finally, I would like to suggest that the Pure Land tradition, represented by several of the contributions in this collection, may have a unique role to play in the construction of a Buddhist environmental ethic. In this world where the morning newspaper brings us an endless litany of depressing stories of human cruelty to other humans and to the natural world, utopian thinking has gone out of fashion. But is it not true to say that when we imagine a world where human beings can live in harmonious and respectful relationships with all living things, along with the physical warp and weft of the cosmos itself, we are imagining something like a paradise? As you may know, our word paradise comes from a Persian word that means a "garden." One of the most important untold stories in Buddhist tradition, in my opinion, is the influence of the concept of a Pure Land on the idealized landscapes that are so often (and often so inaccurately) referred to as "Zen gardens." I wonder whether this could be a time for Buddhists to rediscover the utopian aspiration embedded in this concept—to purify this buddha-field and turn it into a Pure Land.

Notes

1   That essay was published as "Is There a Buddhist Philosophy of Nature?" in *Buddhism and Ecology: The Interconnection of Dharma and Deeds*, ed. Mary Evelyn Tucker and Duncan Ryūken Williams (Cambridge, MA: Harvard University Press, 1997), 327–49.

2   Roderick Frazier Nash, *Wilderness and the American Mind* (New Haven, CT: Yale University Press, 1967), 20–21, 192–93.

3   Y. Murota, "Culture and Environment in Japan," *Environmental Management* 9 (1986): 105–12.

4   Stephen R. Kellert, "Concepts of Nature East and West," in *Reinventing Nature? Responses to Postmodern Deconstruction*, ed. Michael E. Soulé and Gary Lease (Washington, DC: Island Press, 1995), 107.

5   Donald Richie, *The Inland Sea* (Tokyo: Weatherhill, 1971), 13; quoted in Kellert, "Concepts of Nature," 115.

6   In other settings the Dalai Lama has spoken more explicitly about the need to respect the natural environment, as in his speech at the "Forum 2000" Conference, in Prague, Czech Republic, September 1997. This speech is found on the website of the Government of Tibet in Exile (http://www.tibet.com/DL/forum-2000.html).

7   http://www.earthsangha.org [Ed. The Earth Sangha statement the author cites has apparently been revised; for their current statement on the relation between Buddhism and environmentalism, see http://www.earthsangha.org/depth/gb.html (accessed September 3, 2009).]

8   http://www.fwbo.org/index.html [Ed. Nick Wallis/Rijumati, "Buddhism and the Environment," http://www.fwbo.org/articles/buddhism_environment.html (accessed September 3, 2009).]

9   I comment more fully on the important of this sense of distinction in "Is There a Buddhist Philosophy of Nature?"

10 John Elder, "Dust of Snow: Awakening to Conservation," *Tricyle* (Fall 2003): 50–53.

11 William Cronon and Wendell Berry are discussed by John Elder in "Dust of Snow," 51.

12 See Marja-Leena Heikkila-Horn, *Buddhism with Open Eyes: Belief and Practice of Santi Asoke* (Bangkok: Fah Apai, 1997).

13 Paul Ricoeur, *The Symbolism of Evil*, trans. Emerson Buchanan (New York: Harper & Row, 1967), 351.

14 Ibid., 348.

15 Loori in *Buddhism and Ecology*, 177.

16 Doug Cochida, "Zen Practice and a Sense of Place," in Badiner, ed., *Dharma Gaia* (Berkeley: Parallax Press, 1990), 106–11.

17 Steven C. Rockefeller, in *Buddhism and Ecology*, 320.

The Early Buddhist Tradition
and Ecological Ethics

■ ■ ■

Lambert Schmithausen

PRELIMINARY CONSIDERATIONS

In writing this paper[1] I do not conceal that I am most concerned about what is called the "ecological crisis" or the destruction and deterioration of nature. I also readily admit that personally I sympathize with the attempts among adherents of contemporary religions to support what is often called "ecological ethics," in other words, an ethics based on the conviction that humankind is responsible for the preservation of nature, that is, of intact ecosystems and biodiversity—a conviction I do indeed share though I shall not be attempting here to prove its validity. Such a conviction seems to presuppose that intact nature and biodiversity are regarded as a value, and in my opinion they ought to be regarded as a value not only from an anthropocentric point of view, that is, because they may be indispensable (or at least useful or enjoyable) to human beings (though this is doubtless better than nothing), but rather, and primarily, for their own sake, in their own right. And what we need today, in view of the damage already done, is not just protection of nature as a kind of byproduct but rather active protection and even restoration of nature based on the acceptance of the intrinsic value of natural beauty and diversity, and of the fact that other species—both animals and plants—have no less right to existence than human beings.[2]

Yet, as a scholar, and moreover as one whose field is philology and the history of ideas, I cannot avoid asking to what extent ecological ethics is, and has always been, an element of the religious tradition concerned—forming part of its body of teachings or doctrinal system and expressing itself in the actual behavior of its adherents—or to what extent and in what way ecological ethics is, at least, in tune with, and susceptible of being integrated into, said tradition, in my case Buddhism. Such a question may also suggest itself to thoughtful or hesitating believers, or to an attentive observer of the countries where Buddhism is dominant. For the ecological situation in some Buddhist countries is indeed far from being satisfactory. It may well be that this has come about in spite of Buddhism, due to other reasons, including Western influence. But it cannot be excluded *a priori* that Buddhism, or rather certain facets of Buddhism, may somehow be co-responsible for the situation.

In fact, among Buddhists as well as Buddhologists there seems to be considerable disagreement with regard to whether Buddhism does or does not favor an ecological ethics.[3] This disagreement exists also with regard to the more conservative forms of Buddhism, that is, Theravāda and similar but now extinct schools like Sarvāstivāda, and with regard to the text corpus some redaction or other of which constitutes their respective canonical basis. It is this corpus of canonical texts, especially its, roughly speaking, pre-abhidharmic layers, that I have in mind when speaking of the "early Buddhist tradition." Since Theravāda is the only living representative of this tradition, the Pāli canon will naturally be the most frequently (but not exclusively) adduced source.

Especially among Buddhist authors, both Asian and Western, many have come to adopt positions that favor an ecological interpretation of early Buddhism, though often in a more or less anthropocentric perspective.

A prominent example of a mainly nonanthropocentric perspective is the American Buddhist Joanna Macy.[4] According to her, the original, genuine teaching of Buddhism is a theory of universal interconnectedness, mutual conditioning, or radical interdependence of all phenomena, which comes close to the modern general systems theory, and, by dismantling the separate, continuous ego-self, leads to identification with and responsibility for the whole world, humans as well as all other beings. The more so since one aspect of universal interconnectedness is, for her, the relationship of all beings in terms of the modern theory of evolution.[5] Macy prefers evolution to the traditional Buddhist doctrine of rebirth, with which, she thinks, the Buddha himself, too, was not much concerned.[6] Nor has she any sympathy for the idea of nirvāṇa as an escape from the world, because this would imply a devaluation of the world and a weakening of our feeling of responsibility. Accordingly, she emphasizes that, in contrast to a certain tendency among Theravāda Buddhists and especially Western interpreters, original Buddhism (as well as early Mahāyāna) is not escapist but world-affirming, aiming at an awakening which "puts one into the world with a livelier, more caring sense of social engagement."[7]

Another example is the Japanese scholar Noritoshi Aramaki.[8] As I understand him, he maintains that the Buddha, in contrast to the Jainas, said yes to bodily existence and hence to the food chain and to nature as it actually is, and that it is due to this affirmative attitude to bodily existence that *ahiṃsā* is considerably less strict in Buddhism than in Jainism.[9] Accordingly, Aramaki, too, seems to reject the idea that in early Buddhism nirvāṇa aims (at least ultimately) at escape from this world.[10]

But there are also opinions to the contrary. For example, Ian Harris[11] has tried to collect evidence, mainly from the Pāli nikāyas and vinaya, showing that the Buddhist attitude toward nature is predominantly negative. He admits that "it is not inconceivable that historical scholarship may, in the future, reveal that early Buddhists did live in harmony with their surroundings" and that "their doctrinal position may well have contributed to this harmony." But he stresses that this does not mean that they were "environmentalists" in the sense of a "conscious attempt to critically appraise and counteract the adverse by products of the scientific enterprise," and he argues that the transformation of "the traditional attitude of good natured benevolence and decorum directed toward a radically unstable natural environment... into an ethic based on the ultimate value of nature" as advocated by some contemporary Buddhist authors means "a significant doctrinal shift," nay, "the transformation of a... traditional system of thought" into "liberal Christianity."[12]

While Harris appears to argue from a Christian background, Noriaki Hakamaya[13] emphatically rejects all kinds of ecological interpretations of Buddhism from what he claims to be the Buddhist point of view. For him, true[14] Buddhism negates nature. To be sure, for Hakamaya "nature" mainly means the creative origin and true essence of things and beings, as the basis of the latters' life in the sense of a substantial soul or Self,[15] and negating this does look much like traditional Buddhism. But for Hakamaya not having a soul seems to mean, in the case of natural beings including animals, not to be living, sentient beings at all, at least from the metaphysical point of view. Only in the case of the human being does lack of a substantial soul not imply insentience because human beings alone can think. If I understand Hakamaya correctly, he takes this to be the essential message of the twelve-membered formula of dependent origination, connecting it with the Cartesian *cogito ergo sum*.[16] Thus, man is the master of this world.[17] Yet we should not destroy it and should even have compassion for animals (for according to Hakamaya there is no reason why a thinking person should be insensitive to violence), but in any case for Hakamaya human interests come first.[18]

It would thus seem that the sources for our knowledge of early Buddhism are not sufficiently explicit and unambiguous on the issue of ecological ethics; for otherwise such a wide divergence of opinions would hardly be explainable. Actually, in former times environmental problems, if existing at all, were hardly understood as such, and at any rate did not exist in such a conspicuous form as today. Hence, we cannot expect the early texts to contain fully explicit statements with regard to this issue.[19] But on the other hand even in those times there must have been some attitude toward nature. Hence there may well have been some kind of spontaneous, unreflected ecological ethics, or at least evaluations and attitudes that offer a suitable basis on which it might be established today. For today the Buddhist tradition, like any other, cannot avoid facing the problem. If it is to remain a living tradition, it has to supply answers to new vital questions,[20] and it may have to accommodate its heritage to the new situation by means of explication, reinterpretation, reorganization, or even creative extension or change. One of these questions is doubtless whether or not an ecological ethics is required (or at least desirable), and I for one do not see how it could be answered in the affirmative unless intact nature and natural diversity are accorded a positive value.

From a traditional Buddhist point of view, it might, however, be argued that, to be sure, nature ought to be preserved as intact as possible, but that from the Buddhist point of view an explicit ecological ethics, based on imparting value to nature, is superfluous, because a behavior that keeps nature intact is the spontaneous, automatic outflow of the moral and spiritual self-perfection to be accomplished by every person individually; or that such an ethics would even be doomed to ineffectiveness because the present state of nature is a kind of automatic objective reflection, or collective karmic result, of the moral and spiritual state of (human) beings, and that it cannot therefore be influenced directly by ecological activism.

To the latter argument I should reply that at least in early Buddhism the karma doctrine as well as the idea that the physical world is somehow dependent on humanity's moral behavior are not meant to justify fatalism but, on the contrary, intended to encourage endeavor on the part of the individual. To be sure, what is encouraged is, in the first place, moral and spiritual endeavor, but since karma is explicitly regarded to be only one cause among others,[21] there is also room for direct influence on one's own circumstance, as well as on the global situation. Actually, this is shown by the present, actively and directly man-made, destruction and pollution of nature. Hence, there is no reason why it should not be equally possible, to a certain extent at least, to counteract this destruction in an equally direct manner. That the individual feels comparatively helpless with regard to what happens in the world at large does not mean that active environmental commitment is absolutely futile.

As for the first argument, I do not deny that the spiritual perfection of individuals may have an automatic ecological effect. But at least as far as early Buddhist spirituality (as I for one understand it from the texts) is concerned, I shall try to show that what follows from it spontaneously would seem to be, above all, only a largely "passive" ecological attitude, emerging as a kind of byproduct, hardly an "active" one based on positive value perceived to inhere in intact nature and in natural diversity as such, which is, however, what is most required in the present situation. Besides, even if spiritual perfection were to culminate, automatically, in ecological behavior and action, it may not be possible any longer to wait until the spiritual perfection of a majority of people has sufficiently advanced or even reached completion. It would, of course, be so much better if people behaved and acted in such a way spontaneously, due to spiritual perfection, but will there ever be enough perfected people, and do we indeed have that much time left? As in the case of the moral commitments (like not killing living beings) that are taken up right at the beginning by both monk and lay person, it may be necessary to motivate as many ordinary, imperfect people as possible to commit themselves to ecological behavior, and even action, here and now.[22]

Hence, in my opinion the present situation requires an ecological ethics based on according a positive value to nature intact and to natural diversity. The aim of this paper is to investigate—once more but still in an admittedly preliminary way—the early Buddhist tradition from the point of view of the actual or possible relation of this tradition to an ecological

ethics. Though this may not be my job, I have also dared to include a suggestion how and on what conditions such an ethics, if desired, could best
be established in such a way that the essentials of tradition are not jeopar-
dized. Thus, my investigation comprises three levels: (1) description of the
pertinent early Buddhist teachings and attitudes; (2) their critical evaluation from the point of view of ecological ethics; and (3) my own constructive suggestions.

Unfortunately, even mere description is not without problems because
it involves selection or condensation and is hardly separable from interpretation. Actually, divergence of opinion with regard to the early Buddhist attitude to nature or ecological ethics is partly due to fundamental
disagreement with regard to the understanding and interpretation of central teachings and attitudes of early Buddhism and to the exegesis of the
pertinent texts. Such disagreement is no doubt favored not only by the
ambiguity of some texts but also by a certain complexity if not heteroge-
neity of the corpus of canonical texts, showing as they do different layers
and strands. Thus, divergent interpretations may also result from emphasis
on different strands or teachings, and may be reinforced by declaring some
to be original, authentic, or true, while others are regarded as later or even
as deviations. But in the absence of a commonly recognized stratification
of the earlier portions of the canonical texts, what is considered original
or true Buddhism is easily influenced by the interpreter's own thinking
or predilection. I therefore prefer, for the present purpose—which is not
concerned with the origin or development of early Buddhism but with
the attitude, to nature, of the tradition, and especially its authoritative
canonical texts, as a whole[23]—to deal with this tradition simply as one
made up of several strands, or rather spiritual and didactic levels and contexts, which, to be sure, are not entirely unrelated but ought not to be
mixed up by oversystematization either, and therefore will be discussed
separately, one by one.

To be sure, I too presuppose, to some extent, the validity of my interpretation, and understand some of these strands or contexts to be more
central to early Buddhism than others (and I must, for the time being,
confine critical discussion of divergent views to a few very preliminary
hints, mostly in notes). But I have at least tried my best to let my descrip-
tion/interpretation not be influenced by my personal concern. I understand and acknowledge that believers may feel the need for, and hence

tend to create the myth of, an identity of their reinterpreted, reorganized, or creatively extended or changed tradition with the original one, and may not like, or may even strongly resent, the scholar pointing out differences. But as a historian of ideas bound to the modern historical sense, I feel obliged to clearly keep these levels apart[24] (and even believers should perhaps not lose sight of the fact that unacknowledged historical facts may easily become a weapon in the hands of critics). I therefore ask the reader to distinguish sharply between, on the one hand, my description of what I understand to be traditional Buddhist views and, on the other, my critical evaluation of these views in terms of ecological ethics and, finally, my constructive suggestions for how, on this basis, active ecological ethics in the modern sense might be established. The first may be found historically correct or not, the second adequate or not, the third acceptable or not, or even superfluous. But in any case these diffcrent levels should be kept apart and judged separately.

Nature in the Context of the Ultimate Evaluation of Existence

Let me, then, start with what I for one cannot but understand to be the ultimate evaluation of existence in early Buddhism, ubiquitous as it is in the sermons and closely connected with, and emphasized in, the central spiritual context of detachment and release.[25]

The first Noble Truth, which according to tradition[26] was part of the Buddha's first discourse, is well known: birth, old age, disease, dying,[27] separation from dear things or persons, etc.—all this is *dukkha* (Skt. *duḥkha*): painful, disagreeable, ill, entailing suffering. Life is connected with, or at least constantly threatened by, pain, suffering,[28] and is inexorably, sooner or later, ended by death.[29] Even the superficially pleasant[30] things that are the objects of desire often involve more suffering and disadvantage than pleasure.[31] It is only in certain states of meditative concentration that this situation can be temporarily surmounted.[32] But in a more basic sense, the whole world (*loka*),[33] all conditioned things (*saṅkhāra*),[34] all constituents of a person as well as of the external world,[35] and even the states of meditative concentration[36] are unsatisfactory or ill (*dukkha*),[37] in an objective sense,[38] just on account of their being impermanent (*anicca*) and subject to decay (*vipariṇāmadhamma*).[39] As such, they are not one's Self (*attan*) nor one's own (*attaniya*, *mama*, etc.)[40]—because this would imply lasting and free disposal of them[41]—but something alien (*para*, *añña*),[42] and hence of no real value and concern, just like grass, pieces of wood, or leaves (*tiṇa-kaṭṭha-palāsa*) in a park.[43]

This evaluation seems to start from human existence, but it is, of course, equally applicable to animal life. I for one do not remember any canonical text that affirms the food chain universe in the same way as Vedic and Hindu sources[44] sometimes do. Eating may have to be accepted as inevitable for survival,[45] but this does not exclude that it is at the same time detested,[46] and that the natural situation of killing and eating the weaker and of the domination of the strongest is deeply abhorred, not only in society,[47] but also in nature.[48] Therefore, I do not think that it is correct to derive, from the acceptance of the necessity of body and food for human existence (which is usually considered to be the only one in which liberating insight can be attained), an ultimately positive evaluation of nature characterized by the food chain. Even the less violent aspects of nature—vegetation, landscape, and the elements—though hardly if ever viewed in terms of suffering or struggle for survival, cannot claim ultimate value in view of the fact that they too are ultimately ill or unsatisfactory (in an objective sense) just on account of their impermanence.[49]

Therefore, the ultimate analysis and evaluation of existence in early Buddhism does not seem to confer any value on nature, neither on life as such nor on species nor on ecosystems. The ultimate value and goal of early Buddhism, absolute and definitive freedom from suffering, decay, death, and impermanence, cannot be found in nature.[50] But neither is it found in a civilized or artificial world. For the goods and achievements of civilization, too, are, apart from usually benefiting only a minority, often a cause of suffering for others, especially for animals, and are, at any rate, impermanent. Even from an optimistic outlook technological progress will never succeed in abolishing suffering completely, let alone impermanence, to which even god Brahman and the luminous divine beings who abide in still higher spheres are subject.[51]

Thus, the ultimate analysis and evaluation of existence in early Buddhism does not motivate efforts for preserving nature, not to mention restoring it, nor efforts for transforming or subjugating it by means of technology. It only motivates the wish and effort to liberate oneself (*vimutti*) from all constituents of both personal existence and the world—a goal to which this analysis is itself conducive by arousing weariness (*nibbidā*) and detachment (*virāga*).[52] And, at least if compassionateness (*kāruññatā*) and caring for others (*anukampā*) are sufficiently strong,[53] as in the case of the Buddha, it may motivate the person who has attained liberation (or is on the way to it) to help others to do the same,[54] by teaching[55] or just by being a model.[56] It goes without saying that in view of the ultimate evaluation of existence as unsatisfactory the need to liberate oneself (or others, for that matter) from it is considerably increased by the fact that one's existence in the world is, in early Buddhism, generally understood as perpetuating itself through a virtually endless series of rebirths (*punabbhava*) and redeaths—either in this world or in (ultimately impermanent and hence unsatisfactory[57]) yonder heavens and hells—that is, as *saṃsāra*.[58] Definitive release from *dukkha* does not, then, merely mean freedom from frustration, sorrow, and fear arising from wrong attitudes[59] or even (by access to certain forms of meditative concentration) from physical pain in this life, but, above all, release from rebirth[60] and its implications (aging and dying) and imponderabilities.

ORIGINATION IN DEPENDENCE AND ECOLOGICAL ETHICS

In order to attain liberation, it is necessary to gain insight into, and eliminate, the forces by which one's existence in the world (or, more precisely, reiterated existence, rebirth) is kept going. According to the second Noble Truth, the main cause is desire (*taṇhā, tṛṣṇā*).[61] Freedom from rebirth is hence attained by extinguishing desire, especially desire for (further) existence.[62] According to other texts,[63] desire is, in its turn, ultimately rooted in non- or misunderstanding (*avijjā, avidyā*). Desire is hence removed through the removal of *avijjā* by means of insight. This causal nexus is elaborated in the twelve-membered formula of origination in dependence (*paṭiccasamuppāda, pratītyasamutpāda*),[64] which—similar in this regard to the karma doctrine—is thus concerned, at least originally, with the destiny of individual beings[65] (primarily, doubtless, human beings), pointing out that the causes for rebirth as well as, for that matter, for liberation are found within each individual itself, so that it is the individual's own business to make a change or go on as before. I for one fail to see how this analysis of the presuppositions of individual bondage and liberation could, without a radical reinterpretation, provide a basis for ecological ethics based on an intrinsic value of natural diversity and beauty.

To be sure, the canonical texts also contain applications of the principle of origination in dependence that are not expressly, or not at all, related to rebirth, as, for example, psychological or physio-psychological explanations of how feelings[66] or desire[67] arise, or the explanation of how unwholesome behavior like violence, quarrel, and lies originate from desire.[68] In some sermons, people's moral status or morally qualified actions are regarded as influencing even the situation of the external world,[69] and the external world has, in its turn, certain influences on living beings.[70] But it is, as far as I can see, only later on (especially in Chinese Huayan Buddhism)[71] that origination in dependence was even developed into a principle of universal interdependence and interrelatedness. As such it seems, to be sure, to resemble the structural principle of scientific ecology (though closer scrutiny would seem to be required). But as far as I can see even such a principle does not necessarily entail an ecological ethics as I understand it.[72] To be sure, universal interrelatedness would mean that any change I (or we) bring about has influence on everything in the world including myself (or ourselves). But does this preclude that one (or humankind) might try (and to a certain extent even successfully try) to exploit the causal network for one's (or humankind's) own advantage, at the cost of others, as in modern technology? And even if universal interdependence and interrelatedness were of such a kind that this won't work, at least not in the long run, wouldn't it at best entail an anthropocentric ecological attitude—one that preserves intact ecosystems and biodiversity only because and to the extent they are indispensable for the survival of human beings, or at least for their happiness, or spiritual perfection— unless it is supplemented by attributing a positive value to nature as it is, in its own right?

Anyway, the idea of a mutual dependence, interconnectedness, or interrelatedness, here and now, of all things and beings does not seem to be expressed in the canonical texts of early Buddhism.[73] They only teach that not only suffering and rebirth but all things and events, except nirvāṇa,[74] arise in dependence on specific (complexes of) causes and conditions, which in their turn have also arisen in dependence on causes and conditions, without any primary, absolute cause at the beginning. There are, to be sure, instances of explicitly stated mutual causality,[75] but they are special cases.[76] This still holds good even when, in the abhidhamma, most of the elements of the twelve-membered formula of origination in dependence are stated to condition one another mutually,[77] for this statement is only made in the context of a drastic abhidhammic reinterpretation of this formula as referring to one single moment of mind (*ekacittakkhaṇa*).[78] Even the aforementioned occasional references to the influence of human moral behavior on the external world, which inevitably has repercussions on people, are still a far cry from universal interrelatedness. What seems to come closest to the latter is the idea that in the course of the beginningless *saṃsāra*, all living beings have already been one another's relatives.[79] But this idea is hardly meant to imply that there is a causal interdependence between all living beings here and now. It does have an ethical significance, but, as I shall point out later, hardly a deliberately ecological one.

Early Buddhist Spirituality and Ethics in Relation to Ecological Ethics

But let us first to the cessation of suffering and to the fact that the decisive factor for this is the elimination of desire, or greed. Greed is no doubt one of the foremost causes of environmental destruction: especially greed for consumer goods or objects of social prestige, but also greed for sexual pleasures or propagation if it leads to an excessive growth of human population. Hence, there can be no doubt that the elimination and even diminution of greed is ecologically beneficial.

This holds good for other Buddhist virtues as well. For example, for being content with little,[80] being moderate in food,[81] and making full use of things,[82] as antidotes against luxury, overconsumption, and wastefulness,[83] and for mindfulness (*sati*)[84] and vigilance (*appamāda*) as antidotes against thoughtless and careless behavior. And it holds no less good for the practice of dismantling the notions of ego, self, and mine, especially with regard to one's body and mental factors as well as with regard to external phenomena, which leads to detachment[85] and to the elimination of egoism, possessiveness, and conceit.[86]

But it should be kept in mind that such attitudes are spiritual practices and ascetic virtues, especially of the monk, and, primarily at least, intended to increase his own spiritual perfection or purity. *De facto* they may have contributed to a sound ecology, but at least in early Buddhism they do not seem to have been motivated, expressly and primarily, by considerations of ecological ethics in the sense of consciously preserving species and ecosystems as such. To expressly motivate them by this purpose means to adapt them to a new situation, which is legitimate but requires attributing a positive value to nature-as-it-is.

Likewise, renouncing sexual intercourse and propagation, as demanded of monks and nuns, may, perhaps, have had an attenuating effect on population growth but was hardly motivated by such a purpose. The same holds good for the fact that even in the case of lay followers, early Buddhism, as far as I can see, does not push for maximum propagation.

The most pertinent elements of early Buddhist spirituality and practice in our context are doubtless the attitudes of not killing or injuring living beings (*ahiṃsā*, etc.), friendliness (*mettā*, *maitrī*), compassion (*karuṇā*) or compassionateness (*kāruñña*, *kāruññatā*),[87] caring or sympathy (*anukampā*), and concern (*dayā*, *anuddayā*).

Noninjury (*ahiṃsā*) appears to have started, in the Brāhmaṇa period, as a way of protecting oneself from the vengeance of injured animals (and plants) in the yonder world,[88] and probably also from the vengeance of their congeners in this very life.[89]

Friendliness (*mettā*), too, has a Vedic background of self-protection, though not so much from revenge as from spontaneous aggression. For it is derived from Sanskrit *mitra*, which in early Vedic sources means "alliance," especially between different tribes.[90] Such an alliance implied a peace treaty and, usually, some form of cooperation, and could even develop into friendship, just as the ally (also *mitra*) could eventually become a veritable friend, and it is this nuance which became the primary meaning of the word in the later language. At least in later Vedic texts we can find the idea that an alliance or peace/friendship treaty could even be concluded with natural beings.[91] In Buddhism, the emphasis is on cultivating a mental attitude of friendliness or even loving kindness[92] toward all living beings, but the idea of the protective function of alliances or peace treaties[93] has remained alive even in connection with the Buddhist attitude of friendliness (*mettā*), which is in fact considered to serve the purpose of calming, or protecting oneself from, dangerous creatures.[94]

On the other hand, compassion (*karuṇā*), caring (*anukampā*), and concern (*dayā*, *anuddayā*) do not seem to derive from, or have the function of, self-protection;[95] for compassion is usually an attitude primarily directed toward feeble, suffering creatures, not so much toward strong and dangerous ones, and caring (*anukampā*) is an emotion one normally feels for beloved persons like one's children.[96] Significantly enough, Harris[97] does not mention compassion and caring in this context.

His treatment of friendliness (*mettā*) as a spiritual exercise also would seem to require a few corrections. He states that "there is little evidence in the canon, or its associated commentaries, to suggest that *mettā* may be extended to other beings simply as an expression of fellow-feeling"[98] and that Buddhaghosa even discourages meditators "from extending loving kindness to animals or other non-humans."[99]

The latter assertion would seem to be based on a misunderstanding of the passage adduced,[100] which merely discusses the question with what kind of persons one should start the exercise. To be sure, animals do not play a prominent role in Buddhaghosa's treatment of the matter, and it is interesting that what is dealt with in detail is rather *mettā* practiced by animals (actually the Buddha in former existences) toward wicked human beings.[101] But nevertheless in the unlimited form of the exercise referring to all living beings,[102] animals are, of course, included among its objects, belonging as they do to the category of "beings in evil states of existence" (*vinipatika*).[103]

As for the other assertion, namely that there is little evidence in the canon and its commentaries that loving kindness may be extended to other beings simply as an expression of fellow-feeling,[104] it is counterevidenced by Visuddhimagga 9.10, where friendliness or loving kindness toward all sentient beings is based on the "Golden Rule," that is, on the awareness that like oneself other sentient beings, too, seek happiness but dislike pain, want to live but are afraid of death.[105] What else is this than fellow-feeling? And there are plenty of canonical passages arguing similarly for not killing and not injuring.[106] And what about Buddhaghosa[107] advising the meditator to consider, for the sake of arousing loving kindness, the fact that in the beginningless *saṃsāra* all beings have already been one's father, mother, and so on?[108] Actually, in a later publication,[109] Harris himself states that this kind of interrelatedness "leads to a strong feeling of solidarity with all beings."

To be sure, in many passages the exercise of friendliness, etc., is said to be rewarded by rebirth in heaven.[110] Besides, an important (and in early Buddhism probably the most important) function of this exercise, too, is the spiritual purification of the meditator's mind,[111] and as the first of the four unlimited [meditations] (*appamāṇa*) *mettā* starts, as is well known, a series culminating in equanimity or imperturbability (*upekkhā, upekṣā*).[112] However, I do not think that these features contradict or annul the above-mentioned genuinely ethical aspect.[113] Proclaiming friendliness, etc., as a means for attaining heaven is, rather, simply another thread of the texture, another strategy for stimulating people[114] to practice this kind of exercise. And cultivating friendliness, and so on, for the sake of purifying one's own mind does not mean that it has no impact on the meditator's practical behavior.[115] And that the exercise of the four unlimited meditations culminates in equanimity or imperturbability (*upekkhā*) may, to be sure, mean that *upekkhā*, which is very much akin to detachment, is the state that comes closest to liberation.[116] But although there seems to be a certain tension between *upekkhā* and the other states[117] (and although it does not seem to be possible to dwell in different states at the same time, just as one cannot dwell in different jhānas simultaneously), the culminating position of *upekkhā* can hardly mean that the preceding states, or sympathy and concern for that matter, are, at least in the end, once and for all superseded by *upekkhā*. On the contrary, the example of the Buddha himself shows that even in the liberated person *upekkhā* is not considered to prevent compassionateness, friendliness, sympathy, and concern for others from reemerging.[118]

Yet, and in this regard I agree with Harris,[119] even in their primarily ethical form—that is, when they are not, or at least not in the first place, cultivated for the sake of one's own advantage, nor even for one's own spiritual purification, but simply as the expression of some kind of fellow-feeling, friendliness, compassion, sympathy, and noninjury—these qualities do not yet constitute ecological ethics. For they are, primarily at least, directed toward individuals.

To be sure, the Vedic precursor of friendliness (*mettā, maitrī*), alliance (*mitra, mitradheya*), is primarily concluded with other tribes, and in the case of animals, species or classes may be regarded as corresponding to tribes. In the verses of the *Ahirājasutta* or *Khandhaparitta*,[120] friendship (*metta*, neuter)[121] is in fact declared to exist, on the part of the monk, with what is termed families of snake-kings (*ahirāja-kula*)[122] in the prose, and with what one may call rough classes of animals—those having no feet, two feet, four feet, and many feet.[123] And even in the preceding prose part of the sutta, where *metta-* (adj.) qualifies "mind" (*citta*) and obviously has the usual Buddhist meaning of "friendliness" or "benevolence," it is still extended toward these families of snake-kings. It is tempting to develop this feature into an ecological interpretation of *mettā*, that is, into a concept of *mettā* as entailing an appreciation and protection of species as such.[124] But historically the transition from an alliance or a peace or friendship contract with wild animals (or nature) to a concept of *mettā* explicitly including in its aim the protection of species as such is, as far as I can see, problematic. Alliances or friendship contracts with tribes, or species of animals for that matter, are hardly made because of a positive evaluation of these tribes and species as such or of their diversity, but rather because these tribes or species are composed of dangerous individuals (or, of course, because one needs allies against others). And it seems doubtful that this idea was, in the course of its transformation into the Buddhist attitude of friendliness, at any point developed in such a way as to take classes or species of animals not merely as groups of individuals but as deserving to be valued (or at least accorded a right of existence) as species.

Another interesting context to be taken into account in this connection is the Buddhist ideal of kingship. For according to the *Cakkavattisīhanādasutta*[125] the ideal king is expected to protect both social groups of people and "quadrupeds and birds" (*miga-pakkhī*), which in this context might well refer to the animal population as a collective unit,[126] or, in analogy to the social groups, even to two rough classes of animals. There may in fact be a possibility that social groups as well as the animal population are to be protected as such in order to maintain the "resources" of the kingdom or, from a less profane point of view, to keep the cosmos in order (a notion which may lend itself to ecological reinterpretation). But this is hardly an originally Buddhist idea,[127] and rather evokes a Vedic or Hindu background.[128] From a typically Buddhist ethical point of view, protection would rather refer to the totality of individuals constituting the social groups and the animal population.

Likewise, Aśoka's Fifth Pillar Edict stating that he in fact put various species of wild animals[129] under protection may, to be sure, suggest some kind of conservationist intention.[130] But similar prescriptions are found in the (definitely non-Buddhist) Arthaśāstra,[131] the classical Indian treatise on politics. They are thus not specifically Buddhist either. Rather, they seem to be inspired by the Hindu Dharma texts,[132] the motives of which require special investigation. This does not of course exclude that Aśoka's prohibition of killing these species was not also, and perhaps in the first place, motivated by the Buddhist attitude toward animals that had first led him to recommend unrestricted abstention from killing animals.[133] But from this point of view it may well be that even in the Fifth Pillar Edict he aims not so much at conservation of species as at minimizing the killing (and injuring) of individual animals, by prohibiting at least unnecessary, useless, and disproportionate[134] killing[135] and by enjoining, for this purpose, complete protection of such species as were (harmless and) not edible or, for religious or other reasons, not usually eaten or killed for satisfying some other need.[136]

Thus, on the whole the Buddhist attitude of *ahiṃsā*, and still more obviously that of friendliness, compassion, and so on, is, albeit unrestricted (that is, encompassing all living beings), yet primarily directed toward individuals. Hence, in the case of animals too, nonviolence, friendliness, sympathy, concern, and compassion envisage the sentient individual, the concrete subjects of life and of sensations (especially pain),[137] not species or ecosystems, nor even individuals as representatives of species. The value at stake in this spiritual context[138] is the life (and happiness) of the individual, not the transindividual continuity of the species or of life as such, or of nature as a whole.

To be sure, in a world where ecosystems are still intact and no species threatened by extinction, not to kill or injure individuals, that is, just letting natural beings in peace, is probably the best thing one can do from the ecological point of view; the more so since noninjury is not prescribed merely with regard to "useful" animals but with regard to all animals including such as are noxious or a nuisance to human beings;[139] and still more so when, as with the Jainas and, to a certain extent, even in early Buddhism,[140] also plants and even the elements are included. But even so the primary, conscious motivation is not an ecological one, one expressly aiming at the full preservation of species or ecosystems. The early Buddhist concept of noninjury may admit of a gradation in terms of the intensity of suffering caused by killing or injuring different kinds of animals, or in terms of the amount of effort and aggressiveness involved on the part of the perpetrator,[141] but it would hardly make a difference of value between individuals belonging to ecologically detrimental, overrepresented species on the one hand and such as are on the verge of extinction on the other. It would even come into conflict with ecological considerations in cases where such considerations might favor the killing of certain animals, for example, such as belong to species artificially introduced into another continent where they may severely disturb the balance and endanger native species.

Occasionally, however, an ecological element is in fact introduced even in the context of noninjury; for example, when the vinaya rule prohibiting monks from injuring plants is motivated by pointing out that they are the abode of insects and other animals;[142] or when even lay persons are enjoined not to pollute water inhabited by tiny animals;[143] or when a disciple endowed with supranormal power is dissuaded by the Buddha from turning the Earth upside down because this would jeopardize or derange the animals living on her.[144] Such cases show that there was, albeit only sporadically, an awareness of the fact that animals may also be killed, injured, or caused to suffer in an indirect way, by destroying their habitat, and that this too ought to be avoided. But even in these cases what counts is the (indirect) protection of individual animals, not of species.

The *de facto* ecological importance of not killing animals lies, above all, in the fact that it is the basic commitment also for lay Buddhists. Of course, the effect depends on how seriously such a commitment is observed. To be sure, there is always some gap between norm and reality,[145] even in traditional Buddhist countries, let alone countries that have been influenced by modern Western norms or ways of behavior. But there are also aspects inherent in the Buddhist understanding of not killing and not injuring which may have contributed to the ecological problems in some Buddhist countries and ought to be clearly envisaged (and balanced).

The most important of these aspects is the tendency of Buddhism to keep life practicable. This tendency is in tune with the principle of the Middle Way: no license, but no exaggerated self-mortification and squeamishness either. This allows the monks to concentrate on their spiritual perfection, and the lay people to observe the moral essentials and accumulate good karma, without being bothered by excessive and irremediable qualms. In this sense, for Buddhist monks, noninjury is not as strict as for Jaina monks (who are, for example, not even allowed to drink fresh, unboiled water because it is regarded by them to be alive, whereas Buddhism has discarded this idea and the ensuing restriction).[146] As for lay people, their life is kept practicable[147] by confining noninjury, by and large, to animals, whereas plants may be utilized more or less freely,[148] and there is a tendency to ignore and, later on, even deny their sentience.[149] Even so, problems remain—for instance, peasants, when ploughing, can hardly avoid killing dew-worms, and so on, and they may have serious trouble with animals destroying the harvest. Still more difficult is the situation for fishermen, hunters, or butchers, especially in areas where meat or fish is an indispensable element of diet. In such cases, tensions between norm and reality are inevitable. The reaction of early Buddhism (to be inferred from the traditional situation in Theravāda societies) seems to have been to ignore the tension or live with it (or, at best, try to compensate for it by meritorious deeds) as far as agriculture is concerned, but to avoid occupations directly and primarily based on killing animals and leave them, as far as possible, to people outside or on the margin of the Buddhist society.[150] In Mahāyāna (and tantric) Buddhism, however, there is a tendency to solve the problem by providing means for annulling bad karma,[151] such as purificatory rites, or by turning to a supramundane savior like Amida Buddha. To be sure, considerations of practicability are unavoidable, still more so in view of the modern knowledge about protozoa. But one ought to be aware of the danger that in order to facilitate practicability one may easily arrive at reducing inhibitions too much, to the extent of entirely undermining the commitment not to take life, including its *de facto* ecological effects.

Another problem is that (in contrast to Jainism) Buddhism, in tune with its ethics of intention and at the same time in favor of practicability, stresses avoiding intentional killing,[152] which somehow overlaps with direct killing.[153] This is an extremely important point in the context of ecological ethics since most of our contemporary pollution and destruction of nature is unintentional (often even unforeseen) and indirect. As I have already pointed out, there is occasional awareness of the problem in the sources, but on the whole such awareness appears to have been somewhat underdeveloped. This becomes obvious also from the unrestrained way pesticides have been used in most Buddhist countries,[154] or from the lack of inhibition in using cars.

The issue of unintentional and indirect injuring is extremely important also in connection with the modern system of consumption.[155] For example, modern consumers of meat and fish do not themselves do the killing and can even be sure that the animal is not killed for them personally. Nevertheless, as buyers they keep the system going and are hence indirectly responsible for the killing and also for the (often much worse) tortures and ecological ravages that are often connected with the rearing of animals or with catching them (for example, by drift-net fishing).

Anyway, we can state that there are a considerable number of elements in Buddhist spiritual and everyday practice which, if taken seriously, *de facto* contribute to the preservation of a sound natural environment. But they do not establish unimpaired nature and maximum diversity of species as a value in itself (and hence may not be sufficient for motivating active conservation or even restoration). Nor does it—as I have tried to show above—appear possible to establish such a value on the level of the ultimate evaluation of existence in early Buddhism.

INTRAMUNDANE EVALUATIONS OF NATURE

However, the situation may change if we descend to the level of intramundane evaluation. For even though we have to admit that the world as a whole is ultimately ill, unsatisfactory, it obviously includes conditions of relatively increased or reduced suffering, and perhaps also conditions which favor or impede spiritual progress. From these points of view, it would seem possible that preference is given either to nature or to civilization. Actually, the early Buddhist sources do suggest preference, but it varies; there are obviously different, almost contradictory strands.

One strand is unambiguously pro-civilization. The ecologically orientated reader may indeed be somewhat shocked when finding, in quite a few places in the Buddhist canon, a cliché describing ideal intramundane conditions in terms of a thoroughly civilized world: densely populated, one village close to the other, with eighty thousand wealthy, big cities full of people.[156] At the same time, wild nature is often abhorred as dangerous, weird, and disagreeable,[157] and wild animals, especially beasts of prey, as something one does not want to come into contact with.[158]

This view reflects the ideal of a world thoroughly adapted to human beings. It is openly hostile to wild nature and hardly offers any basis for its protection. It is rather a primarily anthropocentric strand regarding nature as something to be warded off,[159] manipulated,[160] and, as the above cliché suggests, even dominated, and it may even have favored the rather uncritical adoption of the nature-dominating modern Western civilization by some Buddhist countries.

But it is not specifically Buddhist. Rather, it seems to have been the common ideal of peasants and townspeople in early India[161] as elsewhere.[162] As such, it has been adopted—or perhaps, rather, tolerated—by Buddhism and made use of in certain didactic contexts. Actually, it accords with or has been adapted to Buddhist cosmological principles insofar as the ideal situation is regarded to be connected with moral (not technological) progress,[163] whereas the breakdown of civilization and natural calamities (like drought) are considered to be caused by human immoral behavior.[164]

Even passages like the verse that declares planting groves and parks, but also constructing wells and dams, to be particularly meritorious[165] seem to refer rather to cultivation, not to reestablishing nature. As far as the "pro-civilization strand" has an ideal of nature, it is indeed cultivated nature, nature shaped by human beings according to their wants and predilections: groves, gardens, well-constructed ponds.[166] Sometimes, even the trees are imagined to consist, ideally, of precious metals and jewels.[167] Such an attitude need not necessarily create ecological problems, but will inevitably do so if interference with nature is too violent or too extensive and neglects the needs and rights of our fellow beings, as nowadays.

Yet even in the context of this strand one may occasionally come across passages in which real nature forms part of the ideal surroundings: trees, flowers, birds, ponds and rivers with fishes and tortoises; and sometimes there is even a stress on diversity[168] or even completeness[169] of species. But even in such passages mostly those elements of nature and biodiversity are selected that the human being finds beautiful and innocuous.[170] Even so, these passages would seem to have been influenced by, or participate in, another basically secular but more literary strand of evaluating nature, viz. the poetic description, and even romanticization, of natural beauty—a strand that has been much more influential in connection with what I am going to call the "hermit strand" to be dealt with below.[171]

There are, however, also texts (like the *Aggaññasutta*[172]) where the process of civilization is rather negatively evaluated and understood as the result of moral decadence. But this does not entail, in this strand, a positive evaluation of nature, let alone wilderness. The primeval, unspoiled state is, on the contrary, described as one of pre- or trans-natural, "ethereal" existence. It seems to fit in with this view that in other sources[173] a positive intramundane development—due to a collective progress in morality and spiritual practice—is depicted as characterized by the disappearance of both nature and civilization. First, animals—at least wild animals[174]—vanish from this Earth (because after having consumed their karma they are reborn as humans). After some time, human beings, too, disappear, because all of them are reborn in a luminous heaven due to having practiced suitable meditation. Finally, even plants and the whole Earth vanish.

This concept gives the impression of a kind of intramundane reflection or echo of the ultimate Buddhist analysis of existence, entailing a pointed awareness of the dark aspects of civilization as well, and conceiving an ideal state, even on the intramundane level, as something radically transcending both nature and civilization.

On the other hand, there are plenty of canonical texts that show an essentially different attitude toward wild nature and would seem to constitute yet another strand, which I call the "hermit strand."[175] It too is not specifically Buddhist, a similar ideal occurring also in Hindu sources.[176]

The hermits are monks (or, occasionally, nuns[177]) who, for the sake of meditation and spiritual perfection, retire from the noisy bustle and allurements of the cities and inhabited places into solitude,[178] and they find it, primarily, in the wilderness (*arañña*, Skt. *araṇya*), under trees,[179] in mountain caves or woodlands, or at least in the open air (*abbhokāsa*).[180]

That the reasons why hermits prefer the wilderness are primarily solitude and undisturbedness becomes clear from the fact that among the places suitable for meditation we find also empty houses and charnel grounds (*susāna*). This may even indicate that in these texts too wilderness is a rather dangerous and weird place,[181] and this is explicitly confirmed in some passages, for example, by pointing out the danger of being threatened by poisonous or wild animals.[182] But the hermit may even render the dangers constantly threatening his life spiritually fruitful by systematically contemplating them in order to intensify his spiritual effort.[183] Or he tries to overcome his fear by appropriate meditation,[184] or has already succeeded in doing so.[185] Nor do the texts suppress the fact that life in the wilderness involves various hardships, like being pestered by gadflies and mosquitoes,[186] or at least forgoing the comforts of civilization and culture.[187] But what the hermit should learn, or has already learned, is precisely to endure such things without becoming displeased[188] and to abandon all wants and desires.[189]

In this way, wilderness can, in spite of its dangers and inconveniences, be evaluated positively. Having become free from fear, irritation, desire, and possessiveness, the hermit will be truly happy precisely in the solitude of the wilderness and may even enjoy the beauties of nature,[190] in spite of their impermanence,[191] and without falling prey to the emotions or destructive patterns of behavior they arouse in worldly people.[192] In a sense, the bliss of meditative absorption and spiritual release experienced by the hermit radiates to the surroundings in which it has been (or may be) attained and imparts a positive value to them.

That the wilderness is especially suitable for spiritual perfection does not of course mean that this perfection will be attained there automatically. As one text[193] puts it, in the wilderness there also live people who are anything but spiritually advanced: uneducated, foolish people; greedy people with evil desires; and madmen. Without the right spiritual attitude and effort, life in the wilderness is futile. Occasionally,[194] the suitability of the wilderness for spiritual perfection is even restricted by stating that it holds good for some persons only, while others may attain spiritual perfection more easily in inhabited places or cities. And truly liberated persons are said to be not affected at all by any sensations, be it in inhabited places or in the wilderness.[195]

In another sermon[196] the monk is recommended a kind of middle way: On the one hand, he is exhorted to patiently endure heat and cold, hunger and thirst, gadflies and mosquitoes, and physical pain. On the other, he is allowed to counteract them by making modest use of the basic achievements of civilization like clothes, lodging, and medicine, and is even advised to avoid dangerous places and dangerous animals.

A similar inhomogeneity in the evaluation of wild nature can also be observed in connection with nuns. In the *Bhikkhunīsaṃyutta*[197] nuns are reported to have fearlessly retired into dark forests and attained spiritual perfection. In the vinaya,[198] however, they are prohibited from living in the wilderness because of the danger of being raped.[199]

Thus, the intramundane evaluation of nature in the canon is rather ambivalent. To be sure, in those early days the wilderness was still far-spread and cultivated land limited, as one sūtra[200] puts it. There was still enough room for hermit life. Nowadays, however, the expansionist dynamics of the pro-civilization attitude—visible already in the old sources—has almost completely succeeded in putting an end to wilderness and leaves little room for solitary, quiet life in unspoiled nature. Yet, as mentioned before, it is precisely undisturbed, unspoiled nature—the wilderness— that is usually regarded as the most favorable environment for spiritual progress and true happiness. This seems to imply an intramundane, positive evaluation, and what is positively evaluated here is not so much individual animals and plants but rather the whole ambience. The ambiance is valued primarily, to be sure, as a place of solitude and silence, but, at least occasionally (as in some verses of the *Theragāthā*), also in its beauty, as the harmonious unity of landscape, plants, and animals. This seems to coincide, to some extent, with what we call "nature" in the sense of an ecosystem, along with the species of animals and plants belonging to it. If this is correct, this strand would indeed furnish a viable basis for ecological ethics including active protection and even restitution of ecosystems, and it seems that monks influenced by this strand have been playing an increasingly important role in the ecological movements in at least some Buddhist countries.[201]

To be sure, the motivation would still be a subtly anthropocentric one: to preserve and even restitute intact natural areas as places most suitable for humanity's spiritual perfection. But one could add that animals, too, would profit from an increase of human spiritual perfection because such would entail a reduction of ill-treatment of them by humans. Besides, nowadays even many Buddhists who are not hermits are probably inclined to expect maximum secular happiness for all sentient beings not from a nature-destroying civilization but from a harmonious coexistence with nature (and there is no reason why a purely intramundane evaluation belonging to the past should be kept if it runs counter to the requirements of the present).

THE STATUS OF ANIMALS

Still, even against this attempt to establish ecological ethics on the intramundane level, one serious objection can be raised: the objection that the positive evaluation, in the "hermit strand," of (wild/intact) nature as an ambiance might seem to have, more or less, lost sight of suffering in nature. The more so since in many canonical texts, and mostly in those that may be characterized as rational discourse, animals and existence as an animal are so negatively evaluated that efforts to preserve them appear highly problematic.

According to these texts, animals are, firstly, intellectually inferior. Though they have some capacity for thinking (*manasikāra*), they lack the faculty of insight (*prajñā*).[202] Hence they cannot understand the Buddhist doctrine and cannot attain liberation, unless they are, in a later existence, reborn as human beings, which is regarded to be possible but very rare.[203]

Secondly, animals are not just subject to suffering like humans, but subject to much more suffering; their existence is considered to be extremely unhappy,[204] not only because they are exploited and tortured by humans[205] but also in nature itself, where the weaker one is threatened and devoured by the stronger,[206] and, moreover, because at least many of them live on disgusting food or in uncomfortable places.[207] In contrast to rebirth as a human, rebirth as an animal is hence usually regarded as an evil rebirth.[208]

Thirdly, animals are considered to be (at least for the most part) morally inferior or even wicked,[209] because of their promiscuity, including even incest,[210] or precisely because the stronger devours the weaker.[211] The latter argument is, by the way, adduced as a reason why rebirth of an animal as a human is so rare.

Such a negative evaluation of animals and animal existence is no doubt extremely unfavorable as a basis for an active ecological ethics. To be sure, the commitment not to take life prevents Buddhists from killing animals once they are there. But if animal existence is in fact such an unhappy state, why should we make any effort to perpetuate it? If the presence of many animals and few humans means that the world is in a bad condition,[212] should we not welcome the present growth of human population[213] and decrease of (at least wild) animals, and should we not be glad if, for some reason or other, animals were to disappear entirely from this world, just as there are none (at least no real ones) in the later Buddhist paradise Sukhāvatī?[214] Would it not be rather cruel and selfish to preserve them for our own spiritual progress, let alone our happiness, if even by an increase of our spiritual perfection we cannot essentially ameliorate their somber situation because it is inherent to their status?

On the one hand, one could, from the traditional Buddhist point of view, rejoin that the number of beings to be born as animals cannot depend on external factors like man-made pollution, deforestation, and so on, but is solely determined by the previous karma of those beings themselves. This would mean that a decrease in the total number of animals would have to be either merely apparent or somehow the result of a preceding large-scale moral and spiritual improvement, and can also in future be achieved only in this way. Hence, at least as long as such a large-scale improvement has not taken place, there may be good reason to argue that in the sense of the Golden Rule it is part of everybody's moral duty to preserve the world in an agreeable condition not only for future generations of humans but also for the beings to be reborn as animals. This would, by the way, even coincide with one's own interests since—in view of the complexity of karmic processes—few persons can exclude the possibility that either they themselves or their friends and relatives may be reborn in one of these groups, so that protection of intact ecosystems would even amount to protecting what may be one's own future abode.

On the other hand, apart from this, the idea of the extreme unhappiness of animals would, too, seem to be a widespread preconception of the peasants and townsmen of those days, seen in Jainism and Hinduism as well[215]—a preconception that may be rooted in frequent bad treatment of domestic animals and in the pro-civilization strand's fear of wilderness. To that strand we can probably also attribute the idea of the wickedness of (at least certain wild) animals. Both of these ideas seem to have been adopted or utilized by Buddhism for didactic purposes. Their main aim is not to make a statement on animals but to warn against the evil consequences of bad karma and to underscore the necessity of maximum moral and spiritual effort.[216] I suggest that in an age where establishing an ecological ethics has become imperative, they ought to be de-dogmatized by being relegated to their specific didactic contexts. For, though animals have doubtless to suffer, the assumption that they have to suffer more than humans appears unwarranted, at least as long as their natural situation is not additionally aggravated by man.

Actually, in another strand of the Buddhist tradition—in the jātaka (together with its commentary) and related texts—animals are often viewed quite differently.[217] I admit that this view is a more popular one and not specifically Buddhist either, but it is not therefore necessarily less appropriate, and it has exercised a considerable influence on the feelings and attitudes of lay Buddhists.[218] As is well known, in these texts animals are described as being both unhappy and happy, stupid and prudent, bad and good. They are even susceptible to religious admonition.[219] To be sure, these texts largely anthropomorphize animals. But in not regarding them as particularly unhappy and wicked creatures they seem to come closer to the truth.

The evaluation of animals in these texts shows some affinity to the hermit strand. In fact, this strand stands out quite frequently in the jātaka and related texts; in a pre-Buddhist setting, to be sure, but nevertheless mostly in connection with ascetics exemplifying such virtues as the Buddhist compilers too wanted to inculcate. In some passages,[220] nature around the hermitage (assama, āśrama) is described as, and expressly called,[221] lovely and beautiful, abounding in a variety of blossoming and fruit-bearing trees spreading delicate odors, and inhabited by various kinds of birds and quadrupeds, and embellished by ponds and rivers with clear water and full of lotus-flowers, fishes, and other aquatic animals. The emphasis on variety of species (which are enumerated in great detail)[222] is conspicuous.

This kind of description of nature around the hermitage is obviously closely related to the romanticizing strand of nature description in secular poetry mentioned above. It is current in non-Buddhist literature as well,[223] and in the jātaka similar descriptions can also be found of the forest inhabited by animal heroes.[224] There can be little doubt that it too depicts nature mainly from a human aesthetic point of view.[225] Even the inclusion of fierce animals like lions, tigers, bears, boars, and crocodiles does not contradict this since they would rather appear to be envisaged—from afar, so to speak—in their majestic beauty. Hence, this is a positive evaluation of intact nature and biodiversity, but a tacit omission of the violence and suffering involved in nature as it actually is.

Yet some passages show that suffering and violence in nature may not simply have been ignored. For example, one passage[226] stresses that in the forest around the hermitage there is plenty of food also for the animals (thus suggesting that in nature food is often scarce). As for violence, the idea is rather that around the hermitage there is an exceptional situation in that violence has been neutralized or overcome[227] by the (nonviolent) spiritual power or irradiation of the hermit, especially by his practice of friendliness or loving kindness (mettā). This is so not only in the sense that by practicing loving kindness the hermit protects himself from the aggressiveness of dangerous creatures, that is, renders them nonaggressive toward himself. Rather, by his spiritual power[228] and irradiation of friendliness or loving kindness,[229] the hermit affects, so to speak, the animals around him so that they abandon their natural mutual enmities to become friendly and nonaggressive even toward one another. Thus there is peace not only with nature but also within nature.[230]

To be sure, this is a vision of an ideal state of nature, disclosing dissatisfaction with nature as it actually is, that is, as involving violence and suffering. But at the same time it does not regard animals as hopelessly miserable. It presupposes that as animals they may be happy and good, and may even advance spiritually, at least under the influence of human spiritual perfection.[231]

Such a view of animals would tally well with arguing for ecological ethics for the sake of maximum spiritual progress and intramundane happiness of all living beings, not merely of human beings. I do not know to what extent a modern Buddhist is ready to subscribe to such a view of animals; but it would anyway be sufficient to abandon the idea that animals are wicked and the idea of their irremediable, extreme unhappiness, and to admit that under natural conditions animals—though, to be sure, not living in a paradise and by no means free from suffering—may, after all, not be so extremely unhappy, at any rate not more than an average human being.

CONCLUSION

My impression is that early Buddhism, at least its primarily monastic tradition as we know it from the canonical texts, was, on the whole, impressed not so much by the undeniable beauty of nature as by its equally undeniable somber aspects: the struggle for life, killing and being killed, devouring and being devoured, greed, suffering, and especially by the ubiquity of decay and impermanence. But the reaction is not effort toward a violent transformation or subjugation of nature but rather effort toward transcending it spiritually. On the ultimate level, early Buddhism does not merely negate nature (as Hakamaya puts it) but rather all mundane existence, nature as well as civilization.

Spiritually, this entails, above all, detachment, including abstention from all self-assertive violence. The world of the food chain and of struggle for survival and power is, as far as I can see, not appreciated by early Buddhism, neither emotionally nor morally. Usually it is simply avoided, kept at a distance as much as possible: theoretically, by a tendency to restrict sentience to animals; practically, by avoiding killing, living on almsfood, and ultimately by attaining *nirvāṇa*. Occasionally, it is said to be partially neutralized by radiating friendliness or by exceptional spiritual power. According to some (non-Theravāda) sources, violence in nature is, in individual cases, accepted but at the same time neutralized by means of self-sacrifice (as in the story of the hungry tigress,[232] or that of king Śibi and the dove[233]).[234]

Thus, early Buddhism does not, on the whole, romanticize nature. I am far from taking this to be a weak point, provided that the same sober and critical attitude is applied to civilization. Nor do I take it to mean that it is altogether impossible to establish an ecological ethics on the basis of the early Buddhist tradition. For, apart from the fact that many of the attitudes connected with or conducive to detachment as well as friendliness, compassion, and so on, are *de facto* ecologically beneficial, it may not be impossible to establish a value-based ecological ethics in a similar way as the value-based ethics of *ahiṃsā*. In the latter case, individual life is established as an inviolable value although it is something that on the level of ultimate evaluation of existence one wants to get rid of, or at least does not strive to retain. This prevents a Buddhist from the short circuit of misinterpreting the ultimate valuelessness of life as permission to destroy life willfully (by killing living beings, including, normally, oneself), or even to kill out of compassion (as is, however, occasionally allowed in Mahāyāna and tantric Buddhism).[235] Should it not be equally justified to establish—in line with the evaluation of nature in the "hermit strand"—nature too, on the intramundane level, as a value to be preserved, in spite of its ultimate valuelessness, in order to prevent the latter from being misinterpreted by deriving from it the permission to exploit and destroy nature relentlessly for our own short-term advantage or for any other reason? And would it not be reasonable, at least for lay persons, to supplement this abstention from damaging with circumspect active engagement for conservation and even restoration of nature, just as abstention from taking individual life is supplemented with cautious help motivated by compassion and loving kindness?

Notes

1   The present paper is a revised and annotated version of a lecture I had the honor to present at the Universities of Colombo and Peradenia in February 1994. It is an elaboration and reconsideration of parts of my *Buddhism and Nature: The Lecture Delivered on the Occasion of the EXPO 1990*, rev. ed., Studia Philologica Buddhica Occasional Paper Series, VII (Tokyo: The International Institute for Buddhist Studies, 1991), to which the reader is referred for more details, documentation, and pertinent literature. I take the opportunity to thank all those who by their questions and critical remarks caused me to rethink various issues, as well as to my friends M. Maitrimurti, S. A. Srinivasan, E. Steinkellner, and A. Wezler for valuable suggestions. It is not their fault that the result is still preliminary in many regards, but since I shall not have a chance to improve on it in the near future I submit it for discussion as it stands, hoping that it will at least contribute to an increasing awareness of some of the problems involved in the issue.

2   I admit, of course, that *in concreto* there are numerous cases of conflict, some hardly soluble, especially if microbes, like small pox or malaria viruses, are taken into consideration. Yet, even microbes would seem to have essential functions in the ecological balance (e.g., limiting populations in number or distribution), so that human beings, if they—understandably, from their point of view—decide to extinguish some of the microbes, may have to compensate for this by voluntary self-restriction.

3   For a survey and an attempt at a typology see Ian Harris, "Getting to Grips with Buddhist Environmentalism: A Provisional Typology," *Journal of Buddhist Ethics* 2 (1995): 173–90, http://www.buddhistethics.org/2/harris2.html (accessed September 3, 2009).

4   Cp. esp. Joanna Macy, *Mutual Causality in Buddhism and General Systems Theory* (Albany: State University of New York Press, 1991), and idem., *World as Lover, World as Self* (Berkeley: Parallax Press, 1991) [German translation: *Die Wiederentdeckung der sinnlichen Erde* (Zurich and München: Theseus, 1994)]. Cp. also Ian Harris, "Buddhist Environmental Ethics and Detraditionalization: The Case of EcoBuddhism," *Religion* 25 (1995): 199–211, 201, 205 ff., 211 n. 55. As for linking Buddhism with ecology, cp. Aldous Huxley, esp. *Island* (1962; repr. London: Grafton Books, 1976), 247–49. Like Macy, he approves of a world-affirming, engaged form of Buddhism (Mahāyāna, with strong Far Eastern and tantric features) and criticizes Hīnayānists or *śrāvaka*s as escapist "*nirvāṇa*-addicts" (*Island*, 87), but as far as I can see he is less explicit as to what, in his opinion, original Buddhism was like.

5   See note 79.

6   Macy, *Mutual Causality*, 163.

7   Joanna Macy, "The Greening of the Self," in Allan Hunt Badiner, ed., *Dharma Gaia: A Harvest of Essays in Buddhism and Ecology* (Berkeley: Parallax Press, 1990), 61.

8   Noritoshi Aramaki, "Shizen-hakai kara Shizen-saisei e—Rekishi no Tenkai ni tsuite" (From Destruction of Nature to Revival of Nature: On a Historical Conversion), *Deai* 11, no. 1 (1992): 3–22.

9   Ibid., 9–11.

10   Ibid., 8 ff.

11   Ian Harris, "How Environmentalist Is Buddhism?" *Religion* 21 (1991): 101–14; cp. also idem., "Causation and *Telos*: The Problem of Buddhist Environmental Ethics," *Journal of Buddhist Ethics* 1 (1994): 45–56, http://www.buddhistethics.org/1/harris1.html (accessed September 3, 2009).

12 Harris, "How Environmentalist Is Buddhism?" 111.

13 See Noriaki Hakamaya, "Shizen-hihan to-shite no Bukkyō" (Buddhism as a Criticism of Physis/Natura), *Komazawa-daigaku Bukkyōgakubu Ronshū* 21 (1990): 380–403, and idem., "Nihon-jin to animizmu" (The Japanese and Animism), *Komazawa-daigaku Bukkyōgakubu Ronshū* 23 (1992): 351–78. For a critical discussion of the former paper, see my *Buddhism and Nature*, §§ 61 ff., to which Hakamaya has replied in the second paper, pp. 365 ff. and 378. A detailed response to this reply would, however, exceed the limits of this paper. For the time being, I can only repeat that, according to my understanding, Hakamaya's Cartesian view of animals is absolutely incompatible with both the canonical texts and the later Buddhist tradition, disastrous in its ethical consequences (as can be seen in modern Western animal mass production and animal experiments, based on the Cartesian premises), and plainly counterintuitive at that. For a very useful summary of the larger framework of Hakamaya's (and S. Matsumoto's) "Critical Buddhism," see Paul L. Swanson, "'Zen Is Not Buddhism': Recent Japanese Critiques of Buddha-Nature," *Numen* XL, no. 2 (1993): 115 ff., esp. 126 ff. Cp. also Harris, "Buddhist Environmental Ethics," 199 ff.

14 Not "genuine," as I misunderstood in *Buddhism and Nature* § 63.2; cp. Hakamaya, "Nihon-jin to animizmu," 366 ff.

15 Hakamaya, "Shizen-hihan to-shite no Bukkyō," 380, and "Nihon-jin to animizmu," 378.

16 Hakamaya, "Nihon-jin to animizmu," 369.

17 Hakamaya, "Shizen-hihan to-shite no Bukkyō," 399.

18 Hakamaya, "Nihon-jin to animizmu," 378.

19 On the problem of anachronism, see P. Pedersen in Ole Bruun and Arne Kalland, eds., *Asian Perceptions of Nature: A Critical Approach*, Nordic Institute of Asian Studies, Studies in Asian Topics, no. 18 (Richmond: Curzon Press, 1995), 266 ff. and 268.

20 Asian Buddhists, and Hindus too for that matter, sometimes argue that they are not obliged to search in their own tradition for answers to the problems provoked by modern technology because these problems have been created not by them but by the West. But since almost all of their countries have, for whatever reason, come to join the business, they have also come to share the problems, whether they like it or not, and hence have to come up with solutions. Of course, it is up to them whether they prefer to develop these solutions on the basis of their own tradition or to borrow them from the West, just like the problems.

21 *Saṃyuttanikāya* (Pali Text Society edition, hereinafter *S*) IV 230 ff.; cp. also *Aṅguttaranikāya* (Pali Text Society edition, hereinafter *A*) II 87 and III 131.

22 Cp. also Macy, *World as Lover*, xii (*Die Wiederentdeckung der sinnlichen Erde*, 13). At the same time, Luis O. Gómez (on p. 46 of "Nonviolence and the Self in Early Buddhism," in Kenneth Kraft, ed., *Inner Peace, World Peace* [Albany: State University of New York, 1992], 31–48) is certainly right in stressing that in Buddhism action cannot be separated from self-cultivation and that the first thing to do—before engaging in public activism—is to adapt one's own lifestyle to ecological requirements. But this, in its turn, requires a corresponding mental attitude and *motivation* (cp. *Dhammapada* [Pali Text Society edition, hereinafter *Dhp*, quoted by verse number] 1–2: *manopubbaṅgamā dhammā ...* ; *A* II 177: *cittena ... loko nīyati ...*).

23 Joanna Macy, e.g., may take my paper, should she find it worth reading, as an attempt to establish ecological ethics on the even more difficult basis of what she would call an

escapist deviation, in parts of the Buddhist tradition, from the original teaching. Personally, I do indeed appreciate her creative adaptation of Buddhist teachings to the requirements of the ecological crisis we are faced with, and I wonder if the Buddha, were he among us today, would not teach in a similar way. All the more it is that I regret that, as a historian of ideas, I cannot help expressing reservations with regard to the extent to which she not only identifies her own understanding of Buddhism with the teaching of the *historical* Buddha but also interprets the transmitted canonical texts accordingly, even such as clearly point to another direction (cp. also note 53), and often in a way which I for one cannot but find unacceptable from the philological point of view. For a few examples, see notes 58, 73, 74, and 76.

24 This would even hold good for traditional elements that are both time-bound and marginal to the message of a religion (as for example, certain geographical or mythological conceptions that were current at the time of the rise of Buddhism), but are hard to accept for modern, especially Western, people, and are therefore liable to be reinterpreted or replaced. Even in such cases, the historian has to insist on the difference, but at the same time has to be aware of the fact that maintaining such conceptions in a cultural ambience where they are common belief is different from sticking to them, as something to be taken literally, in the completely different context of the modern world.

25 It may well be that the strand I have called the "ultimate evaluation of existence" is a kind of (perhaps somewhat overemphasized) negative corollary to a more original spirituality that focused less on the sufferings, dangers, and imperfections of the world and existence in it than on the possibility of attaining, in this very life, a state in which one is, in some fundamental sense, no longer subject to, and afraid of, its threats and frustrations. But I for one find it hard to determine to what extent such focusing on the positive goal of "*nirvāṇa* in this life" actually involved an evaluation of nature substantially different from that of the strand focusing on the unsatisfactoriness of existence and the world where it takes place. To be sure, a person who directly focuses on blissful or at least peaceful meditative states may have fewer problems with enjoying a pleasant natural surrounding than one who tries to overcome attachment by contemplating the all-pervasive unsatisfactoriness of the world. But even the former could hardly attribute *ultimate* value to animal existence unless he or she either puts up with the suffering of animals or takes them to be like perfect saints, unaffected by pain and free from fear and worry —an idea which will hardly be found in any text of early Buddhism. Thus, if these two strands differ in their attitude toward nature, this difference may not be one of ultimate evaluation but rather one of emphasis or explicitness motivated by a difference of spiritual approach.

26 *Vinayapiṭaka* (Pali Text Society edition, hereinafter, *Vin*) I 10. For the text-historical problems of this text see Tilmann Vetter, *The Ideas and Meditative Practices of Early Buddhism* (Leiden: Brill 1988), XXVIII ff.; also, idem., "Bei Lebzeiten das Todlose erreichen," in Gerhard Oberhammer, ed., *Im Tod gewinnt der Mensch sein Selbst* (Wien: Österreichischen Akademie der Wissenschaften, 1995), 213 ff.

27 For grammatical reasons (Wackernagel and Debrunner, *Altindische Grammatik* II [1896; repr. Göttingen: Vandenhoeck und Ruprecht, 1957–c. 1987], 2 § 82), I prefer to take *maraṇa* as an action noun ("dying"; cp. Vetter, "Bei Lebzeiten," 222 ff.), but I do not deny that nonetheless death as a state of which one is afraid is also envisaged.

28 *Suttanipāta* (Pali Text Society edition, quoted by verse number unless otherwise indicated, hereinafter *Sn*) 574: *maccānaṃ jīvitaṃ . . . dukkhena saṃyutaṃ*. Cp. *Theragāthā* (Pali

Text Society edition, quoted by verse number, hereinafter *Th*) 709 ff. and *Upasenasūtra* (edited in E. Waldschmidt, *Von Ceylon bis Turfan* [Göttingen: Vandenhoeck und Ruprecht, 1967], 339–44) §§ 14 ff. For a long list of all kinds of painful and disagreeable events or experiences, see *Milindapañha* (Pali Text Society edition, hereinafter *Mil*) 196 f. The concept of "life" (*jīvita, āyus*) does not appear to be applied to (final) *nirvāṇa* (after death), whereas expressions like *amata/amṛta* ("[state] without dying"), may, to be sure, refer to a spiritual state attainable in this life but would seem to be inapplicable to (saṃsāric, or biological) life as such.

29 *Sn* 575 ff.; *Dhp* 135, 148; *Udānavarga* (F. Bernhard, ed. [Göttingen: Vandenhoeck und Ruprecht, 1965], hereinafter *Uv*) 1.8 ff.; *A* III 71 ff.

30 This aspect is by no means denied because otherwise attachment to things would be inexplicable: cp., e.g., *S* II 171 ff. (14.32–34), III 27 ff. (22.26–28), IV 7 ff. (35.13–18).

31 E.g., *Majjhimanikāya* (Pali Text Society edition, hereinafter *M*) I 91 f. (*app'-assādā kāmā bahudukkhā* . . .), 130; *Dhp* 189; *Sn* 60 ff.

32 Cp. the formula of the four *jhāna*s/*dhyāna*s (e.g., *M* I 21 ff.), which are sometimes designated as "agreeable states in this life" (*diṭṭhadhamma-sukhavihāra*, e.g., *M* I 33; *A* II 23, 36).

33 *A* I 258 (*loko anicco dukkho vipariṇāmadhammo*); cp. *S* I 133 (*sabbo ādīpito loko* . . .).

34 *A* III 443.

35 E.g., *Vin* I 13 f. and *S* III 22 (22.15: the five *skandha*s), II 170 (14.31: the four elements; cp. 14.35–36), IV 1 ff. (35.1 and 4: internal and external *āyatana*s).

36 Thus explicitly texts like *M* I 435 ff., III 108; cp. *M* I 89 ff. Such an evaluation may, however, not have been acceptable to all strands of early Buddhism (cp. notes 25 and 39).

37 Occasionally, more drastic expressions are used, like "afflicted" (*upadduta, upassaṭṭha*: e.g., *S* IV 29; *Th* 1133), "aflame" (*āditta*: *Vin* I 34; *S* IV 19 ff.; cp. *S* I 133; *Th* 712), "[like] hot ashes" (*kukkuḷa*: *S* III 177), "disease" (*roga*: *S* II 175, III 167, 189), "ulcer" (*gaṇḍa*: *S* III 167, 189), "comparable to a murderer with his sword raised" (*A* III 443), etc. In contradistinction to some other schools (the Gokulikas according to *Kathāvatthu-aṭṭhakathā* 58,1; cp. also *Abhidharmakośa* (Prahlad Pradhan, ed. [Patna: K. P. Jayaswal Research Institute, 1967], hereinafter *AKBh*) 330,9 ff., *Kathāvatthu* II.6 stresses that this should not be taken to mean that all *dharma*s are exclusively painful or arouse none but such feelings and to exclude that at least some of them (in spite of their impermanence) possess also agreeable features (cp. also *S* II 170, 173 f., IV 10 ff., etc.).

38 As I understand it, in (this strand or spiritual context of) early Buddhism, "illness" or "unsatisfactoriness" (*dukkhatā*) is ascribed to both internal and external things or constituents-of-existence on the mere ground of their impermanence. This means that *dukkha* in this sense is an intrinsic, objective, "ontological" characteristic of things. Therefore, it would not seem to be taught as qualifying things only on condition that a person is subject to attachment to them, so that for an awakened person free from attachment impermanent things (especially things of nature) would no longer be *dukkha* (and would therefore be open to positive evaluation in an ultimate sense). It is rather precisely because one has, once and for all, realized the intrinsic ultimate unsatisfactoriness of the constituents of a person as well as of external things that attachment to and identification with them is entirely abandoned and cannot arise again. On the other hand, it may well be precisely this freedom from attachment and possessiveness due to comprehension of their impermanence and ultimate unsatisfactoriness that enables the awakened person to adequately appreciate beautiful, pleasant things on the intramundane level

(as will be elaborated below in connection with the "hermit strand"), in spite of their impermanence and ultimate unsatisfactoriness, simply because such a person takes (and even systematically contemplates) them as they actually are, viz. as impermanent, subject to decay, and not one's self or one's own, and does not approach them with egoistic or unwarranted expectations, and hence is not subject to distress and frustration (or *dukkha* in the psychological sense of *domanassa*) at their disappearance or decay (e.g., *S* II 275 [21.2]; *[Mahā-]Vibhāṣā[-śāstra]* [*Taishō Shinshū Daizōkyō* vol. 27, hereinafter *Vi*] 540c25–27 [sūtra quotation]).

39 It ought to be kept in mind that awareness of unsatisfactoriness based on impermanence is cultivated for the sake of detachment from the constituents of the person and the world. For this reason, the logical consequence that even liberating insight itself would, on account of its being, as a state of mind, impermanent, turn out to be *dukkha*, i.e., unsatisfactory, may not have been recognized from the outset. In later abhidharma, some schools have decided to except the states of supramundane liberating insight even from objective, "ontological" *duḥkhatā*. In view of the fact that at least most of these schools nevertheless understood these states as impermanent mental events (cp. already *S* II 60; *A* V 9 ff.), this decision implied that the "ontological" *duḥkhatā* could no longer be grounded on mere impermanence but required a different basis. At the same time, it would seem to have enabled the Yogācāra conception of the Buddha as a continuum of *mental* factors (*cittas* and *caittas*) free from *all* kinds of *duḥkhatā* and continuing forever. Cp. Lambert Schmithausen in *Zeitschrift der Deutschen Morgenländischen Gesellschaft*, Supplement III.2 (1977): 918 ff.

40 See note 35; cp. also *S* III 33 ff. (22.33–34), IV 81 ff. (35.101–2), 128 ff. (35.138–39).

41 *Vin* I 13.

42 *S* III 167 (22.122), IV 50 (35.80).

43 *S* IV 128 f., cp. *Th* 717; *Upasenasutra* § 17.

44 E.g., *Manusmṛti* 5.28–30; *Kauṣitaki-Upaniṣad* 2.9. For further details see Brian K. Smith, "Eaters, Food, and Social Hierarchy in Ancient India," *Journal of the American Academy of Religion* 58, no. 2 (1990): 177 ff.

45 Cp., e.g., *Dīghanikaya* (Pali Text Society edition, hereinafter *D*) III 130; *S* IV 104 (*yāvad eva imassa kāyassa ṭhitiyā*).

46 *S* II 98 ff. (food compared to the flesh of one's only son); *A* IV 46, 49, etc. (notion that food is disgusting, *āhare paṭikūlasaññā*).

47 Cp. *Sn* 935–36, and *Mahāniddesa*; *D* II 58 ff.

48 Expressly so *M* III 169 (cp. *Taishō Shinshū Daizōkyō* [Buddhist Tripiṭaka in Chinese, hereinafter *T*] vol. 1, 761b24 f.) and *S* V 456 (cp. *T* vol. 2, 108c15–17); cp. also *Mahāniddesa* (p. 408) on *Sn* 936b; *T* vol. 3, 467b18 ff.

49 *Th* 1133; *A* IV 100 ff.; *S* II 170 (14.31), 174 ff. (14.35–36); *T* vol. 1, 137c10 ff.; cp. *Buddhism and Nature*, n. 68. The impermanence of vegetation and landscape is emphasized also at *Śrāvakabhūmi* of Ācārya Asaṅga (K. Shukla, ed. [Patna: Kāśīprasādajāyasavāla-Anuśīlanasaṃsthānam, 1973], hereinafter *ŚrBh*) 483,2 ff. Cp. also the drastically negative evaluation of nature in a canonical text quoted in *Vi* 541a14 ff., where Śāriputra is provocatively addressed by a drunken non-Buddhist ascetic with a verse in which the latter states that after having satiated himself with meat and wine, he now perceives the herbs, trees, and mountains on the earth to be like a mass of gold; Śāriputra replies that he, in his turn, having satiated himself with the transphenomenal state (*ānimitta*) and having always cultivated concentration on emptiness (*śūnyatāsamādhi*, i.e., on all dharmas being

neither self nor mine), he perceives the herbs, trees, and mountains on the earth to be like a mass of saliva.

50 Cp. *Dhp* 188 ff. (*Uv* 27.31 ff.), pointing out that nature does not offer ultimate safety and liberation from suffering. The above statement is not of course intended to deny the fact that even while still alive released persons do no longer suffer from the adversities or fleetingness of nature in the same way as unreleased persons do (cp. note 38). But this is, like the fact that released persons are no longer afraid of death (cp. Vetter, "Bei Lebzeiten," 219 ff.; *Th* 707 ff.), due to their spiritual detachment and/or to the certitude that they will soon also be free, once and for all, from all physical pain, vicissitudes, and impermanence (cp. note 60). Their happiness, or serenity, is hence not at all the merit of nature, and they would, essentially, also be happy, or serene, in any other surroundings (cp. *Udāna* [Pali Text Society edition, hereinafter *Ud*] 2.4), even the most polluted one.

51 *A* IV 104 ff. As for the impermanence and decay of edifices, goods, and artifacts, see *ŚrBh* 482,14 ff., 483,16 ff.

52 Cp., e.g., *S* IV 1 ff.; *A* III 71 ff., III 443: *sabbaloke ca me mano nābhiramissati, sabbalokā ca me mano vuṭṭhahissati, nibbānaponaṃ ca me mānasaṃ bhavissati*, IV 50: *sabbaloke anabhiratasaññā*, referring to the "manifold [things] of the world" (*loka-cittesu* [v.l. *ocitresu*], cp. *Th* 674; *S* I 22); *T* vol. 1, 137c 12–14, etc.

53 I for one find it hard to deny that the overwhelming majority of the canonical materials suggests that in early Buddhism it was just a *matter of course* to strive, in the first place, for one's *own* self-perfection and release (cp. *D* III 61; *A* II 68: *ye te samaṇabrāhmaṇā … ekam attānaṃ damenti, … ekam attānaṃ parinibbāpenti*). According to tradition (*Vin* I 4 ff.; *M* I 167 ff.; cp. J. Sakamoto-Goto in *Journal of Indian and Buddhist Studies* XLI, no. 1 [1992]: 474–69) even the Buddha himself, after his awakening, i.e. after attaining (spiritual) release (*vimutti*: *Vin* I 1; *M* I 167), first hesitated to teach (cp. *D* II 35 ff.: same story for the former Buddha Vipassin; cp. also *Vin* III 8: some of the former buddhas weary of teaching in detail); and when after all he did decide to do so, he started, once again according to tradition (*Vin* I 9 ff.), with instructions on how to transcend death, suffering, and rebirth, and how to become detached and released from all elements of personal existence. I find it problematic to denounce this matter of striving for one's own release as "selfish," since others are not, of course, grudged release, and every serious Buddhist wishes all living beings well. Nor is release attained, let alone maintained, at the cost of others. On the contrary, release implies not only that the released person is forever safe from the world, but also that the rest of the world is forever safe from that person. According to the "logic" of *ahiṃsā* (see p. 182 with notes 88 and 89) attaining absolute safety presupposes bestowing absolute safety. In fact, even in this life the arhat is, on account of his spiritual perfection, simply "incapable" (*abhabba*) of intentionally killing (or, for that matter, injuring) any living being (*D* III 133), and after his death, even unintentional killing is excluded because he is not reborn and hence no longer in the world. Moreover, several passages stress that he who wants to take care of others has first to take care of himself (e.g., *A* III 373), in the sense of spiritual self-perfection, or that caring for oneself is at the same time caring for others, and vice versa (*S* V 169). The latter case is explained as referring to forbearance, non-injury, friendliness, and sympathy, which at the same time serve one's own spiritual perfection (cp. *Sāratthappakāsinī* III 227). Hence, striving primarily for one's own self-perfection and release does not exclude, and to a certain extent even involves, caring for others.

The problem is, however, to what extent caring for others includes not just nonviolence and benevolent *spirituality* but *active* help, especially in the case of monks and nuns. There are, to be sure, occasional references to everyday cases of active help motivated by compassion (e.g., *Vin* III 62: a monk freeing an animal caught in a trap), but the most important action for the benefit of others is teaching them the path to liberation, and exhorting them to practice it. As the above-mentioned traditional account of the Buddha's hesitation shows, such an activity is, however, neither a necessary requirement for nor an automatic outcome of a person's release, but requires the conviction that there is a sensitive audience and sufficiently strong compassion toward other living beings (*sattesu kāruññatā*: *Vin* I 6; *M* I 169; cp. *D* II 38). It would thus seem to have been originally understood as a kind of gratuitous extra, which is, to be sure, occasionally recommended to monks (e.g., *Vin* I 21; *S* I 105) and duly appreciated as superior to mere concern with one's own release (e.g., *A* II 95 ff., I 168; cp. *A* II 179), yet not in isolation from the latter but only as a supplement to it (ibid.; *Dhp* 158). It seems that it was only later that reflection on the special case of the Buddha led to conceiving his career as aiming, from the outset, at both his own and others' release, and that it was only with the rise of Mahāyāna that this difference was developed into a critical attitude toward striving primarily for one's own release, now devalued as inferior and "selfish" in contrast to buddhahood as the higher ideal. But as is well known it is only in one strand of somewhat later Mahāyāna (viz. the *ekayāna* current) that such private release was considered impossible, whereas other Mahāyāna currents like Yogācāra continued to admit that both kinds of release are possible (so that even bodhisattvas may need exhortation not to enter "private" *nirvāṇa*: e.g., *Daśabhūmikasūtra* [J. Rahder, ed. (Paris: P. Guethner, 1926), hereinafter *DBhS*] 66,19 ff. [8.K]), though Buddhahood does, of course, have a much higher status.

In view of this situation, the assumption that the doctrine of nonexistence of a self—let alone the early canonical spirituality of understanding the constituents of one's personality or any elements of existence not to be self or mine—excludes striving, or at least successful striving, for private release, appears to me highly problematic. Whatever the logical cogency of this assumption *for us*, it need not have been perceived, from the outset, by the Buddhists themselves, and only unambiguous textual evidence could prove that it really was. As far as I can see, the "spiritual practice of not-self" is, in the early canonical texts, confined to the context of weariness (*nibbidā*) of and detachment (*virāga*) and release (*vimutti*) from the constituents of one's personality as well as other elements of existence (e.g., *S* III 21 ff., IV 1 ff.), but still coexists, somehow, with the (commonsense) notion of a "person" (*puggala*) as the subject of bondage and liberation. I for one do not recall having come across any canonical passage suggesting that the idea of not-self explodes the idea of private release. Nor do I know of unambiguous canonical evidence proving that the spiritual practice of not-self was regarded to result in compassion or friendliness. (L. Cousin's [Buddha-L electronic discussion group, November 1995] reference to *M* III 76 and 251 does not convince me, because the notion of *sammādiṭṭhi* and *sammāsaṃkappa* underlying the two passages would seem to be different [cp. E. Frauwallner, *Geschichte der indischen Philosophie*, vol. 1 (Salzburg: O. Müller, 1953), 185], and because III 76 may not intend a sequence of causes and effects but a sequence of steps, the later ones supplementing those preceding; for III 251, even this much is problematic [cp. Nyanatiloka, *Buddhist Dictionary* (1950; repr. Kandy: Buddhist Publication Society, 2004), s.v. "magga"].) In the canonical texts, the idea of not-self does not even seem to be used for grounding everyday ethical behavior like desisting from killing living beings (but cp. *ŚrBh* 378,15 ff. where it serves to counteract the notion of "enemy"). The purpose of grounding ethical behavior is rather achieved by the Golden Rule (see note 113), i.e., by empathetic analogy of self and others. In Mahāyāna Buddhism, it is primarily this analogy that is, in the form of "[the idea] that others (or: all living beings) are like oneself" (*ātmaparasamatā, sarvasattveṣv ātmasamacittatā*, etc.: e.g., *Mahāyānasūtralaṃkāra* [S. Lévi, ed. (Paris: H. Champion, 1907), hereinafter *MSA*] 14.30cd; *Bhāṣya* on 9.76 and 17.46; *Bodhicaryāvatāra* of Śāntideva [P. L. Vaidya, ed. (Darbhanga: Mithila Institute, 1960), hereinafter *BCA*] 8.90[ff.]), extended also to the context of soteriology. Occasionally this idea is now indeed, in contrast to the spiritually unwholesome egocentric belief in an individual self, designated as the "view of a vast self" (*mahātmadṛṣṭi, MSA* 14.37) comprising all living beings (cp. *BCA* 6.126; cp. also the explanation of *sabbattatāya* at *VisM* 9.47 [which, however, in view of *Udāna* 3.10, cannot be the original meaning of this expression]). It may, moreover, be grounded on the fact that all living beings are pervaded by one and the same true nature (*tathatā, dharmadhātu: MSA* 14.30; *Bhāṣya* on *Madhyāntavibhāga* 2.14; *Pañjikā* on *BCA* 6.126), which may be called their (common, true) self or essence (*ātman*) and is at the same time identified with their being devoid of an (individual) self or essence (*nairātmya*) (*MSA* 9.23; cp. 14.30 with Sthiramati's commentary [*Tanjur*, Peking, mi 304b6 ff.]). It is only in Śāntideva (*BCA* 8.101 ff.) that I have noted an argument for altruistic (salvific) action directly starting from the nonexistence of a self, in the sense that since there is no self (not even in the form of an aggregate) to which suffering could be ascribed or by which it could be owned, there is nothing on the basis of which one could distinguish between one's own and others' suffering. But in other texts (e.g., *DBhS* 55,6–8 [7.A(2)]) the relation between lack of self (*nairātmya*) and compassion, etc., is rather felt to be one of a tension, which, however, is bridged over by the bodhisattva because he needs both as *complementary* elements of his spiritual practice. And at *DBhS* 17,26 ff. (1.QQ–SS) it is the awareness that the *other* living beings are merely a mass of disagreeable or unsatisfactory factors without self but do not realize this that arouses compassion on the part of the bodhisattva. Thus, the matter is rather complex, and surely in need of closer investigation. See, for example, the discussion on the parallel problem of emptiness and compassion in the Buddha-L electronic discussion group (October–November 1995).

54 Such a "return to the world" out of compassion does not of course imply in any way a change in the *evaluation* of mundane existence or of the world, let alone nature. This holds good even for Mahāyāna Buddhism (not, perhaps, Far Eastern Mahāyāna, but at least Indian Mahāyāna, cp., e.g., *DBhS* 3.B, E–G, 6.O); for here, too, the motive of bodhisattvas or buddhas to remain, voluntarily, in the world is not preservation of nature but, primarily, to *save* other living beings from *saṃsāra* and lead them to *nirvāṇa* or buddhahood (e.g., *DBhS* 1.SS, 2.X–CC, 3.G, 5.F–H), and only secondarily to *reduce* their sufferings, or improve their existence, on an *intramundane* level (which theoretically may, but need not, include preservation of nature).

It should also be noted that especially in Mahāyāna the buddhas are often regarded to exist in a more or less supramundane sphere or dimension, and to descend to this world only in the form of mere apparitions (*nirmāṇa*) (cp. P. Harrison in *Ōtani Gakuhō* 74 [1995]: 1 ff.—an idea which does not at all suggest a revalorization of the natural world. And even the ideas of the Buddha's relics being alive (cp. G. Schopen in *Religion* 17 [1987]: 203 ff.) or of his physical presence in the monastery (idem. in *Journal of Indian*

Philosophy 18 [1990]: 181 ff.) have quite obviously no ecological significance but are motivated by purely religious needs.

55 E.g., *A* II 96 ff.; *Vin* I 21.

56 E.g., *M* I 23 (cp. *A* I 60 ff.; *S* II 203) with *Papañcasūdanī* I 129. In a sense, *every* released person, unless totally isolated, *automatically* helps others by being a model, and this is, according to *Mil* 195 ff., the reason why the Buddha has prohibited the monks from committing suicide (but cp. the exceptions referred to in note 59).

57 Cp. the statement that all forms of becoming or existence (*sabbe bhavā*), which include those in the heavenly spheres, are impermanent and (hence) unsatisfactory: *Ud* 3.10; *A* II 177; cp. *Th* 260.

58 E.g. *Itivuttaka* (Pali Text Society edition, quoted by page number, hereinafter *It*) 17; *D* II 30 ff.; *S* II 101 ff. (12.64), 104 (12.65), 185 (15,10). I do not deny the possibility of Buddhist spirituality without belief in rebirth, but—whatever the situation may have been in the very beginnings of the Buddha's teaching (cp. Vetter, "Bei Lebzeiten," 219 ff.)—in the canonical texts of early Buddhism the idea of rebirth, already indicated in the second Noble Truth (*taṇhā ponobbhavikā*, Skt. *tṛṣṇā paunarbhavikā* or °*ki*), is essential and ubiquitous, as Macy (*Mutual Causality*, 162) herself admits. And she is hardly right in taking *S* II 26 ff. as evidence for her assumption that "the Buddha did not consider it relevant or useful to reflect on the possibility or character of other existences" (*Mutual Causality*, 163). The purport of the text is rather to make it clear that by understanding origination in dependence one has no longer any *doubts* and abandons idle speculation as to whether at all, how precisely, and in what form rebirth has taken or will take place, but, on the contrary, *knows* that it is a fact, how it works, and how it can be brought to an end.

59 This is doubtless an important aspect (cp., e.g., *S* III 1 ff.), but not the only one, as Isshi Yamada asserts in "Premises and Implications of Interdependence" (in Somaratina Balasooriya et al., eds., *Buddhist Studies in Honour of Walpola Rahula* [London: Gordon Fazer, 1980], 290 n. 55): ". . . Non-attachment . . . is not escaping from life, but is detaching oneself from one's own deception of Self. This is the meaning of the doctrine of Anātman." For the basic formula of the spiritual practice of not-self is quite unambiguous in stating that the elimination of the notions of "I," "mine," and "Self" with regard to the *skandha*s as well as sense-objects entails weariness of and detachment and liberation from these elements themselves, which have been recognized as impermanent and unsatisfactory (*rūpasmiṃ* etc. *nibbindati, nibbindaṃ virajjati, virāgā vimuccati*), the final result being that there is no further rebirth (*Vin* I 14; *S* IV 1 ff., etc.; cp. also *Sn* 1068). Passages like *S* I 22 do not contradict this but rather want to make clear that this liberation cannot be attained by physically removing the objects of desire but only by eradicating desire itself.

   For a saint comparing life to a burden, a disease, poison, a place of execution, and a burning house, see *Th* 709 ff. and *Upasenasūtra* §§ 14–17. There may even have been cases (not condemned by the Buddha) of arhats committing suicide in situations of excessive physical pain (*S* III 119 ff., IV 55 ff. = *M* III 263 ff.; cp. also *S* I 120 ff. with *Sāratthappakāsinī* I 183,4 f.), but the interpretation of these cases poses intricate problems (cp. D. Keown in *Journal of Buddhist Ethics* 3 [1996]: 8–31).

60 E.g., *M* III 187 = *A* I 142; *S* II 5, 24 f.; *A* IV 105; *Ud* 33 (3.10), 71 (6.7), 74 (7.1), 93 (8.9: final cessation of the *skandha*s); *Mil* 197,20 ff. Even the *Mettasutta* (*Sn* 143–52) ends up with detachment and overcoming rebirth; similarly *A* II 176 f. The certitude of

the released person that he/she is no longer subject to rebirth and redeath and hence has virtually transcended all kinds of *dukkha* constitutes a state of sublime happiness, which may be called "*nirvāṇa* in this life" (*M* III 187).

61 *Vin* I 10; *S* V 421. Desire is expressly characterized as "leading to rebirth" (*pono(b) bhavika*, Skt. *paunarbhavika*).

62 Cp., e.g., *A* IV 105 (*ucchinnā bhavataṇhā . . . , n' atthi dāni punabbhavo*).

63 E.g., *A* V 116 ff. (*avijjā* as the "nourishment" of *bhavataṇhā*).

64 E.g., *S* II 1 f. or *Vin* I 1.

65 Actually, the stereotyped twelve-membered formula appears to be, basically, a juxtaposition of two different analyses of the process of rebirth (cp. Frauwallner, *Geschichte der indischen Philosophie*, 197 ff.; Vetter, *Ideas and Meditative Practices*, 45 ff.): a more archaic second half (from *taṇhā* to being [re]born, aging, and dying), preserved separately at *S* II 84 ff. (12.52–57) and in the Sarvāstivāda version of the *Mahānidānasūtra* (*T* vol. 1, 578b21–579a1 etc., corresponding to *D* II 55–58: cp. Vetter in *WZKS* 38 [1994]: 144; cp. also *S* II 52 ff. where *jarāmaraṇa* is traced back until *vedanā*), and a more advanced first half (from *avijjā* to vedanā), which is related to (and may even be based on a reworking and extension of) *D* II 62 ff. (where vedanā is traced back to *vijñāna*). This fact also explains why the canonical texts do not explicitly refer the twelve-membered formula to *three* different existences, as abhidharma sources often do: what was originally intended was just the explanation of rebirth, not of two different rebirths. But the decision to juxtapose two different descriptions of the same process, linked together by the item "feeling" (*vedanā*), automatically resulted in a concatenation that almost inevitably came to be understood as a sequence, now covering three different existences. Since the Abhidharmikas are well aware of the fact that the different descriptions of the two rebirth processes are not intended to point out an actual qualitative difference of these processes but merely emphasize, each time, different aspects, the abhidharmic interpretation is not a case of serious misunderstanding, much less serious, in my view, than the interpretation proposed (with considerable polemic vehemence) by Japanese scholars like K. Mizuno (*Primitive Buddhism* [Ube: Karinbunko, 1969]) and I. Yamada ("Premises and Implications") or by J. Macy (who explicitly refers to Mizuno). I cannot help feeling that the interpretation of the Japanese scholars is heavily influenced by the wish to show that original Buddhism is, basically, in agreement with Mahāyāna Buddhism (as understood in the Far East, at that), and also with modern requirements. This amounts to a pattern (also shared by Macy) according to which abhidharma is a degradation, while Mahāyāna has recovered the original teaching of the Buddha, especially the original meaning of *pratītyasamutpāda*, which is (in line, it seems, with Huayan) understood as *inter*dependence. Even the twelve-membered formula is, apart from being marginalized, dissociated as much as possible from its specific reference to rebirth. A detailed criticism of this view would, of course, by far exceed the limits of this paper. For the time being, I can only state that in the textual evidence adduced I have, so far, not found anything to convince me, and give one example (for another one, cp. note 67): In a discussion of *M* I 261 ff., Yamada ("Premises and Implications," 267 ff., esp. 270 ff.), referring (ibid. n. 8) to a number of famous Japanese scholars, distinguishes between a "natural" and a "reversal" sequence of the twelve-membered *paṭiccasamuppāda* formula. The "reversal" sequence is the one starting from *avijjā* and ending in "aging-and-dying" and is understood by Yamada as referring to rebirth. But the "natural" sequence he interprets, quite surprisingly and without philological arguments, as referring to *conceptual inter*dependence in

a Madhyamaka and partly even Hegelian sense: The dependence of "aging-and-dying" on "being born" means that the former presupposes the latter as its conceptual opposite, and "being born" presupposes "becoming" (*bhava*) as "the dialectically conceived 'unity of opposites' which includes both '*jarāmaraṇa*' and '*jāti*.'"

This conceptual dependence is, of course, a mutual one, i.e., *inter*dependence, so that "the three factors are simultaneous." I for one fail to see how all this can be gleaned from the text itself, which any unbiased reader cannot but understand as the simple attempt to retrace, for didactic reasons, the visible effect, viz. aging-and-dying (involving suffering), step by step to its basic condition, viz. *avijjā*, the result of the investigation being thereafter summed up by restating the causal chain in its actual sequence from cause to effect. Perhaps Yamada was misled by a misunderstanding of the problematic term *akālika* (on which cp. J. Bronkhorst in *Studien zur Indologie und Iranistik* 10 [1984]: 187 ff.), which he takes to mean "timeless" also in the sense of "simultaneous" (p. 275); but this is altogether arbitrary. Another point is that he renders the question introducing the so-called "natural" sequence as "When what condition is not, are becoming-old and dying not?" but this must have been taken by Yamada from another source (like *S* II 7). *M* I 261 ff. has "Is aging-and-dying actually dependent on being born or not: what do you (*vo*, cp. *T* vol. 1, 768a13) think about this?" But even if Yamada's version of the question were accepted it would not be sufficient to support his view because the interpretation of the formula *asmin satīdaṃ bhavati* (in contrast to *asyotpādād idam utpadyate*) as referring to *conceptual inter*dependence is a Madhyamaka idea (cp. *Ratnāvalī* I.48) that we are not entitled to superimpose on the canonical texts without strong evidence.

66 E.g., *A* I 176; *D* II 62 ff. (although, strictly speaking, the latter passage, by stating that *viññāṇa* descends into the womb, presupposes its preexistence, hence *re*birth).

67 E.g., *S* II 72 or IV 86 (sense-perception arising in dependence on sense-faculty and sense-object, the concomitance of the three is "contact," dependent on which there is feeling, entailing, in its turn, desire). In other texts (e.g., *S* II 73 f. or IV 87), this series is extended up to aging-and-dying. The parallelism of this sequence with the twelve-membered formula has misled Japanese scholars (e.g., Mizuno, op. cit. [see note 65], 142 ff.; Yamada, "Premises and Implications," 272) to interpret *nāmarūpa* in the twelve-membered formula as sense-objects, although such a use is rare (but cp. *S* II 24) and is impossible in passages like *D* II 63 where *nāmarūpa* (lit. "name and form [or figure]") clearly means the living individual either under his physical aspect or as a psycho-physical being, from the proto-embryonic phase onward. Apart from this, the "psychological" chain starts with the explanation of how *actual* perception of an object arises, whereas *vijñāna* in the rebirth-focused twelve-membered series is, originally, rather the latent, subtle *faculty* of perception which enters the womb at the moment of conception, keeps the body alive during life, and leaves it at death (cp., e.g., Frauwallner, *Geschichte der indischen Philosophie*, 1: 204 ff.; D. Kalupahana, *Causality: The Central Philosophy of Buddhism* [Honolulu: University Press of Hawaii, 1975], 117 ff.; L. Schmithausen, *Ālayavijñāna* [Tokyo: International Institute for Buddhist Studies, 1987], 7; Vetter, *Ideas and Meditative Practices*, 49 ff.; W. S. Waldron, "How Innovative Is the *Ālayavijñāna*?" *Journal of Indian Philosophy* 22 [1994]; 201 ff.)

68 *D* II 58–61.

69 *D* III 59 ff. (see below, notes 162 and 163); more explicitly: *T* vol. 1, 137b16 ff. According to a somewhat later text, the *Saddharmasmṛtyupasthānasūtra*, people's moral behavior and piety causes the righteous *nāga*s to send seasonable rain so that crops thrive (*T* vol.

17, 105c23 ff. and 29 ff., 106c29 ff.), whereas immoral and impious behavior strengthens the unrighteous *nāga*s who send unwholesome rain, thunderstorms, and hail (106a29 ff., c24 ff.).

70 E.g., *S* IV 230; *A* II 87, III 131 (feelings caused by change of season or weather, *utupariṇāma*).

71 Cp., e.g., Francis A. Cook in J. Baird Callicott and Roger T. Ames, eds., *Nature in Asian Traditions of Thought* (Albany: State University of New York Press, 1989), 213 ff.

72 Cp., in this connection, also the remarks in Harris, "How Environmentalist Is Buddhism?" 104. Harris ("Causation and *Telos*," 53) even argues that a totally "symmetric" causality as implied in universal interpenetration would render change inexplicable and, hence, ecological ethics both impossible and pointless. This argument seems to presuppose *total simultaneous* interdependence, in the sense that everything is totally constituted and determined by, and at the same time, in its turn, constitutes and determines, everything else. Yet as far as I can see the above consequence would not follow in the case of "weaker" forms of interdependence or mutual causality (e.g., all entities, or chains of entities, merely *influencing* and thereby gradually changing one another to a certain, and perhaps different, extent). But as I am going to point out, this problem does not concern *early* Buddhism. On the other hand, in my opinion, too, the early Buddhist view of the world is dysteleological in the sense that on the *ultimate* level the world is fundamentally and incurably ill. But this does not preclude the existence *and establishment* of better or, for that matter, worse conditions on the *intramundane* level. What creates problems (cp. also Ian Harris, "Buddhism," in Jean Holm, ed., *Attitudes to Nature* [London: Pinter Publishers, 1994], 11) even on the intramundane level is the introduction of a—not specifically Buddhist (cp. A. Mette, *Indische Kulturstiftungsberichte und ihr Verhältnis zur Zeitaltersage* [Mainz: Verlag der Akademie der Wissenschaften und der Literatur, 1973])—view of automatic cyclical cosmic ups and downs. To be sure, at least according to later Buddhist sources these cosmic ups and downs are conditioned by corresponding ups and downs of the moral and spiritual attitude of human beings (cp. Mette, 14), but precisely on account of the cyclical automatism of this process this amounts, *de facto*, to a kind of determinism of moral and spiritual rise and decline, which is difficult to reconcile with the moral and spiritual freedom of the individual that is fundamental to early Buddhist ethics and soteriology.

73 Cp. note 65. It is not of course sufficient to base the assumption of universal mutual causality in the canon on a hyperetymological interpretation of terms, as Macy does. According to her (*Mutual Causality*, 54), *paṭicca* expresses the feedback central to mutual causality, and *paṭiccasamuppāda* she paraphrases as "the being-on-account-of-arising-together" (*Mutual Causality*, 34, 57), and explains it by adducing Buddhaghosa's definition of *paṭiccasamuppāda* as "that according to which co-ordinate phenomena are produced mutually" or "according to which phenomena arise together in reciprocal dependence." But apart from the fact that Buddhaghosa's explanation is a commentarial sophistication belonging to a much later period, a careful perusal of the corresponding paragraphs of his *Visuddhimagga* (ed. Henry Clarke Warren, rev. Dharmananda Kosambi [Cambridge: Harvard University Press, 1950], 17.15 ff., esp. 17.17–20) reveals that the passage quoted (probably *Sāratthappakāsinī* II 6,27–29) has been misunderstood by her. It rather means that [the group of factors that constitute] the condition-aspect (*paccayākāra*) is called *paṭiccasamuppāda* because it produces united factors (*sahite dhamme*), i.e., factors which never occur without one another (*aññamaññam avinibbhoga-vutti-dhamme*: *VisM*

17.18), and that they do so in dependence on one another (*aññamaññaṃ paṭicca*), i.e., in cooperation and when they are complete (*VisM* 17.18, 20)—hence, complex cooperating causes (cp. also Kalupahana, op. cit. [see note 67], 56) and complex effects, without mention of mutuality or interdependence of *cause and effect*. Apart from this, it is not probable that the prefix *sam-* was, from the outset, intended to convey such a heavy meaning. Even a later author like Candrakīrti (*Prasannapadā* 5,4) does not press it in this way, stating that *pad* with the prefix *sam-ud-* simply means "arising" (*prādurbhāva*). The original function of *sam-* in *samutpāda* was hence more likely merely to underline the completion of the action (see L. Renou, *Grammaire Sanskrite* [Paris: A. Maisonneuve, 1946], 145).

74 Liberation (*vimutti*) in the sense of a spiritual event is, of course, dependent on a cause, as *S* II 30 makes clear (cp. also *Uv* 26.9: *sahetuṃ parinirvānti*). But the canonical texts sometimes refer to another dimension of *nirvāṇa* that they call "unconditioned" or perhaps rather "without conditioning" (*asaṅkhata*: *Ud* 8.3; *Th* 725), a realm (*āyatana*) where there are no elements, no celestial bodies, where there is neither this world nor the yonder one, neither arrival nor departure, neither dying nor being born nor pain (*Ud* 8.1; cp. 1.10; *S* I 15; *D* I 223), where both the sense-faculties and the apperception of sense-objects cease (*S* IV 98: *se āyatane . . . yattha cakkhu ca nirujjhati rūpasaññā ca nirujjhati*, etc.). J. Macy (*World as Lover*, 61 f., 74 f.; *Die Wiederentdeckung der sinnlichen Erde*, 84 and 98) struggles hard to get these passages out of the way because such a *nirvāṇa* would be a refuge to which one could try to withdraw from this imperfect world instead of realizing the latter to be the only one available and hence to try one's best to preserve or even improve it. In *Mutual Causality*, 134 f., she rejects the usual understanding of *āyatana* at *Ud* 8.1 as "sphere" in favor of "gateway" or "faculty" and takes the passage to refer not to *nirvāṇa* as "an objective self-existent, supernatural essence or realm" but to "the means by which we perceive, or the way in which we perceive." But the *Critical Pāli Dictionary* (Copenhagen: Royal Danish Academy of Sciences and Letters, 1924–2001, hereinafter *CPD*) makes it clear that the basic meaning of *āyatana* is "dwelling-place," "region." Hence, it is reasonable to start from the metaphor of a "realm" or "sphere," which is not only supported by its being referred to by the locative *yattha* (cp. also *Ud* 1.10, etc.) but also by the use of unambiguous metaphors like *pada* or *sthāna* in parallel contexts like *It* 37 and 39 or *Uv* 26.24–27. Another question is whether this "sphere" or "state" should be understood as an "objective, self-existent essence," but at any rate I for one find that an unbiased understanding of *Ud* 8.1 suggests that it is beyond the world and beyond *saṃsāra*, and hence beyond becoming and conditioning, as is clear from *Ud* 8.3 as well as *It* 37 ff. and 38 ff. There is no reason to follow Macy in rejecting the traditional understanding of *asaṅkhata* as "unconditioned" (perhaps in the more specific sense of "not produced by a volition or desire for some form of individual existence") or "without conditioning" in favor of a hyperetymological rendering "uncompounded"; for where there is no birth, arising, making/causing, there can hardly be conditioning. Cp. also passages like *M* I 500 and II 299 documenting the quasi-synonymity of *saṅkhata* and *paṭiccasamuppanna* and their equivalence to "impermanent" (*anicca*), and *It* 37 where this "sphere" (*pada*) is qualified as "unoriginated" (*asamuppanna*) and expressly termed an "escape from this" (*tassa nissaraṇaṃ*), viz. the born, originated (*samuppanna*), and conditioned (*saṅkhata*) body which is full of diseases and not worth being pleased with (for *nissaraṇa* c. gen. see examples in *Pali Tripiṭaka Concordance* s.v. *nissaraṇa*).

75   E.g., *nāmarūpa* and *viññāṇa* (*S* II 104 ff., 113 f.; *D* II 32, 63); *āyu* and *usmā* (M I 295).
     In a weaker sense, one might add instances of "spiral" causality (of the hen and egg type)
     where, just as in the twelve-membered *pratītyasamutpāda* formula, the effect (or medi-
     ate effect) of a cause is, in its turn, the cause or presupposition of *another* instance of the
     initial cause. One has to distinguish mutual dependence of cause and effect from mutual
     cooperation of causes in engendering a common effect (cp. note 73).

76   There is no reason for assuming that mutual causality, though stated explicitly only in
     the case of *nāmarūpa* and *viññāṇa*, has to be presupposed as being *implied* throughout
     the twelve-membered chain, as Yamada ("Premises and Implications," 274) and Macy
     (*Mutual Causality*, 56) do. The latter bases herself on the *pe* at *S* II 114 that, however,
     merely stands for the full enumeration of the remaining members of the chain but does
     not of course extend reciprocity to them (as is confirmed by *D* II 32 ff.). *Sn* 728 ff.,
     adduced by Macy (*Mutual Causality*, 55) in support of mutual causality, is not con-
     clusive; for the text only states that *avijjā*, etc., are *somehow* conditions of suffering but
     does not waste any words on the relation of these conditions to each other; as for *upadhi*
     (wrongly equated by Macy with *nidāna*), see *CPD* and Norman's translation of *Sn* 728
     and his note on *Sn* 33–34. With regard to contact, feeling, and desire, mutual depen-
     dence is expressly denied at *S* II 141 (14.3) and 148 (14.10).

77   *Vibhaṅga* 141–43, 158 ff.

78   *Vibhaṅga-aṭṭhakathā* 207; Nyanatiloka, *Guide through the Abhidhamma-piṭaka* (Kandy:
     Buddhist Publication Society, 1971), 35 f. Cp. also *AKBh* 133,1 ff.; *Vi* 118c7 ff.; *DBhS*
     49,10 ff. (6.F).

79   *S* II 189 f. An appealing ecological reinterpretation of this idea is offered by Y. Kajiyama
     in *Buddhism and Nature: Proceeding of an International Symposium on the Occasion of
     EXPO 1990* (Tokyo: The International Institute for Buddhist Studies, 1991), 40; cp. also
     ibid., 55 f. J. Macy (*World as Lover*, 202; *Die Wiederentdeckung der sinnlichen Erde*, 238)
     seems to reinterpret it in terms of the modern theory of evolution, whereas this theory
     was decidedly rejected by the German Buddhist H. Hecker in a lecture entitled *Über die
     Natur*, delivered at Roseburg on September 19, 1992.

80   *santuṭṭhi*, *appicchatā*, etc. (e.g., *D* I 71; *M* I 13).

81   *bhojane mattuññatā* (e.g., *A* I 114).

82   E.g., *Vin* II 291.

83   Cp., e.g., L. De Silva in Klas Sandell, ed., *Buddhist Perspectives on the Ecocrisis* (Kandy:
     Buddhist Publication Society, 1987), 15 ff., and in Martine Batchelor and Kerry Brown,
     eds., *Buddhism and Ecology* (London: Cassell, 1992), 21 ff. The passages referred to by
     De Silva are, to be sure, very appealing, but it may not be superfluous to have a closer
     look at some of them in order to clarify to what extent they are actually motivated by
     ecological concerns:

        1. *D* III 188 (*bhoge saṃharamānassa bhamarasseva iriyato / bhogā sannicayaṃ yanti
     vammiko v' upacīyati*) is taken by De Silva to show that "man is expected to make legiti-
     mate use of nature so that he can rise above nature and realise his innate spiritual poten-
     tial." But actually the passage does not mention rising above nature nor spiritual potential
     but just accumulation of wealth, and what is explicitly said in the text is merely that by
     assiduously collecting one bit after the other, just like a bee, one (viz. a layman) will finally
     come to assemble a large amount. To be sure, the commentary (*Sumaṅgalavilāsinī* III
     951), when explaining the bee simile, refers to the fact that the bee does not harm the
     flower when collecting the honey from it, and this may be justified in view of *Dhp* 49.

But even the commentary does not explicitly apply this aspect of the simile to the main theme, and even if one does so the passage may refer to a cautious attitude not toward *nature* but rather toward other *people* or society, i.e., to social, not ecological ethics. This is at any rate true of *Dhp* 49 (cp. also *Dasaveyāliya* 1.2–3) where the bee simile is used to illustrate how the *monk* should behave on his almsround in the village (*gāme*): just as a bee collects honey from a flower without damaging it, so the monk should not become a burden or nuisance to his lay supporters, or even ruin them—and thereby also himself—economically. It is, of course, possible to deliberately extend the principle of concern for others and circumspect use of resources to the treatment of nature. But even this would not yet be an ecological attitude in my sense (viz. protecting nature as a whole for its own sake), but rather an anthropocentric one motivated by long-term human utilization of natural resources, or, at best, by concern for fellow beings as *individuals*.

2. Likewise, the simile of a person who, in order to eat a few fruits (*A* IV 283 and *Manorathapūraṇī* IV 138), shakes a fig tree (*udumbara, Ficus glomerata*) so violently that many more fruits than needed fall down, in its context merely illustrates unsound economy (living beyond one's means: *app'āyo samāno uḷāraṃ jīvikaṃ kappeti*). Still, if taken by itself, it may well be understood as recommending circumspect use of natural resources. But one can hardly derive from it an ecological ethics in the sense of protecting nature as a whole for its own sake.

3. Similarly, an ecological ethics deduced from a generalization of the idea that felling or injuring a tree whose shade or fruits one has enjoyed is a case of ingratitude or disloyalty (*A* III 369; *Jātaka* [Pali Text Society edition, hereinafter *Ja*] IV 352; *Petavatthu* 2.9.3 and 5; cp. *Buddhism and Nature,* n. 38) would be an anthropocentric one, since the motive for not destroying nature would be the *service* rendered by nature to *human beings*, not the intrinsic value of nature as such. The same would also hold true for an extension of the social principle of benefit for benefit recommended in the *Sigalovādasutta* (*D* III 189 ff.) to the ecological sphere (in the sense of "treat nature well, and nature will treat you well," as such not of course a bad thing).

84 Cp., e.g., Detlev Kantowsky, *Von Südasien lernen* (Frankfurt and New York: Edition Qumran im Campus Verlag, 1985), 135 ff.
85 E.g., *Vin* I 13 ff. (cp. note 53); *M* I 138 ff., III 19 ff.; *S* III 22, 49 f., 67 ff., IV 1–3, 24–26; cp. also *A* III 444 (*sabbaloke atammayo*).
86 E.g., *M* III 18 ff; *S* II 252 ff., III 79–81, 103, 136 ff., 169 ff.; cp. *A* III 444, IV 53.
87 For the difference in usage see Harvey B. Aronson, *Love and Sympathy in Theravāda Buddhism* (Delhi: Motilal Banarsidass, 1980), 14 ff., 20.
88 Hanns-Peter Schmidt, "The Origin of *Ahiṃsā*," in *Mélanges d'Indianisme à la mémoire de L. Renou* (Paris: E. de Boccard, 1968), 643 ff.
89 Cp. *Vin* I 220, prohibiting monks from eating the flesh of tigers, etc., because congeners might attack them.
90 Cp., especially, Hanns-Peter Schmidt, "Indo-Iranian *Mitra* Studies: The State of the Central Problem," in *Études mithriaques, Acta Iranica* 1978, esp. 368 ff. and 385 ff.
91 Cp. *Śatapathabrāhmaṇa* 3.8.5.10 f. (alliance with water and plants) or 4.1.4.8 (god *Mitra* being the ally or friend of all beings, including animals). As for a Buddhist text still very close to this idea, see the *Ahirājasutta* (cp. 184–85 and note 120).
92 The latter rendering is justified when *mettā* is exemplified by mother-love (*Sn* 149 ff. [cp. note 104]; *VisM* 9.72). But in view of *mettā* being derived from *mitra* I normally prefer the rendering "friendliness."

93 Cp. also the reciprocity of the "gift of safety" (*abhaya*, lit. "freedom from fear-and-danger") at *A* IV 246 (*pāṇātipātā paṭivirato . . . sattānaṃ abhayaṃ dattvā . . . abhayassa . . . bhāgī hoti*).

94 E.g., *Vin* II 194 ff., II 109 f. = *A* II 72 (*Ahirājasutta*, prose; cp. below p. 184); for the protective effect of *mettā* cp. also texts like *S* II 264; *A* IV 150; *VisM* 9.71–72; *Cullaniddesa* and *Sn* 42 (p. 142, no. 239.B); cp. also Aronson, op. cit. (see note 87), 48 ff.; Harris, "How Environmentalist Is Buddhism?" 107, and "Buddhism," 18 ff.; Gómez, "Nonviolence and the Self," 37.

95 *Vi* 427a15 ff. raises the question whether, like *maitrī, karuṇā* and the other *apramāṇas* also protect from danger, and answers this in the affirmative, but has then to solve the problem why such a function is not mentioned in any *sūtra*.

96 This observation I owe to M. Maitrimurti.

97 Harris, "How Environmentalist Is Buddhism?" 106 ff.

98 Ibid., 107, 7–9.

99 Ibid., 106 and n. 47. Similarly, though more cautiously, Harris, "Buddhism," 18.

100 *VisM* 9.3–4.

101 *VisM* 9.30–34.

102 *VisM* 9.50.

103 *VisM* 9.51 ff. At M III 169, *vinipātagata* must refer to animals. *VisM* 13.93, where Buddhaghosa refers each of the expressions *apāya, duggati, vinipāta*, and *niraya* to a different *gati*, connecting the animals with *apāya*, is a typically commentarial attempt at differentiating canonical quasi-synonyms (as at least the first three terms would seem to be) and hence no strong counterevidence.

104 Cp. Perry Schmidt-Leukel, "Das Problem von Dewalt und Kieg in der buddhistischen Ethik," in *Rundbriefe "Buddhismus heute"* 5 (November 1991): 7. Cp. also the *Mettasutta* (*Sn* 143–52) where *mettā* toward all living beings (*sabba-bhūtesu*: 149c; *sabbalokasmi*: 150a; *sabbe sattā*: 145d and 147d; *ye keci pāṇabhūt'*, mobile as well as stationary: 146ab) is compared to the love of a mother toward her only son. There is no explicit reference to self-protection in the *Mettasutta* (a fact from which Gómez ["Nonviolence and the Self," 40] seems to derive that it was not, originally, used for this purpose), but the commentary ascribes such a function to it, and in Theravāda countries it is actually one of the texts used in the paritta ceremony (cp., e.g., R. Gombrich, *Precept and Practice* [Oxford: Oxford University Press, 1971], 205, who seems to think that it was "intended from the very first to serve such a purpose").

105 Cp. also ŚrBh 427,21 ff.

106 *Sn* 705; *Dhp* 129 ff.; *Ud* 5.1 = *S* I 75, V 353 ff.; cp. *Buddhism and Nature* nn. 17 and 172. As I understand these passages, they do not indicate that the reference points "self" and "other" are changed *through* compassion and non-violence (Gómez, "Nonviolence and the Self," 44) but are rather intended to *motivate* non-violence, etc., by pointing out the analogy or likeness (*attānaṃ upamaṃ katvā*; not "identification") between self and others. And as far as I can see, at least in early Buddhism this grounding of ethical behavior on the *analogy* between self and others has nothing to do with the Buddhist spirituality of no-self (*anattā*), as Gómez ("Nonviolence and the Self," 42 ff.) seems to suggest (cp. also note 53). Actually, it is common to Buddhist, Jaina, and Hindu sources: cp., e.g., *Āyāraṃga* 1.2.3.4 (Walther Schubring, ed. [Hamburg: de Gruyter, 1966], p. 8,23–25) and 1.3.3.1 (p. 15,18 ff.); *Uttarajjhayaṇa* 6.6 (*Jaina Āgama Series*

vol. 15, p. 109 § 167); *Dasaveyāliya* 6.10 (ibid., p. 40 § 273); *Tattvārthādhigamasūtra* 7.5; *Mahābhārata* (critical edition, hereinafter refered to as *MBh*) 13.132.55, 13.116.21 ff., cp. 12.237.25 ff.

107　*VisM* 9.36. Cp. *Buddhism and Nature* n. 221; cp. also *ŚrBh* 379,8 ff.

108　Cp. p. 181 and note 79.

109　Harris, "Buddhism," 14; cp. also 17.

110　E.g., *D* I 251, II 250 ff.; *M* II 194 ff.; *A* II 128 ff., V 342.

111　E.g., *A* I 201, III 290 ff., 446; *D* III 247 ff. Cp. also *ŚrBh* 429,1 ff. (context: *maitrī*): *api tu tān etarhy anukampe yaduta svacittaniṣkāluṣyatām avyāpannatām upādāya . . . (sva°* added with ms.). Cp. also *M* I 284 ff. (*appamāṇas* conducive to tranquillity, *vūpasama*). For the purificatory function of *ahiṃsā* cp. Harris, "Buddhism," 17.

112　E.g., *D* III 49 ff., 78, 223 ff.; *M* I 38; *S* IV 296; *A* I 196 ff., V 344 ff.

113　Likewise, the genuinely ethical aspect of abstention from taking life if it is based on the "Golden Rule" is not annulled by the fact that it *also* serves spiritual purification or is motivated by fear of being reborn in an evil existence that is the karmic consequence of killing (e.g., *S* IV 342; *A* IV 247, V 289) and, in a sense, the ethicized pendant of the older idea of the vengeance of the victim. Cp. also Schmidt-Leukel, "Das Problem von Dewalt und Kieg," 9 (but ignore the misleading analysis of *upādāna*).

114　Perhaps primarily lay people from the Brahmanical fold, or even Brahmins specifically, since it is particularly god Brahman's world they are said to be conducive to.

115　Even if *mettā/maitrī* does not necessarily entail active help (cp. *AKBh* 272,13 on its being, nevertheless, meritorious), it still prevents, by counteracting hatred and malevolence, the practitioner from injuring others (cp., perhaps, *S* IV 351 ff.).

116　It seems that the *appamāṇa*s were, originally, more closely related, or even conducive, to liberation (cp. Vetter, *Ideas and Meditative Practice*, 26–28; R. Gombrich in *Asiatische Studien* 38.4 [1994]: 1082; A. Skilton, *A Concise History of Buddhism* [Birmingham: Windhorse, 1994], 35).

117　The relation between equanimity or imperturbability on the one hand and friendliness and compassion on the other is doubtless a crucial one for understanding Buddhist spirituality (and the differences between its various forms), but a detailed discussion of this difficult and controversial issue would exceed the limits of this paper.

118　Cp., e.g., *Vin* I 6 (after his awakening the Buddha, after some hesitation [see note 53], decided on teaching because he has *compassion* with living beings); cp. also *Vin* II 195 (the Buddha tames a wild elephant by suffusing him with friendliness); cp. also *Vin* I 21 = *S* I 105.

119　Harris, "How Environmentalist Is Buddhism?" 111; "Causation and *Telos*", 18.

120　*A* II 72 f. = *Vin* II 110; cp. *Ja* II 145 f.; cp. also note 94.

121　Cp. *Buddhism and Nature* § 43 and n. 217.

122　Actually, these beings are identified as *nāga*s at *Ja* II 145, and it ought to be kept in mind that *nāga*s are both snakes, i.e., animals, *and* mythical beings (cp., e.g., *Vin* I 87 ff., 219 ff.). At any rate, in the present context friendship with them involves friendship with, or at least protection from, snakes.

123　Cp. also the enumeration of species of animals (snakes, scorpions, centipedes, etc.) in the spell-like prose formula following the verses.

124　Cp. *Buddhism and Nature* § 45.

125　*D* III 61. Cp. also *Ja* V 123 (v. 45) and VI 94 (v. 123).

126 This suggestion I owe to Dr. P. Schmidt-Leukel.

127 Which does not of course prevent Buddhists from adopting or adapting this aim or value on an *intramundane* level.

128 Cp., e.g., J. Gonda, *Die Religionen Indiens* I: Veda und älterer Hinduismus (Stuttgart: W. Kohlhammer, 1960), 163, 172.

129 For a detailed interpretation of Aśoka's animal list, see K. R. Norman, "Notes on Aśoka's Fifth Pillar Edict," in *JRAS* (1967): 26–32 (= *Collected Papers* I 68–76).

130 Cp. Gómez, "Nonviolence and the Self," 34.

131 Cp. *Kauṭilīya-Arthaśāstra* (3 vols., R. P. Kangle, ed. [Bombay: University of Bombay, 1960–1965]) 2.26; cp. also 13.5.12 ff., and Helmut Scharfe, *Investigations in Kauṭalya's Manual of Political Science* (2nd rev. ed. of *Untersuchungen zur Staatsrechtslehre des Kauṭalya* [Wiesbaden: O. Harrasowitz, 1993]), 252 ff.

132 Cp. L. Alsdorf, *Beiträge zur Geschichte von Vegetarismus und Rinderverehrung in Indien*, Abhandlungen der Akademie der Wissenschaften und der Literatur in Mainz, Jahrgang 1961, no. 6 (Wiesbaden: Franz Steiner Verlag, 1962), 50 ff.; Scharfe, op. cit. (see note 131), 257.

133 *Rock Edicts* IV A and C, IX G, XI C; cp. also I B (though Alsdorf, op. cit. [see note 132], 52 ff., suggests that *idha* refers to the capital only; but cp. also Ulrich Schneider, *Die Grossen Felsen-Edikte Aśokas* [Wiesbaden: Otto Harrasowitz, 1978], 120), *Pillar Edict* 7 NN, and the interpretation suggested by C. Caillat (in *Bulletin d'études indiennes* 9 [1991]: 9 ff.) for *Rock Edict* XIII M–N, and her reference to the Aramaic edict of Kandahar (ibid. 12 and n. 14). [Ed. Electronic version of English translation: http://www.cs.colostate.edu/~malaiya/ashoka.html, accessed October 23, 2009.]

134 Cp. especially killing pregnant and young animals or sucklings.

135 A different approach is the prohibition of killing and injuring on special days (cp. *Kauṭilīya-Arthaśāstra* 13.5.12), which in Aśoka's mind may have served as a kind of reminder and temporary ritual enactment of the *ideal* of nonviolence even for such people as were unable to come up to it in their daily lives.

136 This is explicitly stated for quadrupeds and suggested by Dharmaśāstra parallels for at least some of the animals expressly enumerated (cp., e.g., the birds at the beginning of Aśoka's list with *Manu* 5.12). The fish named in the edict are regarded as inedible according to R. Thapar, *Aśoka and the Decline of the Mauryas*, 2nd ed. (repr. Oxford and New York: Oxford University Press, 1998), 71 n. 3 (referring to Hora).

137 Cp., e.g., *Dhp* 129–32; *S* V 353.

138 Life—both human and animal life—as a value would seem to contradict the ultimate Buddhist evaluation of existence as well as the idea of the special unhappiness of animal life. But this is just one of the cases of different spiritual or didactic levels and contexts to be kept apart.

139 Cp. *Buddhism and Nature* §§ 39.3 and 42. One reason, at least, for the inclusion of dangerous and noxious animals into *ahiṃsā* and *mettā* is, of course, the historical background indicated above, viz. their original function of avoiding revenge and protecting from aggression (see above, p. 182).

140 *Buddhism and Nature* §§ 10.1–11.2; my *The Problem of the Sentience of Plants in Earliest Buddhism* (Tokyo: The International Institute for Buddhist Studies, 1991), 5 ff., 23 ff., 46 ff., 58 ff.

141 Cp. *Buddhism and Nature* n. 244.

142 *T* vol. 23, 75a23 ff., 776b18 ff.; cp. also *Paramatthajotikā* II, vol. I 154,23 ff., where the addressee is a brahmin; cp. *Problem of the Sentience of Plants* § 5.2 and n. 204.

143 *Vin* I 225; *Sn* 14; *S* I 169; cp. *Problem of the Sentience of Plants* § 11.1.

144 *Vin* III 7.

145 On the problem of the relationship between norm and actual behavior cp., e.g., P. Pedersen in Bruun and Kalland, eds., *Asian Perceptions of Nature*, 264–66. Cp. also *Buddhism and Nature* § 4.2.

146 Cp. *Problem of the Sentience of Plants* §§ 16.1–4, 25.2–3, 38.3.

147 Cp. also Gunapala Dhammasiri, *Fundamentals of Buddhist Ethics* (Singapore: Buddhist Research Society, 1986), 174 ff.

148 Cp. *Problem of the Sentience of Plants* § 26.2; cp. also *Buddhism and Nature* § 11.1.

149 Cp. *Problem of the Sentience of Plants*, esp. §§ 24 ff.; *Buddhism and Nature* §§ 9–10.

150 E.g., Mudagamuwe Maithri Murthi, *Das Verhalten der ceylonesischen Buddhisten gegenüber Tieren und Pflanzan* (master's thesis, Hamburg, 1986), 28 ff., 48, 53, 56; M. Spiro, *Buddhism and Society* (Berkeley and Los Angeles: University of California Press, 1982), 45; Gombrich, op. cit. (see note 104), 245, 261.

151 Cp. *Buddhism and Nature* §§ 14.3–5 and 60. Cp. also N. Hakamaya, "Akugō-fusshoku no Gishiki-kanren-kyōten-zakkō" (Sūtras Concerned with Rites for Extinguishing Evil), I in *Komazawa-daigaku-bukkyōgakubu-kenkyū-kiyō* 50 (1992): 274–47; III in ibid. 51 (1993): 337–298; II in *Komazawa-daigaku-bukkyōgakubu-ronshū* 23 (1992): 442–23; IV in ibid. 24 (1993): 434–13; V and VI in *Komazawa-tanki-daigaku-kenkyū-kiyō* 23 (1995): 95–127, and 24 (1996): 67–91.

152 The *Saddharmasmṛtyupasthānasūtra* (*T* vol. 17, 2b22 ff.) mentions various cases of killing that are not regarded as an evil deed, e.g., when one unintentionally crushes a worm or ant while walking, or when one lights a fire for some other reason and an insect jumps into it.

153 Cp. *Buddhism and Nature* § 37.

154 Cp. *Buddhism and Nature* § 12 and Sandell in Bruun and Kalland, eds., *Asian Perceptions of Nature*, 155 f., pointing out that when using pesticides Sri Lankan farmers either do not care about the Buddhist norm (declaring insects to be their enemies) or refer to their lack of intention to kill. But cp. also M. Spiro, op. cit. (see note 150), 45, who writes that in Burma the government had difficulties in persuading people to use DDT.

155 Cp. *Buddhism and Nature* § 38.

156 E.g., *D* III 75; *M* II 71 f.; *A* I 159 ff.; cp. *Buddhism and Nature* § 20; Harris, "How Environmentalist Is Buddhism?" 108, and "Buddhism," 21 ff.

157 E.g., *D* I 73; *M* I 276, 3/8; *S* III 108 ff.; *Ja* VI 506 ff.; cp. *Buddhism and Nature* § 20; Harris, "How Environmentalist Is Buddhism?" 108, and "Buddhism," 22 f. This attitude is also found in later texts; cp., e.g., *DBhS* 21,25 ff., contrasting the "*huge* city of omniscience (= Buddhahood)" (*sarvajñatā-mahānagara*) with the "[large] forest (*aṭavī*) of *saṃsāra*."

158 E.g., *Apadāna* (Pali Text Society edition, hereinafter *Ap*) I 271 (334.11). By the way, in the context of the description of nature surrounding the hermitage (see below, p. 196 with note 220), the first line of this verse (enumerating various species of beasts of prey) occurs as an element underlining the beauty of nature.

159 Apotropaic spells and rites, though, to be sure, not entirely alien to settlement-based and perhaps even wilderness-based monks (cp., e.g., self-protection from snake bite

taught to monks in the *Ahirājasutta*: see p. 184 with note 120), would yet mainly seem to be the Buddhist response to requirements from the side of lay people.

160 E.g., by means of ceremonies and spells soliciting rain, as exemplified by the (later) *Meghasūtra* (ed. [in extracts] by C. Bendall in *JRAS* 12 (1880): 286–311; *T* vol. 19, nos. 989 and 991–93).

161 It goes back even to Vedic times: cp. W. Rau, *Staat und Gesellschaft im Alten Indien nach den Brāhmaṇa-Texten dargestellt* (Wiesbaden: Otto Harrasowitz, 1957), 53.

162 For Japan cp. Ulrike Thiede, *Japanibis und Japanische Nachtigall als Beispiele zweier Pole im Naturverständnis der Japaner*, Gesellschaft für Natur- und Völkerkunde Ostasiens, Mitteilungen Bd. 90 (Hamburg: Gesellschaft für Natur- und Völkerkunde Ostasiens, 1982), 118 (". . . da die Natur den Bauern nur als formbare und nutzbare Natur interessiert") and 127 (". . . wird vom Bauern allgemein die Natur in nützliche und nutzlose bzw. schädliche Natur eingeteilt. Die nützliche Natur wird geformt und gepflegt, die schädliche abgewehrt und vernichtet"). For certain South-American Indian societies cp., e.g., A. Gebhart-Sayer, *Die Spitze des Bewusstseins* (PhD diss., Tübingen, 1987), 102, 110, 285 ff.; Mark Münzel, *Medizinmannwesen und Geistervorstellungen bei den Kamayurá (Alto Xingú, Brasilien)* (Wiesbaden: Franz Steiner Verlag, 1971), 27 ff., 99. I am, of course, aware of the fact that much more material is available and that the subject may require differentiation.

163 *D* III 75 (densely populated world during the period of the longest lifespan), 59–64 (period of moral perfection), and 68 (implying that the period of moral perfection is identical with period of the longest lifespan).

164 *A* I 159 ff., II 74 ff.; *D* III 71–73; *Ja* II 124, cp. *Ja* III 110 ff.

165 *SN* I 33; cp. *Buddhism and Nature* § 24 and n. 98. Cp. *MBh* 13.99. Cp. also Aśoka's having trees planted and wells dug along the roads for the use of men and beasts (*pasumunisānaṃ*: *Rock Edict* II D; *Pillar Edict* 7 R–T), "beasts" referring, in view of "along the roads," to draft and riding beasts in the first place, though wild animals may not be excluded (cp. *MBh* 13.99.16–17).

166 E.g., *S* II 106; *M* I 365, III 5, 130 ff.; Harris, "Buddhism," 21. At *S* I 233 (11.15), the evaluation is, at the same time, relativized as intramundane by the reference that a *truly* lovely place is only that where holy men (*arahanto*) live, no matter whether wilderness or inhabited place.

167 E.g., *D* II 171, 182; *Ap* I 333 (396.6).

168 E.g., *D* III 201 f.; *Petavatthu* 2.12.2–4; similarly *Suvarṇabhāsottamasūtra* (Johannes Nobel, ed. [Leipzig: Otto Harrassowitz, 1937]) 164 f. Cp. also *Ap* I 333 (396.1–6) where, however, the trees are said to be made of gold and beset with jewels.

169 *Vimānavatthu* 3.7.4–6. Similarly *Aṣṭasāhasrikā Prajñāpāramitā* (P. L. Vaidya, ed. [Darbhanga: The Mithila Institute, 1960], hereinafter *Aṣṭ*) 240,24 ff. (tree consisting of precious metals or jewels: ibid. 240,14).

170 Cp., in this connection, the description, in the *Kauṭilīya-Arthaśāstra* (Kangle, ed., 2.2.3) of the king's pleasure-grove as containing trees *without thorns*, tame animals, and beasts of prey with *broken claws and fangs*.

171 See pp. 191ff. and especially 196.

172 *D* III 84 ff.

173 Esp. *T* vol. 1, 137b16 ff. (*Dīrghāgama*, probably of the Dharmaguptaka school); cp. also *Yogācārabhūmi* (Vidhushekhara Bhattacharya, ed. [Calcutta: University of Calcutta, 1957]) 34,16 ff., and *AKBh* 178,5 ff., esp. 11 ff.

174 According to *Abhidharmakośa* 178,11 ff., *domestic* animals will only disappear together with human beings.

175 Cp. *Buddhism and Nature* § 25.

176 Cp. Hajime Nakamura, "The Idea of Nature, East and West," in *The Great Ideas Today* (Chicago: Encyclopedia Britannica, 1980), 274.

177 *S* I 128 ff. (*Bhikkhunī-saṃyutta*).

178 E.g., *D* III 195 (. . . *pantāni senāsanāni . . . appasaddāni . . . vijanavātāni . . . paṭisallānasāruppāni*). Against noise also *M* I 456 ff., II 30; *A* III 31; cp. L. De Silva in Sandell, *Buddhist Perspectives on the Ecocrisis*, 21 ff.

179 Cp. the Buddha's awakening under a pipal tree. In spite of the undeniable importance of the positive emotional implications of this element of tradition (which is often adduced as evidence for a pro-nature attitude of Buddhism), it should be noted that the tree is also used as a simile for negative factors, e.g., *S* II 87 ff. (12.55–57) where it illustrates desire (*taṇhā*), and its felling and uprooting the eradication of desire.

180 E.g., *D* I 71; *M* I 269.

181 E.g., *M* I 16 ff. Numinous parks, groves, and trees characterized as dangerous: *M* I 20. Cp. also Harris, "How Environmentalist Is Buddhism?" 108, and "Buddhism," 20.

182 E.g., *A* III 100–2; *Cullaniddesa* and *Sn* 42 (PTS ed. p. 199; Nālandā ed. 265,3 f.); cp. *S* I 219 f.

183 *A* III 100–2. Cp. also S. J. Tambiah, *The Buddhist Saints of the Forest and the Cult of Amulets* (Cambridge: Cambridge University Press, 1984; repr. 1993), 89 ff.

184 Thus in *S* I 219 f. Cp. also the (Mahāyānist) *Ugradattaparipṛcchā* quoted in *Śikṣāsamuccaya* (C. Bendall, ed. [St. Pétersbourg: Imperial Academy of Sciences (1897–1902); repr. 's-Gravenhage: Mouton, 1957], hereinafter *Śikṣ*) 198 ff., esp. 199,3 ff.

185 E.g., *Th* 189–90, 41; *Sn* 42 with *Cullaniddesa* 77 (§ 15, Nālandā ed. 268,11–13); *A* IV 291 (*araññiko . . . bhayabheravasaho . . .*); *S* I 132 (*na taṃ bhāyami*: the perfected nun dwelling in the wilderness is not afraid of Māra, who in this case would seem to represent all kinds of threats—and of course also temptations); *D* III 133 (arhat cannot have fear).

186 E.g., *Th* 31 = 244.

187 E.g., *A* III 108 f.; *S* I 181.

188 *Th* 31 = 244; *A* IV 291 (*aratiṃ abhibhuyya . . . viharati*).

189 E.g., *S* I 130 f., 181; *A* III 219 (*app'icchatā, santuṭṭhi*).

190 *Th* 13; 113 = 601 = 1070, 307–10, 1135–37, 992 = *Dhp* 99. Cp. also Schmithausen, "Buddhismus und Natur," in R. Panikkar and W. Strolz, eds., *Die Verantwortung des Menschen für eine bewohnbare Welt in Christentum, Hinduismus und Buddhismus* (Freiburg im Breisgau: Herder, 1985), 109 ff.; *Buddhism and Nature* § 25.2; Harris, "How Environmentalist Is Buddhism?" 107 and n. 54. But cp. *D* II 102 ff. (= *Ud* 62 ff.) where what the Buddha enjoys as lovely (*ramaṇīya*) is the *city* of Vesālī and its holy places (*cetiya*, which may but need not be trees, groves, etc.: cp. *Encyclopedia of Buddhism* IV,1 104).

191 Cp. also the remarks in note 38.

192 Cp. S. Lienhard, "Sur la structure poétique des Theratherīgāthā," in *Journal Asiatique* 263 (1975): 375 ff., esp. 382 ff.; for destructive behavior cp., e.g., *Jātakamālā of Āryaśūra* (P. L. Vaidya, ed. [Darbhanga: Mithila Institute, 1959], hereinafter *Jm*) 28.13–14.

193 *A* III 219; cp. *M* I 18. Cp. also *Śikṣ* 198,2 ff. (mentioning, in this connection, also wild *animals*, besides robbers and outcasts).

194 *M* I 104 ff. (*Vanapatthasutta*).

195 *Ud* 12 (2.4); *Uv* 30.51.

196 *M* I 9 ff. (*Sabbāsavasutta*). (The importance of this passage for the present context was kindly pointed out to me by Dr. P. Schmidt-Leukel.) Harris ("How Environmentalist Is Buddhism?" 108), however, supposes that the real background of the prohibition is the notion of the "unwholesome influences at work in this tainted environment." This would fit in with the attitude of the civilization-oriented strand to which city- or even village-based monks (and nuns) would by and large seem to belong, in contrast to those who are wilderness-based (*araññavāsin*).

197 *S* I 128 ff.

198 *Vin* II 278.

199 The reason adduced in the *Vinaya* may, to be sure, signalize that the difference is not so much one of evaluation of wilderness as one of concern, the *Vinaya* being concerned not with spiritual practice proper but with matters of discipline and social reputation of the order and its members.

200 *A* I 35.

201 Cp., e.g., Bhikkhu Buddhadasa in Thailand, or the Thai monks practicing tree ordination in order to preserve forests (Harris, "Getting to Grips," 178 ff. with n. 34; cp. also "Monks battle to save the forests," *The Nation* 23, no. 2 [1991]: B2).

202 *Mil* 32,25–27; cp. *Buddhism and Nature* § 21.1 and n. 84; Harris, "How Environmentalist Is Buddhism?" 105 and n. 25.

203 *M* III 169; *S* V 455 ff., 476; *A* I 37. For copious evidence, from Buddhist as well as Hindu and Jaina sources, for the idea that rebirth as a human is difficult to attain cp. M. Hara, "A Note on the Hindu Concept of Man," *Journal of the Faculty of Letters, The Univ. of Tokyo, Aesthetics* 11 (1986): 45 ff.

204 *M* I 74 ff., III 169; *Th* 258; cp. *Buddhism and Nature* § 21.2 and nn. 85–87.

205 *Yogācārabhūmi* 87,14–16.

206 Ibid. 87,13 ff.; cp. *M* III 169. Cp. also *T* vol. 3, 467b18 ff.

207 *M* III 167–69.

208 *A* III 339. Cp. also the hierarchy of forms of existence at *M* II 193 ff. As for *VisM* 13.93, see note 103. Besides, Buddhaghosa justifies his statement that animals are *apāya* but not *duggati* by pointing out that the *gati* of animals includes powerful *nāga*s. Precisely for this reason, the passage hardly implies the attribution of a higher value to existence as an *ordinary*, natural animal.

209 Cp. *Buddhism and Nature* § 21.2 and n. 88, and § 26 and n. 119.

210 *D* III 72.

211 *M* III 169.

212 Thus quite clearly in the Story of the Elder Māleyyadeva (see note 230), 43,1 and 84.

213 Cp. the opinion reported in *Buddhism and Nature*, end of n. 84.

214 Cp. *Buddhism and Nature* § 23.1; Schmithausen, "Buddhismus und Natur," 105 ff.; cp. also *Aṣṭ* 178,28–30.

215 Cp. *Buddhism and Nature* § 39.2, nn. 170 and 171.

216 Thus especially *M* III 163 ff. (*Bālapaṇḍitasutta*).

217 Cp. *Buddhism and Nature* § 27.1; Harris, "How Environmentalist Is Buddhism?" 105, nn. 29 and 30.

218 Murthi, *Verhalten der ceylonesischen Buddhisten*, 7 ff.

219 Cp., e.g., the story of the furious elephant Nāḷāgiri tamed and admonished by the

Buddha (*Vin* II 195 f.; *Ja* V 336 ff., or II 53). A famous example from another Buddhist tradition is, of course, the Tibetan Yogin Milaraspa who is reported to have not only enjoyed the beauty of landscape, vegetation, and animal life—in a detached way due to his awareness of their ultimate emptiness (*rNal 'byor Mi la ras pa'i rnam mgur* [Xining: Qinghai minzu chuban, 1981], 249 ff., 441)—but also to have preached to wild animals and pacified them, so that in his presence the frightened stag becomes fearless and the fierce hunting dog peaceful (ibid., 430 ff.; H. Hoffmann, *Mi-la ras-pa: Sieben Legenden* [München-Planegg: Barth, 1950], 87 ff.; Garma C. C. Chang, *The Hundred Thousand Songs of Milarepa* [Boulder: Shambhala, 1977], I 275 ff.).

220 E.g., *Ja* V 405 ff., VI 529 ff., 533 ff.; *Ap* I 15 ff., 328 ff. (no. 393, vv. 1–5), II 345–47 (no. 402, vv. 1–31), 362 ff. (no. 407, vv. 1–20), 367 ff. (no. 409, vv. 1–20). Cp. also *Ja* VI 496 ff.

221 Cp., e.g., *Ja* V 405 (v. 68b): *rammaṃ*; VI 530 (v. 343), 534 (vv. 376 and 379): *manorame*; 536 (v. 395): *sobhanā, upasobhitaṃ*; Ap I 15 f. (vv. 3–5; 10–13): *sobhayantā, sobhayanti*.

222 Ludwig Alsdorf (*Kleine Schriften*, ed. A. Wezler [Wiesbaden: Steiner Verlag, 1974], 333 ff.) is certainly right in identifying these descriptions, in the *Vessantara-Jātaka*, as an obstruction in the dénouement and in regarding the description of nature by means of a mere enumeration of species of plants and animals as rather primitive from the artistic point of view, but it may be "intolerably boring" only for readers who are unacquainted with the species enumerated and for whom they remain mere names, but not for those in whom each name evokes a colorful vision of the corresponding reality.

223 Cp., e.g., *MBh* 1.64, 3.155.37 ff.; *Rāmāyaṇa* (crit. ed. [Vadodara, India: Oriental Institute, 1992]) 3.69.2 ff.

224 E.g., *Ja* V 416, 420 (*Kunāla Jātaka*; cp. W. B. Bollée's edition and trans. [London: Luzac, 1970], 8 ff., 14 ff., 124 ff.) describing the beauty of forests inhabited by two birds (the second of whom is, however, virtually a sage; besides, ascetics [*tāpasa*: 420,9] are mentioned in passing among the creatures inhabiting that forest). Without any connection with hermits or animal-heroes: *Ja* VI 277 ff.

225 Clearly so in *MBh* 1.64.6 statement that around the hermitage there are no trees without flowers, fruits, and bees, *nor such as have thorns*. Similarly 3.155.65cd.

226 *Ja* V 405 ff. (vv. 264 ff.).

227 For tameness of animals around the hermitage also *MBh* 1.64.18ef; *Rāmāyaṇa* 3.69.8ab; Atindranath Bose, *Social and Rural Economy of Northern India* (Calcutta: Firma K. L. Mukhopadhyay, 1970), 100.

228 *Ja* VI 591,13 ff. (*tejena*). Cp. also Milaraspa (see note 219).

229 E.g., *Ja* VI 73, 520; *Jm* ch. 1.8; cp. *Ja* II 53. Cp. also Śaṅkara, *Yogasūtrabhāṣyavivaraṇa* and *Yogasūtra* II.35 (natural enmity among animals stops due to the yogin's *ahiṃsā*).

230 Cp. also E. Denis (ed.) and St. Collins (trans.), "The Story of the Elder Māleyyadeva," *Journal of the Pali Text Society* 18 (1993): 50 and 88.

231 Cp. also *Ja* VI 29,26–28, and, for a later example, Milaraspa (loc. cit.: see note 219). In these two cases at least, self-protection of the ascetic does not seem to play a significant role. What happens is rather a spontaneous transformation of the character and behavior of the animal under the influence of the perfected person for the benefit of the animals themselves only.

232 *Jm* ch. 1; for parallels cp. D. Schlingloff, *Studies in the Ajanta Paintings: Identifications and Interpretations* (Delhi: Ajanta Publications, 1987), 145.

233 Cp. É. Lamotte, *Le Traité de la Grande Vertu de Sagesse de Nāgārjuna*, tome I (Louvain: Peeters, 1949), 255 ff.; Schlingloff, op. cit., 86 ff.; Marion Meisig, *König Śibi und die Taube* (Wiesbaden: O. Harrassowitz, 1995).

234 Cp. also the readiness of the Bodhisattva to offer his body to the hungry beasts of prey in case self-protection by means of friendliness should not work (*Ratnarāśisūtra* quoted *Śikṣ* 200,15 ff.; J. A. Silk, *The Origins and Early History of the Mahāratnakūṭa Tradition of Mahāyāna Buddhism, with a Study of the Ratnarāśisūtra and Related Materials* [PhD diss., University of Michigan, 1994], 470 ff.).

235 See *Buddhism and Nature* §§ 48 ff., esp. 54 ff.

Index

About the Contributors

— ∎ ∎ ∎ —

DAVID BARNHILL is the author of *Engaging the Earth: American Nature Writers and the World* (forthcoming), and two works on the poetry and literary prose of Basho. He is the co-editor of *Deep Ecology and World Religions: New Essays on Sacred Ground* (State University of New York Press, 2001) and is currently the director of environmental studies at the University of Wisconsin–Oshkosh.

MITSUYA DAKE is the author of several English-language essays in *Pacific World* and *The Pure Land*—professional journals in the academic study of Buddhism—and is currently Dean of Faculty at Ryukoku University; the director of the Buddhism and the Environment Research Unit of the Center for Humanities, Science, and Religion at Ryukoku University; and Executive Director of the International Association of Shin Buddhist Studies.

DAVID ECKEL is the author of *Bhāviveka and His Buddhist Opponents* (Harvard University Press, 2008); *Buddhism* (Oxford University Press, 2002); and *To See the Buddha* (Princeton University Press, 1994). He is currently at Boston University, where he is the winner of the university's prestigious Metcalf Award for Teaching Excellence.

SHINICHI INOUE, now deceased, was formerly the president of the Japanese Miyazaki Bank and a renowned economist who authored *Putting Buddhism to Work: A New Approach to Management and Business* (Kodansha, 1998).

STEPHANIE KAZA is the author of *Hooked: Buddhist Writings on Greed, Desire and the Urge to Consume* (Shambhala, 2005) and *The Attentive Heart: Conversations with Trees* (Shambhala, 1996). She is the co-editor of *Dharma Rain: Sources of Buddhist Environmentalism* (Shambhala, 2000) and currently is a professor of environmental studies at the University of Vermont.

TETSUNORI KOIZUMI is the author of *Interdependence and Change in the Global System* (University Press of America, 1993), the director of the International Institute for Integrative Studies, and was previously Professor Emeritus at Ryukoku University and visiting professor at Ohio State University.

IKUO NAKAMURA is a former professor at Osaka University and is now a member of the faculty at Gakushuin University, Tokyo.

LAMBERT SCHMITHAUSEN is the author of "Maitri and Magic: Aspects of the Buddhist Attitude Toward the Dangerous in Nature" (*Indo-Iranian Journal*, 2000) and *The Problem of the Sentience of Plants in Earliest Buddhism* (International Institute for Buddhist Studies, 1991).

DUNCAN RYUKAN WILLIAMS is the author of *The Other Side of Zen: A Social History of Soto Zen Buddhism in Tokugawa Japan* (Princeton University Press, 2004); editor of *Buddhism and Ecology: The Interconnection of Dharma and Deeds* (Harvard Center for World Religions, 1998); co-editor of *American Buddhism: Methods and Findings in Recent Scholarship* (Routledge, 1998); and currently at the University of California, Berkeley.

About Wisdom

— ∎ ∎ ∎ —

Wisdom Publications, a nonprofit publisher, is dedicated to making available authentic works relating to Buddhism for the benefit of all. We publish books by ancient and modern masters in all traditions of Buddhism, translations of important texts, and original scholarship. Additionally, we offer books that explore East-West themes unfolding as traditional Buddhism encounters our modern culture in all its aspects. Our titles are published with the appreciation of Buddhism as a living philosophy, and with the special commitment to preserve and transmit important works from Buddhism's many traditions.

To learn more about Wisdom, or to browse books online, visit our website at www.wisdompubs.org.

You may request a copy of our catalog online
or by writing to this address:

Wisdom Publications
199 Elm Street
Somerville, Massachusetts 02144 USA
Telephone: 617-776-7416
Fax: 617-776-7841
Email: info@wisdompubs.org
www.wisdompubs.org

THE WISDOM TRUST

As a nonprofit publisher, Wisdom is dedicated to the publication of Dharma books for the benefit of all sentient beings and dependent upon the kindness and generosity of sponsors in order to do so.

If you would like to make a donation to Wisdom, you may do so through our website or our Somerville office. If you would like to help sponsor the publication of a book, please write or email us at the address above.

Thank you.

Wisdom is a nonprofit, charitable 501(c)(3) organization affiliated with the Foundation for the Preservation of the Mahayana Tradition (FPMT).